Praise for The Physician To Finance

"Wow! Amanda and Nick have written a much-needed masterpiece to help medical students and early career physicians obtain financial independence. Their passion to help others shines through in this concise, comprehensive and beautifully illustrated book. This is a definite must read!"

Todd C. Villines, MD, FACC, FAHA, MSCCT, Prior Colonel, US Army Medical Corp
The Julian Ruffin Beckwith Distinguished Professor of Medicine, The University of Virginia

"This book is a must for anyone contemplating going to medical school, currently in medical school or residency, or in practice. In fact, one should probably read this book every year while in college, medical school, residency, fellowship, and the first few years of practice. The information Amanda and Nick share is invaluable, practical, and easy to put to use. Protect your financial future by planning ahead with this book."

David J Norris, MD, MBA
Author of *The Financially Intelligent Physician* and *Great Care, Every Patient*

"Nick and Amanda have provided a first of its kind, truly comprehensive list of personal finance topics. The chapter recaps and well organized charts and graphs effortlessly guide you along the path to financial success."

Paul T Scheatzle DO FAAPMR
Author of *The Journey: Take the Path to Health* and *Fitness. Energize Your Life*

"A deep dive into understanding your finances. *The Physician's Guide to Finance* provides practical advice from surviving medical school's financial minefield to the opportunities and pitfalls of a real paycheck. This is far more than a cursory overview. There is something for almost everyone to learn—don't miss the opportunity."

James Geyer, MD founder of Smart Business Great Medicine

"What a great resource! I wish I had this book 20 or even 30 years ago. I have learned a lot via experiences...some good and some bad. If I had read this book when I was a medical student or resident I think I could have avoided most of the bad experiences! A must read and resource for medical students and residents and a good source of information for many fully trained doctors as well."

Michael J. Stamos, MD, FACS, FASCRS
Dean, School of Medicine | University of California, Irvine (UCI)

"The book is great! I think it is a must-read for all Med students, trainees, and attending. Nick and Amanda have made difficult and confusing topics user friendly and easy to digest. I wish I had this 20 years ago!"

Stephanie Pearson, MD, FACOG
Disabled physician turned insurance broker-CEO and co-founder of PearsonRavitz, LLC

"Amanda & Nick Christian have written a clear, concise, and a deceptively simple look-ing book on personal finance for physicians. Their intimate knowledge of a physician's life and mastery of personal finance shines through. Their focus on early career is right where it should be. I wish I had this book when I was doing my residency!"

"All I can say is BRAVO! I love that this book is organized to follow med students through-out their ENTIRE career. There aren't many people out there willing to tell the truth about the journey and even less willing to show students how to build wealth as they grow. Thank you Nick and Amanda for creating my new favorite student resource. It is definitely a must-have for any med student!"

"I highly recommend *The Physician's Guide to Finance* to every single student considering a career in medicine. Nick and Amanda provide a clear, concise, and realistic roadmap for all medical school students. Their research and personal experiences will assist students at the beginning of their college career and beyond. From financial aid and scholarships to retirement planning and malpractice insurance, Nick and Amanda provide valuable advice for every single step of a physician's journey. This is a must-read for all students entering medical school!"

"Physicians are some of the most highly educated and highly trained individuals in the workforce. But ask any doctor how many lectures they were given on the financial impli-cations of a career in medicine or fiscal responsibility, and you're likely to be met with silence. Nick and Amanda have created an engaging and invaluable resource for phy-sicians at any stage in their career (from applying to medical school to planning for retirement). The insights and guidance contained in *The Physicians' Guide to Finance* are invaluable to medical professionals."

"This is a must read book for any healthcare provider be it straight out of medical school, residency or practicing in the field for many years. Effective financial management is some thing that we as health care providers rarely learn either in medical school or res-idency. I firmly believe Nick and Amanda have done a fabulous job laying down the valuable tools covering a very broad spectrum, from tools for financial aid while in med-ical school to managing retirement accounts as one progresses through his/her medical career. The book is easy to understand with not too many complicated financial jargons. A very practical resource. This is the best investment you'll ever make."

"Finance is not something easy to understand and handle. This book is a great resource for new graduates to understand the basics of finance handling, as it explains in a very simple language. Nick and Amanda have provided highly valuable tips and topics from their own experience and comprehended everything useful in *The Physician's Guide to Finance*."

Arti Khatri, MD Chief Medical Resident
The University of Texas Health Science Center at Tyler

"It has arrived. Nick and Amanda's all purpose financial guide to help you chart your course toward truly being financially free. A resource that you can come to over and over again. From medical school, to residency and into practice. The focus is on getting started early so that you don't end up being stranded. This book is about to change the game for thousands of people desiring to serve in medicine. Read it now!"

Jason M. Valadao, MD, Aviator, Military Physician and Author of
Exceptional Every Day: An Empowering Process to Unlock Your Why and Transform Your Life

"Nick and Amanda have written a financial book I wish I would have had earlier in my medical journey! Distilling finances to the most pertinent information and breaking it in to simple to understand sections makes this book a must read for all healthcare professionals. Their integration of numerous infographics to clarify complex financial topics elevate this book to a new level! Would highly recommend this to individuals in any part of their medical journey."

Alex Sadauskas, MD

"*The Physician's Guide to Finance* describes a 'wealth' of personal finance topics every doctor in practice (or training) should consider. Nick and Amanda's backgrounds in finance and medicine fuse together to create a unique perspective—practical, real-world financial information tailored to those in the medical profession. Truly a helpful resource, worthy of your time to read!"

John Madison, CPA
Founder of Dayspring Financial Ministry and Author of *The Steward Plan*

"As a well-being coach for physicians, I see the stress that results when physicians adopt a lifestyle that requires a continued high income to maintain. Over time, they feel trapped, pressured, and exhausted trying to keep up. *The Physician's Guide to Finance* offers a way out: real-world knowledge about personal finance specifically for physicians. Nick and Amanda Christian share their personal experience and offer valuable insights about every aspect of financial decision-making. If you're a physician, trainee, or the spouse of one, you need this book!"

Diane W. Shannon, MD, MPH, ACC
Well-being Coach for Physicians

"A lot of useful information but short and succinct at the same time. Financial books always seem overwhelming to me, but this breaks it down and makes it easier to digest. Highly recommended!"

Richard Wagner, DO

"This book is an incredible resource and a must-read for all ranging from those considering a medical career to those who are physicians in practice! This book is written in an easy-to-understand fashion with chapter recaps and plenty of diagrams with sections tailored to financial aspects at different times of one's medical career. If you have any questions regarding finance at all, look no further; this is the book for you!"

Adhitya Venkataswamy, DO
Chief Resident at Penn Highlands Healthcare

"This book is informative and insightful, an excellent resource for those interested in pursuing a career as a physician, medical students, as well as physicians. It was enlightening to learn about the unique financial needs medical students face on their journey to becoming a physician, as well as the financial decisions they must consider once they become a physician. I would definitely recommend this book to others, including my own clients."

Andrea N. Johnson, Ph.D.
Financial Consultant and Owner of ANJ Consulting Services

"I personally wish I had read this book prior to beginning medical school. This book is clearly organized and should be incorporated into the curricula of medical school especially for students underrepresented in medicine. I will recommend this book to any medical student and residents looking to build on their personal finances and secure their future as a physician. Thank you Nick and Amanda for being a resource to students."

Kwadwo Sarpong, Medical Student

2021 Edition

The Physician's Guide To Finance

Personal Finance For Medical Students, Residents, and Attending Physicians

Amanda Christian, MD & Nick Christian, MBA

Published by **MONEY** ᴏᴠᴇʀ *Milkshakes*, LLC

DISCLOSURE: This book is intended as educational information and is not intended as legal, accounting, financial, or other professional advice. This book is designed to provide information that the authors believe to be accurate on the subject matter it covers, but it is sold with the understanding that neither the authors nor the publisher is offering individualized advice tailored to any specific portfolio or any individual's particular needs, or rendering investment advice or other professional services, such as legal or accounting advice. A competent professional service should be sought if one needs expert assistance in areas that include investment, legal, and/or accounting advice.

This publication references performance data collected over many time periods. Past results do not guarantee future performance. Additionally, performance data, in addition to laws and regulations, change over time, which could change the status of the information in this book. This book provides historical data solely to discuss and illustrate the underlying principles. Additionally, this book is not intended to serve as the basis for any financial decision, as a recommendation of a specific investment advisor, or as an offer to sell or purchase any security. Only a prospectus may be used to offer to sell or purchase securities, and a prospectus must be read and considered carefully before investing or spending money.

The views expressed within this book are the views of the authors alone. They do not reflect the views of the author's employers. No warranty is made with respect to the accuracy or completeness of the information contained herein, and both the author and the publisher specifically disclaim any responsibility for any liability, loss, or risk, personal or otherwise, which is incurred as a consequence, directly or indirectly, of the use an application of any of the contents of this book.

Editor: Jennifer Sisson
Copy Editor: Melissa Jonsson
Interior Design/Layout by Lorie DeWorken, Mind the Margins, LLC
Cover Design by Casey Fritz

Published by Money Over Milkshakes, LLC

ACKNOWLEDGEMENTS

This book would not be possible without the support, encouragement, and professional editing done by Jennifer Sisson and Melissa Jonsson. Making this book presentable to the masses is primarily due to their effort, and we will forever be in their debt. We also want to acknowledge Lorie DeWorken for making this the prettiest finance book on the market. Her work on the book's interior design far exceeded my hopes to make this an easy-to-read, engaging, and unique reading experience.

A special thanks to Josh Monk, a senior financial advisor and close friend who spent considerable time reviewing the material for the book and providing us with detailed feedback. Thank you for supporting our efforts from day one.

I also want to acknowledge a special group of people who not only responded to a stranger's request but took the time to review and provide feedback for the book based on their areas of expertise. Paul Shronts, Amber Peters (Mizz P.), Jeremy Gilbreath, PhD, MBA, Daniel Lee, MD, Dr. Kyle Hoedebecke, Todd C. Villines, MD, Jessica Schwager, Ashley Shelley, MD, Elizabeth Polfer, MD, Matt Wakeman and Farah Lokey.

CONTENTS

NICK'S DEDICATION

To our beautiful children, James, Sydney, and Charlotte:
May you pursue projects in life that you are truly passionate about.

To my co-author and wife Amanda,
who once sent me the following quote:

"Give someone a book; they'll read for a day.
Teach someone to write a book,
and they'll experience a lifetime of paralyzing self-doubt."
—Lauren DeStefano

Thank you for all the comic relief, support,
and encouragement along the way.

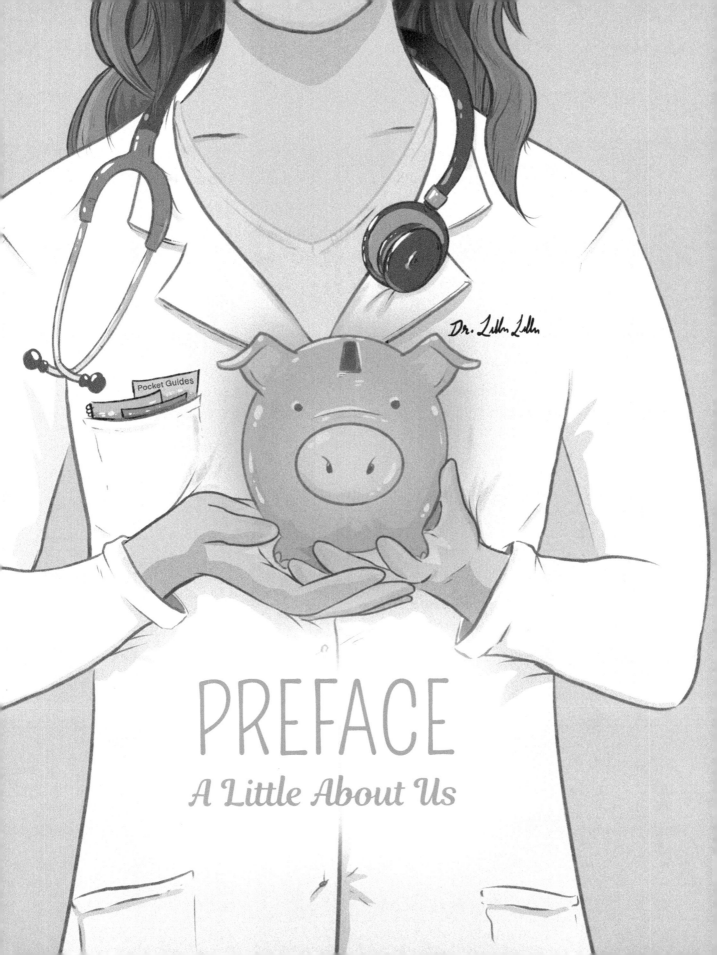

PREFACE
A Little About Us

NICK

When I was a kid, I always wanted to be a businessman. I didn't know what that meant, but I enjoyed walking around with my dad's old briefcase full of Monopoly money and Fruit Roll-Ups. My father was a businessman who traveled the world, and my grandfather before him. I wanted to be like them. By the time I got to college, I had pursued a bachelor's degree in international business. In my spare time, I was learning as much as I could about the stock market.

Professionally, I've spent most of my career working my way up the ladder in different accounting and finance departments both in the U.S. and abroad—initially as a financial analyst, then as a manager, and most recently as a director of finance and data analytics. Somewhere in the middle, I got itchy feet and took two years to complete an MBA in China.

Through the years, my passion for personal finance education has grown through several events in my life. One of the earlier experiences was my freshman year at university when I opened up the mail my first week and had five separate credit card offers between $1,000 and $5,000 each, despite having no credit. A potentially devastating debt trap for incoming freshmen.

I spent both my undergraduate and graduate years learning to analyze financial statements but never the dangers of predatory lending from high-interest credit card companies. I was encouraged to work at large corporate banks, but never did we discuss how these banks were making billions charging overdraft fees that would prey on the most vulnerable of us.

IF I WASN'T BEING EDUCATED ON THESE TOPICS WITH A MASTER'S IN INTERNATIONAL FINANCE, THEN WHO WAS?

The decisive moment came after Amanda and I had children of our own. I volunteered to teach a series of classes at our kid's school about business and finance concepts through the incredible organization Junior Achievement. I had confidently given presentations in front of executive teams for years, but for some reason, I had butterflies in my stomach.

I asked myself, why was I so anxious and excited in front of a room full of 1st graders? I came to realize it was because I cared so deeply about protecting these kids and desperately wanted to make a positive impact on how they understood concepts around money.

I came out of that experience more fulfilled than I had felt in years. That was it. I was hooked. Sharing with others what I've learned about personal finance was what I wanted to do moving forward.

AMANDA

I dreamed of being a physician since I was a child. I wanted to help people in a meaningful way and pursue my interest in science. I attended the University of Chicago, where I received my bachelor's degree in biology. Those were challenging years financially, and I needed to be resourceful in order to stay in school. I participated in the work-study program at the university and obtained Pell Grants for financial support.

During my time in Chicago, I had several odd jobs to make ends meet. I worked full-time in the summers doing research. I also made money tutoring, nannying, house-sitting, and several odd jobs I found on Craigslist. Despite my best efforts, I still graduated with student debt. It wasn't ideal, but I accepted it and moved forward.

After graduating, I spent a few years in San Diego. At first, I got a job working in a loan department for a mortgage company. After about 6 months, I landed the position I was really after: a research position in the pediatric neurology department with the University of California, San Diego.

After a couple of years, I decided to move back home to Oklahoma and apply for medical school as an in-state resident. I was accepted into medical school at the University of Oklahoma, and I completed my OB/GYN residency at Texas Tech University. I have been practicing medicine since 2017, with lots of lessons learned along the way.

Nick and I are excited to share the lessons we've learned around personal finance throughout the years with you!

Why We Wrote the Book

(NICK) Shortly after Amanda was accepted into medical school, we wanted to put ourselves in the best position possible for our future and our finances. Our financial picture was much different back then. We had very little in savings. We both had student debt from our undergraduate degrees and were about to incur considerably more debt to advance our education. And on top of all this, we were both going back to being full-time students—which meant no income.

I wanted to speak with a financial advisor to get us on a solid path. I wanted to know what things we should be doing now to set ourselves up for success in the future. So, I made some phone calls and set up appointments with six different financial advisors over two days.

After two days of meetings, I came away disheartened and disappointed. Most of the advisors I met with were not interested in helping unless we had a few hundred thousand dollars that they could manage. A couple of the advisors cut the meetings short after I had told them we had about $300 in our checking account. Two were kind enough not to appear visibly disappointed when they found out we were not wealthy, but we couldn't afford their services at $200-$300 per hour. All of them ended the conversation by telling me to come back in a few years, and they would be in a better position to help.

That was a key experience that prompted us to write this book. We wanted to create a guide for people in every stage of their careers, from students in school with little to no income to those who have completed their studies and are beginning to reap the rewards of years of hard work. That is why we created Money Over Milkshakes. We wanted to create a casual and comfortable space to discuss all things finance—a space not influenced by advertisers or corporations offering kickbacks to promote their products, just good honest advice. We want this book to be all the advice we never had and didn't know how to find.

This book is written specifically for medical students, residents, and early-career physicians who want to make informed financial decisions for themselves and their families. Although the book is geared towards those in the medical field, the financial tools and resources mentioned are applicable to all. We wrote a book that hits close to our personal experiences, but the basics of personal finance are universal.

How the Book Is Organized

The book is organized into five sections. Our first section is dedicated to those at the beginning of their careers, for pre-medical and medical students alike. The second section is for readers currently in residency. Both sections cover important financial decisions that need to be made in the early stages of your career.

The remaining sections in the book apply to readers at any stage in their career. Sections 3 through 5 will put you in a position to make informed financial decisions with the most helpful financial tools available.

We've also written this book with the following mantra in mind:

SIMPLE, STRAIGHTFORWARD, AND OPINIONATED.

SIMPLE—The financial industry is full of people that will talk over you. Whether the intention is to confuse or impress, you tend to leave these conversations none the wiser. This book makes no assumptions about your prior knowledge of personal finance. We start with basic explanations of the concepts and tools and build from there. Throughout the book, we provide *definitions* when introducing new financial terms.

STRAIGHTFORWARD—Some advisors will make you feel that because of the so-called "complexity" of the investment world, you should throw up your hands and let the professionals handle it. We disagree. The explanations, examples, summaries, and visuals in this book are meant to unpack these financial instruments in a way that will give you control of your finances.

OPINIONATED—We are intentionally opinionated. We'll discuss the products and services we support and those we do not. People are often opinionated in private among our family and friends but take a more impersonal public position. In this book, we invite you to be part of our inner circle; we give you our personal opinions, as well as the experience and research that have led us to those conclusions.

We mention several companies, services, and tools throughout this book. These are our opinions based on our research and personal experiences. Our opinion is not for sale, and therefore we are not paid or sponsored by any company mentioned in the book. This core value also extends to our organization, **Money Over Milkshakes**.

The Path to Financial Freedom

WHAT IS FINANCIAL FREEDOM?

Financial freedom can mean different things to different people. It boils down to the freedom to choose—to choose how you spend your time, to choose what projects you decide to take on, to choose a work-life balance that is most enjoyable to you. When you have reached a point where you can choose whether to work or not, you have reached financial freedom.

Most of us could not get by without a paycheck for a month or two. Financial freedom is having the choice to never receive a paycheck for the rest of your life.

HOW DO YOU ACHIEVE FINANCIAL FREEDOM?

It certainly doesn't just magically happen. Financial freedom isn't something you wake up to on a random Tuesday. Having a good job isn't going to cut it either—even if that job comes with a substantial income. A fat paycheck alone is not enough to achieve financial freedom. You're going to need a plan. That plan needs to be specific and followed by intentional actions. Your plan for financial freedom then guides the everyday financial decisions in your life.

THE PLAN

The academic path to becoming a physician is relatively clear. The education and training required are easy to understand and presented through our education system in a chronological and systematic way.

When it comes to achieving financial freedom, the path tends to be much less clear—but it doesn't have to be. We have worked hard first to provide you with an easy-to-understand pathway to financial freedom. With the plan in place, you can achieve success through organized, actionable steps.

Here's the high-level overview:

1 During your PRE-MED AND MEDICAL SCHOOL years, your focus regarding personal finance should be on understanding your options around student debt and finding opportunities to reduce it. This is what we cover in our first section of the book.

2 In RESIDENCY, the focus shifts to making informed decisions to manage your student debt, preparing for life after residency, and forming healthy financial habits early in your career.

3 In our SETTING YOURSELF UP FOR SUCCESS section, we discuss healthy financial habits that are important to achieving financial freedom. Thoughtful budgeting and a savings plan are two of the topics we dive into. We'll also discuss:

· Non-taxable accounts that will save you money
· Financial decisions around mortgages and real estate
· Using credit cards to your advantage
· Understanding basic tax concepts to lower your taxes

4 In our INVESTING section, I (Nick) share what I've learned after 20 years of investing and talk you through concepts such as *asset allocation* and *portfolio rebalancing*. I'll also discuss an investment strategy that is simple to understand, can save you tens of thousands of dollars over time, and has statistically outperformed 90% of professional money managers over the long term. I also discuss saving and investing options for your children.

5 Our final section, PROTECTING WHAT YOU'VE EARNED AFTER RESIDENCY, covers sheltering your assets from liability, passing on your assets to family through estate planning, and protecting your wealth through life, disability, and umbrella insurance policies.

Asset allocation determines how much of your savings and retirement funds should go towards different investments such as stocks, bonds, and mutual funds.

Portfolio rebalancing is the process of buying or selling your investments to maintain a desired asset allocation.

IS FINANCIAL FREEDOM A REALISTIC GOAL?

This concept of financial freedom may seem unachievable in your current situation. Maybe you're reading this without any money in savings. Or you feel like you're arriving late to the party as far as making smart financial decisions. No matter what stage you are in your career, you can start to improve your financial picture today.

Our approach when taking on a project that may seem overwhelming at first is to take it one step at a time. You may want to read this cover to cover, or you can also consider this an encyclopedia of personal finance topics. Allowing you to pick and choose the subjects that you would like to learn more about. Once you understand the concepts, you can begin to extract value to apply to your own life.

Finally, we'll provide actionable steps throughout the book. You may choose to review the actionable steps in the chapter summaries, or at the end of the book. Take one action item at a time and check them off as you accomplish them. Personal finance education is a continuous journey, and you've chosen a good place to start!

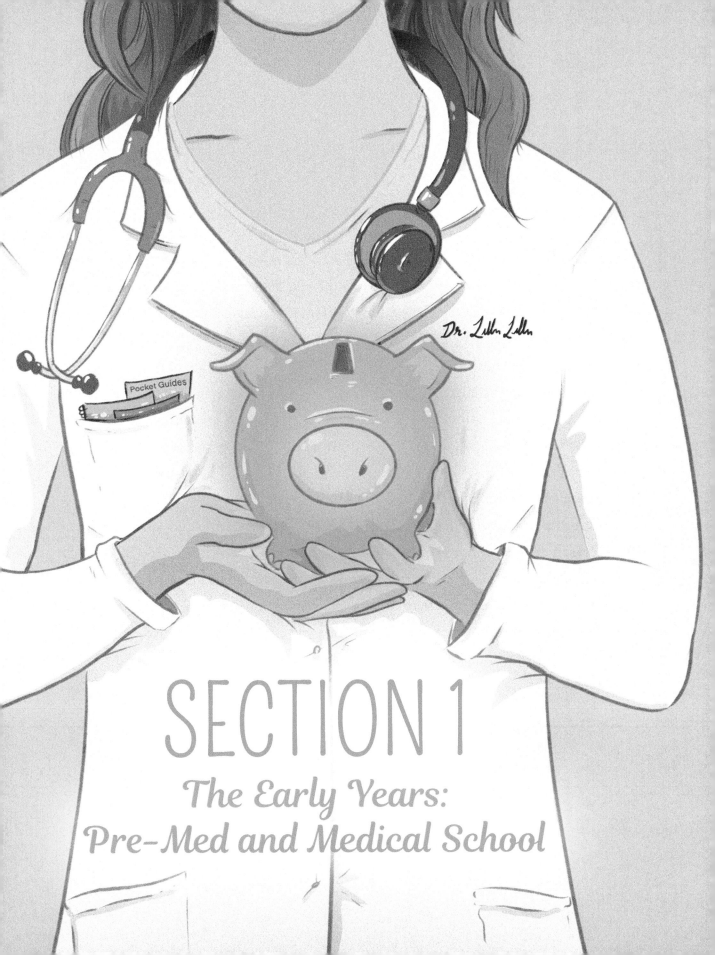

SECTION 1

The Early Years:
Pre-Med and Medical School

It's unfortunate that some of the biggest financial decisions you'll make in your life will be at the earliest part of your career—a time when it's difficult to imagine the needs of your future self. The financial decisions you make during your undergraduate and medical school years will be with you for decades to come.

That's a lot to put on a young student whose passion lies in medicine, not finance. The truth is, the majority of students are ill-equipped to make major financial decisions around debt, loans, and savings. Like many other students graduating from high school, you probably had little to no exposure to personal finance. Teaching personal finance is not often a priority in our education system. If you were lucky, maybe your parents tried to teach you a few things about managing money. Most students are not so lucky.

This section is aimed at giving you a financial head start, arming you with the information necessary to take advantage of low-interest loans, scholarship opportunities, work-study programs, and more. Every $1 of debt you save at this stage in your career is $2 of debt that you have eliminated in the years to come.

As a reminder, if you are currently in residency, you can start the book from our SECTION 2: RESIDENCY. If you're further along in your career as an attending and have a solid plan for your student debt, feel free to start reading from SECTION 3: SETTING YOURSELF UP FOR SUCCESS.

In this section, we will be covering the following:

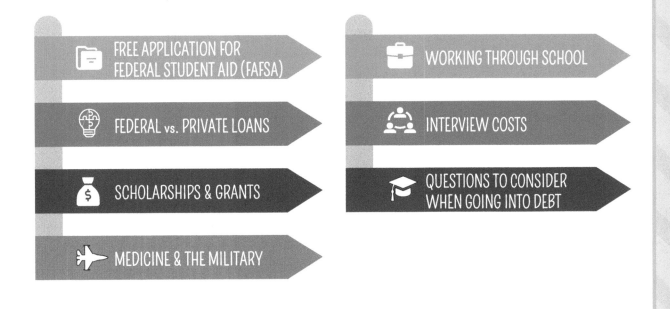

FREE APPLICATION FOR FEDERAL STUDENT AID (FAFSA)

WORKING THROUGH SCHOOL

FEDERAL vs. PRIVATE LOANS

INTERVIEW COSTS

SCHOLARSHIPS & GRANTS

QUESTIONS TO CONSIDER WHEN GOING INTO DEBT

MEDICINE & THE MILITARY

Chapter 1

FREE APPLICATION FOR FEDERAL STUDENT AID (FAFSA)

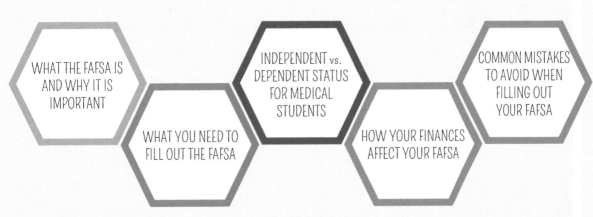

Applying for student aid is often the first major financial choice made by young students. In this chapter, we'll discuss how to apply for financial aid, details to consider, and common mistakes to avoid on the application.

What the FAFSA is and Why it is Important

FAFSA stands for Free Application for Federal Student Aid. This is the application you fill out to apply for financial aid from the federal and state government. Unless you and your family are paying cash for all your classes through undergrad and medical school, you'll want to fill out the FAFSA. Not only is the application necessary for grants and scholarships, but it is also required for federal student loans, many scholarships, and work-study programs.

The application process is open from October 1st through June 30th of every year. Many aid programs are considered on a first-come, first-served basis, so fill out the FAFSA as early as possible. You must fill out a FAFSA for every year you are requesting financial aid.

Don't make the mistake of assuming you won't qualify for aid. In 2018, college students missed out on $2.6 billion of Pell Grants[1] just because they did not fill out their FAFSAs. That was free money—money that would never need to be paid back—that went unclaimed. If you do not qualify for scholarships or grants, you may still be eligible for low-interest student loans.

If you are considering private loans, fill out your FAFSA and apply for federal loans as well to compare whether private or federal loans have the better loan terms. Keep in mind, if you are awarded federal student loans, you do not have to accept the funds, so it only benefits you to apply.

What You Need to Fill Out the FAFSA

The FAFSA is free to fill out and submit. Unless you need translation assistance, you should not be paying someone to fill out the FAFSA for you. Unfortunately, the internet is peppered with companies that will try and convince you to pay them for this service.

All it takes to fill out the FAFSA is some time to gather the documents below and 30-60 minutes sitting in front of a computer. In fact, students can even complete the FAFSA via a convenient mobile app called myStudentAid.

You will need the following information to fill out the form:

- ☐ An FSA ID for both the student and the parent to sign electronically. (If you do not have one, you can create one at studentaid.gov/fsa-id/create-account/account-info)
- ☐ Student's Social Security number
- ☐ Student's driver license number
- ☐ Alien registration number (if you are not a U.S. citizen, go to studentaid.gov/understand-aid/eligibility/requirements/non-us-citizens)
- ☐ Your federal income tax returns for two years prior to the academic year. For example, for the 2021-22 academic school year, you will need your 2019 taxes only. If your financial situation has changed since then, contact the school's financial aid office directly. You can transfer your federal tax return information online into your FAFSA using the IRS Data Retrieval Tool (studentaid.gov/help-center/answers/article/what-is-irs-drt).
- ☐ W2—the tax statement received for your wages from your employer.
- ☐ 1040 form—an IRS tax form used for personal federal income tax returns.
- ☐ Bank statements
- ☐ *Brokerage* statements (for investments such as stocks, bonds, and mutual funds)
- ☐ Records of untaxed income such as welfare benefits, military allowances, veteran benefits, and Social Security payments
- ☐ Records relating to recent circumstances affecting your finances, such as a large amount of medical debt, a death, divorce, or a job loss
- ☐ If you are 25 years or younger, you must be registered with the Selective Service. You can register or verify your status on their website.
- ☐ Title IV Institution Codes for each of the schools you are applying to. Codes can be found at finaid.org/fafsa/tiv/.

Brokerage: an institution that acts as a middleman to connect buyers and sellers of investments such as stocks, bonds, or funds.

Independent vs. Dependent Status for Medical Students

If someone else claims responsibility for you on their tax return (like your parents), you are considered a dependent for tax purposes, regardless of whether you pay for your own expenses. If you are the head of your own household, you are independent. If you are pursuing a master's or doctorate degree, you are considered independent, and your parent's income will not affect your financial aid package. (If you're not certain whether you're a dependent or not, a list of questions to help determine your dependency status can be found at studentaid.gov/apply-for-aid/fafsa/filling-out/dependency.)

If you are a dependent student, you will need all the items in the list above for whoever claims you as a dependent—in most cases, your parent or guardian. If you are independent, you'll only need your own information.

Your Student Aid Report can take up to two or three weeks to arrive after you submit the FAFSA, but in most cases, you'll receive your financial aid results within a week.

How Your Finances Affect your FAFSA

Your responses on the FAFSA will determine your Expected Family Contribution (EFC). This calculation represents how much of your family's resources you are expected to use toward your education without financial aid. The calculation to figure out your financial aid eligibility is as follows:

COST OF ATTENDANCE (COA) – EXPECTED FAMILY CONTRIBUTION (EFC)

=

FINANCIAL NEED

If you would like to get an estimate on how much financial aid you are eligible for, FAFSA has a forecaster tool you can access at fafsa.ed.gov/spa/fafsa4c.

Two main things reduce your financial aid eligibility: income and assets. Income is the money you've made through working, while assets are savings that can be used towards your education. The infographic below breaks these out in detail.

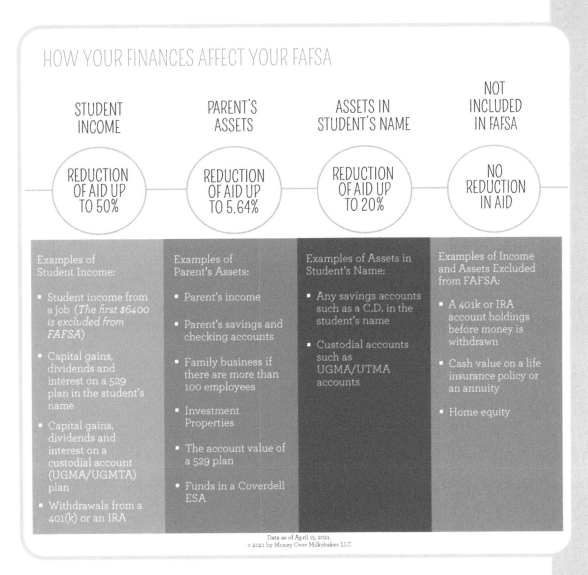

HOW YOUR FINANCES AFFECT YOUR FAFSA

STUDENT INCOME	PARENT'S ASSETS	ASSETS IN STUDENT'S NAME	NOT INCLUDED IN FAFSA
REDUCTION OF AID UP TO 50%	REDUCTION OF AID UP TO 5.64%	REDUCTION OF AID UP TO 20%	NO REDUCTION IN AID

Examples of Student Income:

- Student income from a job (*The first $6400 is excluded from FAFSA*)
- Capital gains, dividends and interest on a 529 plan in the student's name
- Capital gains, dividends and interest on a custodial account (UGMA/UGMTA) plan
- Withdrawals from a 401(k) or an IRA

Examples of Parent's Assets:

- Parent's income
- Parent's savings and checking accounts
- Family business if there are more than 100 employees
- Investment Properties
- The account value of a 529 plan
- Funds in a Coverdell ESA

Examples of Assets in Student's Name:

- Any savings accounts such as a C.D. in the student's name
- Custodial accounts such as UGMA/UTMA accounts

Examples of Income and Assets Excluded from FAFSA:

- A 401k or IRA account holdings before money is withdrawn
- Cash value on a life insurance policy or an annuity
- Home equity

Data as of April 15, 2021.
© 2021 by Money Over Milkshakes LLC

Several years ago, the FAFSA implemented the "prior-prior year" policy, which requires students to use their taxes from 2 years prior. For the 2021-2022 FAFSA, you would need your taxes from 2019. Withdrawals from retirement accounts will not count as income on the FAFSA for two years, so if you can, you should wait until your second semester of your sophomore year before pulling out any money from a 401k or an IRA to maximize your eligibility for financial aid.

SIMPLIFIED NEEDS TEST

If the student's parents' annual adjusted *gross income* (AGI) is less than $50,000 a year or one of your parents is considered a 'dislocated worker' (studentaid.gov/2021/help/parent-dislocated-worker), none of your family's assets are counted against you in your financial aid calculation.

Gross income: the amount of money earned before taxes or other deductions are taken out.

Common Mistakes to Avoid
When Filling Out the FAFSA

PROCRASTINATING. Most aid is on a first-come, first-served basis. You increase your chances of receiving aid the earlier you submit.

ASSUMING YOUR INCOME IS TOO HIGH. Even if you don't qualify for Pell Grants, you may qualify for federal loans.

WAITING TO FILE YOUR FAFSA until your taxes are completed for the current year. FAFSA now requires your taxes from two years prior, so there is no reason to wait.

LIMITING THE NUMBER OF SCHOOLS YOU LIST. If you're at all interested in attending a school, you should list that school. You can list up to 10. Universities cannot see the other schools you have added. If you do not list the school, they will not consider you for grants at that institution.

IF YOUR FINANCIAL SITUATION CHANGES due to medical bills, a reduction in income, or job loss, make sure to update your status using a special circumstance form that you can get from your school's financial aid office.

AVOID TYPOS AND INCORRECT INFORMATION by using the IRS Data Retrieval Tool to automatically upload your most recent tax information. This will save you tons of time.

ENTERING YOUR ADJUSTED GROSS INCOME (AGI) WRONG. AGI is not the same as taxable income. For 2019, your AGI can be found in box 8b on your 1040 or on line 35 on your 1040NR.

USING A TEMPORARY ADDRESS. Use a dependable address that won't change anytime soon. You might list your parent's address if you are unsure.

Chapter 1 Recap
FAFSA

✓ Set an annual calendar reminder for October 1st to submit the FAFSA for every year you plan on receiving aid.

✓ Create an FSA ID for both the student and parents.

✓ To fill out the FAFSA online, go to studentaid. gov/h/apply-for-aid/fafsa or download the MyStudentAid app for Apple devices and Android devices.

✓ If you are male and 25 years or younger, you must be registered with the Selective Service to eligible for financial aid. You can register or verify your status on their website: www.sss.gov.

✓ Gather the Title IV Institution Codes for each of the schools you are applying to. Codes can be found at finaid.org/fafsa/tiv/.

✓ Use the IRS data retrieval tool option in the application to import information from your tax forms and save considerable time.

✓ Use the FAFSA forecaster tool to estimate how much aid you will qualify for.

Scan for a full list of the links and tools listed.

Chapter 2
FEDERAL VS. PRIVATE LOANS

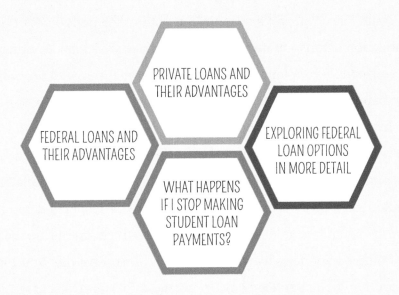

Finding ways to reduce your debt becomes your most important financial responsibility while in school. Selecting the right type of loan is an important part of making that decision. This chapter will compare your federal and private student loan options and the advantages that come with each.

Federal Loans and Their Advantages

Federal loans are offered by the government and administered by the U.S. Department of Education. In general, federal loans have lower interest rates than private loans, and your credit worthiness/score will not directly affect your ability to receive financial aid. If you are exploring student loans, you will want to start with your FAFSA to determine what the government can offer. You do not have to accept the financial aid that is awarded, and you are still free to explore private options.

To begin with, your loans are on a fixed rate, meaning you lock in an interest rate for the life of the loan. The advantage of a fixed rate is in the certainty of knowing there will not be any changes to your rate. There is also no penalty for paying off the loan early, which can happen with a private loan. You will also get a 6-month grace period beginning after graduation before you must start paying back your loan. Another perk to federal loans is your lender will not run a credit check, with the only exception being for Federal PLUS loans for parents and graduates.

In our opinion, the top advantage of federal loans is the support offered on loan payments if you are affected by financial hardship. This is a big one. For example, as I'm writing this, due to the coronavirus pandemic, loan payments on all federal loans will be suspended for at least 17 months, and interest does not accumulate on the loans during that period.

Some additional advantages of federal loans are that you may qualify for the Public Service Loan Forgiveness Program, discussed in detail in CHAPTER 10. When you are in repayment, you have several options to choose from, based on your circumstances.

Private Loans and Their Advantages

These are loans offered by private institutions, such as banks and credit unions. Private loans are not based on financial need but based on your creditworthiness. These institutions will run a credit check, and if you are a dependent student or someone without a strong credit score, you may need the assistance of a co-signer. Loans can have fixed or variable interest rates. You have to be careful with variable rates. The interest rate on your loan is based on the changes in the federal interest rate. Depending on the economy, your rate can change and can be unpredictable over a long period. You could end up with a much higher interest rate than you originally signed on for.

Potential advantages of private loans include qualifying for a higher borrowing limit and, depending on your credit score, possibly qualifying for a lower interest rate. Private loans can also be used as a supplement to fill any financial gaps that federal loans do not cover. Having said that, you'll want to keep in mind that many of the advantages listed for federal loans are the disadvantages to private loans. For instance, there is no guarantee that you'll receive assistance on loan payments during financially challenging times.

If you decide to explore private loan options, you should still complete your FAFSA and apply for federal student loans. While you do not have to accept the loans, you'll want to carry out side-by-side comparisons against your private loan options. At that point, you'll be able to choose which option works best for you.

FEDERAL LOAN ADVANTAGES	PRIVATE LOAN ADVANTAGES
Based on your finances (determined by FAFSA)	Based on your credit worthiness (i.e., credit score)
Support on payments during financial hardships	Lower interest rates with strong credit worthiness
No payments until after you graduate	Fewer limitations on the amount of the loan
6-month grace period on payments after graduation	Variable and fixed interest rate options
Possible loan forgiveness for public service	
Several repayment options to choose from	
No penalty for paying your loan off early	

Here are some questions you should ask when applying for a private loan:

- Can I make pre-payments without being charged a penalty?
- Can I pay off my loan early without penalty?
- Is the interest rate variable or fixed?
- What are the options to defer loans? Can I start payments after graduation?

What Happens If I Stop Making Payments?

If you do not make payments for more than 90 days, your loan servicer will report it to the three national credit bureaus, and your credit score will be negatively affected. If you do not make any payments for more than 270 days, your loan may go into default. This could mean that the entire amount owed would become due immediately. The government could also garnish your wages, and any tax refunds may be withheld and applied towards the student debt. In addition, your school may not release your academic transcript until your federal loan is in good standing.

Bankruptcy is not normally an option for relief, as your student loans will not be forgiven. Now that I have shared all the horrible things that can occur, please note that this can be avoided. If you have federal loans, you can temporarily defer payments on these loans due to financial hardships for up to 3 years. This may not be an option with a private loan.

Exploring Federal Loan Options in More Detail

Federal Direct Loans can be broken down into two categories: Subsidized and Unsubsidized loans. Students who show financial need through their FAFSA application are eligible for subsidized loans. The most important thing to remember about subsidized loans is that the interest does not begin accruing until after you graduate, so you will pay considerably less over time compared to an unsubsidized loan.

With an unsubsidized loan, the interest will begin accruing the moment the loans are dispersed. Interest will start accruing immediately whether you are making payments on the loans or not. Let's say at the end of medical school, you are $200,000 in debt. To keep things simple, let's say half of it is subsidized, and the other half is unsubsidized. Assuming you defer payments through residency, at the end of four years, your subsidized loans will look the same since the government will pay the interest on your loans. That $100,000 won't change. On the other hand, the other $100,000 of debt is in unsubsidized loans. Interest will start accruing immediately. Assuming you're paying 4.30% per year, at the end of four years of residency, you would have added $9,025 to your loan to pay off.

For the 2020-2021 school year, the federal student loan rates have dropped dramatically due to the COVID-19 pandemic and its effects on the economy. Interest rates have been reduced by 1.78%. New Undergraduate Direct loans now have an interest rate of 2.75%, Graduate loans are 4.30%, and Graduate and Parent PLUS loans are 5.30%.[2]

Below is an illustration of the 2020-2021 changes.

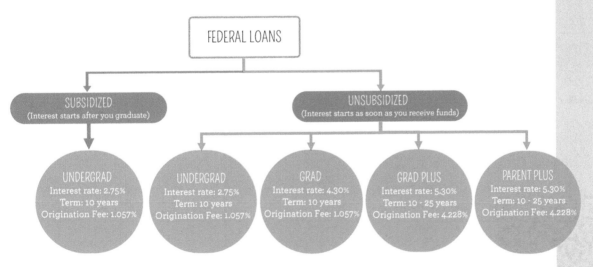

The origination fee is the additional cost for processing the loan. This fee is automatically deducted from your disbursement and must be considered when making comparisons to other loan options.

Chapter 2 Recap

FEDERAL VS. PRIVATE LOANS

✓ Review the pros and cons of private and federal student loans before selecting a loan.

Ask the following questions when applying for a private loan:

✓ Can I make pre-payments without being charged a penalty?

✓ Can I pay off my loan early without a penalty?

✓ Is the interest rate variable or fixed?

✓ What are the options to defer loans during times of financial hardship?

✓ Can I defer payments until after graduation?

Scan for a full list of the links and tools listed.

Chapter 3
SCHOLARSHIPS AND GRANTS

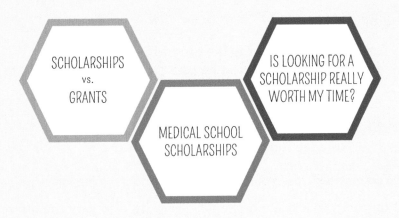

SCHOLARSHIPS
vs.
GRANTS

MEDICAL SCHOOL
SCHOLARSHIPS

IS LOOKING FOR A
SCHOLARSHIP REALLY
WORTH MY TIME?

I wanted to start this chapter by answering the question, "Is researching scholarships really worth the effort?" Filling out scholarship applications and writing essays takes a lot of time and energy. Many students worry about putting in a lot of effort only to receive very little in return.

Here is a scenario to consider. Let's assume after 40 hours of researching and applying for scholarships, and you are awarded $2,000. That might not seem like much. You've likely heard of someone who was awarded $10,000 or $20,000 in scholarships, making smaller awards feel less attractive. However, spending 40 hours on researching and applying for scholarships and being awarded $2,000 gives you a rate of return of $50/hour—a much better rate than many of us have ever made professionally. This makes even the most modest awards well worth your time.

Scholarship vs. Grants

Scholarships and grants support a student's education by granting the student aid (money) based on their need or achievements. Unlike a loan, scholarships and grants are money that the student does not have to repay. Exceptions to this usually come from not honoring the scholarship agreement by:

- Withdrawing from the program early
- Changing your student status from full-time to part-time
- Receiving other scholarships or grants that reduce your need for financial aid
- Not meeting the required GPA

You may also lose your scholarship if you get arrested or present yourself on social media in an offensive way. It's also very important to read all the terms within the agreement. When in doubt, ask your scholarship provider for clarity on the terms and conditions of your scholarship.

Grants are generally based solely on your financial need, while scholarships can be based on:

- Financial need
- Achievements in academics, sports, music, arts, and other areas
- Minority status related to sex, ethnicity, religion, national origin, etc.

It's important to note that medical students are not eligible for either Pell Grants or subsidized loans. Only students in undergrad are eligible.

Medical students are eligible for other grants through programs such as:[3]

- The National Institute of General Medical Sciences (NIGMS) for students interested in pursuing careers in clinical and biomedical research

- The American Association of University Women (AAUW) for female students of color

- The Ford Foundation

- And collegegrants.org has an additional 15 grants for medical students to consider

Medical School Scholarships

It goes without saying that your primary objective in medical school is the successful completion of your education. We would argue that finding ways to reduce your student debt should be your secondary objective. Applying for scholarships is time well spent and an effective way to reduce student debt. In this chapter, we've included some resources on scholarships to support your personal finance objective of reducing your debt.

Start your scholarship search with compilation websites like Fastweb, which has compiled over 25 medical school and pre-med scholarships to consider with direct links for applications. Scholarships.com also provides a list of medical scholarships to review and apply for.

We've listed a few scholarships below that offer $5,000 or more to medical students:

- Physicians of Tomorrow Scholarship (www.ama-assn.org/about/awards/physicians-tomorrow-awards)
- Edith Seville Coale Scholarship (www.zontawashingtondc.org/scholarship-edith-seville-coale-medical.html)
- The Herbert W. Nickens Medical Student Scholarships (www.aamc.org/what-we-do/aamc-awards/nickens-medical-student-scholarships)
- Tylenol Future Care Scholarship (www.tylenol.com/news/scholarship)
- Diverse Medical Scholars Program (nmfonline.org/about-our-scholarships-and-awards/service-learning-programs/united-health-foundationnmf-diverse-medical-scholars-program)
- International Guest Scholarship (www.facs.org/member-services/scholarships/international/igs)

Some medical schools are taking a progressive approach by offering free or substantially discounted tuition to their students. Here is a list of a few programs taking this approach:

- NYU School of Medicine (med.nyu.edu/education)

- Washington University School of Medicine (medicine.wustl.edu/education/financial-support/)

- Cornell Medical School (medicaleducation.weill.cornell.edu/admissions/costs-aid)

- Cleveland Clinic Lerner College of Medicine (portals.clevelandclinic.org/cclcm/Tuition-Financial-Aid)

Additionally, be sure to check local organizations for scholarship opportunities. Community foundations or businesses may offer scholarships to medical students. If you're considering practicing in a rural area, you should also explore state-sponsored programs. On a personal note, a colleague had agreed to return to her rural hometown and, in return, was provided with a monthly stipend of around $2,000 through medical school and residency. Her commitment involved working at a rural hospital for at least four years.

> ## ONE RULE OF THUMB:
> If a scholarship application costs money to apply, it's probably a scam. Ask questions to the scholarship provider should you have any doubts.

Also, be sure to connect with your academic counselor. Scholarship providers often contact academic counselors regarding scholarship opportunities, so counselors will pass along scholarship opportunities if they believe that you are a good fit.

SCHOLARSHIPS AND GRANTS

✓ College students miss out on billions of dollars in Pell Grants each year. Don't assume you won't qualify. Just apply!

✓ When you are not earning income, your financial responsibility is to reduce your student debt as much as possible.

✓ Apply for medical school scholarships, such as those on the list compiled by Fastweb or the list gathered by Scholarships.com.

✓ Since scholarships and grants are awarded on a first-come, first-served basis, add a calendar reminder on the deadlines for the scholarships you plan to apply for.

✓ Set up a meeting with your academic counselor or financial aid office to discuss local scholarship opportunities.

Scan for a full list of the links and tools listed.

Chapter 4

MEDICINE AND THE MILITARY

Although we did not serve in the military, many of our colleagues did. Through our research and support working with medical professionals that have served in the military, we created this chapter to highlight their experiences with military medicine. The requirements for scholarships and service for each branch of the military will vary slightly; however, the general benefits and drawbacks are similar.

Military Medicine Basics

Whether you are considering support from the military for undergrad, medical school, or residency, the general rule is that every year you receive financial support is a year you will owe in military service.

If you are considering financial support from the military in medical school, you can either apply to the Uniformed Services University[4] in Bethesda, Maryland, or attend a civilian medical school and apply for the Health Professions Scholarship Program (HPSP).

MEDICAL SCHOOL OPTIONS

UNIFORMED SERVICES UNIVERSITY MEDICAL SCHOOL

- Monthly salary of $3,200
- Housing allowance up to $2,300 per month
- No medical school debt
- You will owe the military 7 years of service

CIVILIAN MEDICAL SCHOOL WITH HPSP AID

- Monthly salary of $2,300
- No medical school debt
- You may need a cost-of-living loan due to the lower monthly salary
- You will owe the military 4 years of service

As the illustration shows, there is a higher salary associated with attending the Uniformed Services University of the Health Sciences. Your starting rank is O-1. This is a 2nd lieutenant in the Army and Air Force and an ensign in the Navy or Public Health Service.

If you do not have prior military service, your annual base pay during medical school is approximately $40,000/year. Your pay increases with additional years of military service, and the base pay increases 2-3% yearly to account for *inflation*. You will also enjoy a substantial housing allowance of around $2,300 per month as an O-1. If you have some roommates, you can do pretty well, with extra cash to spare.

> *Inflation:* the decreased purchasing value of money over time. Think of the difference in costs to go to the movie theater 75 years ago compared to now.

Since the Uniformed Services University option costs the military more than a civilian medical school, this will result in seven years of required military service. On the other hand, a non-military medical school has a set stipend of around $2,300 a month (as of 2020) through the Health Professions Scholarship Program and requires a year of service for every year of medical school.

In addition to the three branches of the military, medical students from the U.S. Public Health Service also attend the university.

Health Professions Scholarship Program

This is the scholarship program offered to those attending a civilian medical school. This scholarship is available to physicians (M.D. or D.O.), dentists, physician's assistants, optometrists, psychologists, nurse practitioners, pharmacists, and veterinarians. This program is available for service in the Army, Navy, and Air Force. Army and Air Force offer one- to four-year scholarships, while the Navy offers three and four-year scholarships.

Military Residency

Once you graduate medical school, you achieve the pay grade of O-3, the rank of captain in the Army and Air Force, and the rank of lieutenant in the Navy and Public Health Service.

If you complete your residency in a military facility, you will be paid at that rank. For a captain in the Army, that is just shy of $53,000 a year.[5] For comparison, a regular resident's salary can range from $40,000 to $65,000, depending on where the residency is located. In addition to base pay, the resident will receive bonus pay, which can range from $20,000 to $60,000, depending on the medical specialty.

For an HPSP recipient, the commitment is four years of military service *after* residency is completed. So if you have just completed a three-year family residency, you'll have an additional four years on your commitment. If you are working at a military hospital, your time there will count as years of service required, so no additional military service is required if you complete your residency at a military hospital.

General Pros for Military Medicine

BEING PART OF SOMETHING GREATER THAN YOURSELF

The military provides you with an opportunity to serve your country, first and foremost. We emphasize this to begin with since every military physician we spoke to said you should not join the military for the financial perks alone. There must be something more there—a sense of pride and duty.

LITTLE TO NO STUDENT DEBT

To most, this is an extremely attractive perk—the opportunity to finish medical school without any student debt. Once you serve in the military, your GI Bill benefits will pay for additional degrees, or those benefits can often be passed on to your children to pay for college. One of the physicians we interviewed received three master's degrees with essentially no out-of-pocket costs using the GI Bill. Another physician had the military pay for their undergrad degree, had served four years in the military, and subsequently used their GI Bill to pay for medical school. In other words, undergrad and medical school were paid for with a four-year commitment.

FINANCIAL AID WHILE IN SCHOOL

While you're in school, you're receiving a monthly stipend of $2,000 to $3,000, depending on your rank and experience. In addition, your books, equipment, and other fees are paid for. Another financial incentive can come in the form of a sign-on bonus. In some cases, you may receive a sign-on bonus of up to $20,000. This can be considerably more if joining as a residency-trained physician. Your local recruiter can provide the exact amount.

HEALTHCARE AND TAX BENEFITS

A little-known fact is that 25% to 30% of your military income is not taxable. That is thousands of dollars saved that go into your pocket and can be used for investment opportunities. You will also save a considerable amount on healthcare-related expenses. The military offers exceptionally inexpensive medical, dental, and life insurance coverage for you and your family. With the average cost per month for family health insurance being $1,152,[6] that translates into a significant saving opportunity.

RETIREMENT BENEFITS

Military retirement is attractive. Depending on when you entered into service, after 20 years of service, you will receive 40% to 50% of your most recent base pay. We are oversimplifying here, but the longer you serve in the military, the higher your percentage of base pay will be in retirement. Additional information on military pay can be found at militarypay.defense.gov.

The Thrift Savings Plan (TSP) is the retirement plan for federal employees very similar to a 401(k). Like a 401(k) in 2020, you're able to contribute up to $19,500 a year. The military will match 1% of your base pay whether you contribute money or not. On top of that, after two years of service, the military will match an additional 4% for a total match of 5% of your base pay. Your *vesting period* will vary. Essentially it can take two to three years of service for that money to become available to you in your retirement.

Vesting period: the time a person must wait to fully own assets such as company stock or employer match retirement benefits.

OTHER BENEFITS

Here some additional benefits to consider:

- Guaranteed residency spot through the military match, although not necessarily in the specialty of your choosing
- 30 days of PTO annually
- Malpractice coverage is provided for active-duty physicians
- Opportunity to travel
- Military training opportunities such as being a flight med, dive med, battalion surgeon, or an MD on an aircraft carrier

General Cons for Military Medicine

TRADING MONEY FOR TIME

The most important consideration to understand is that you are trading money for time. Time in service to the military. As mentioned, the general rule of thumb is that you will owe a year of service for every year of school paid for by the military. This of course can vary depending on whether you choose the military or a civilian medical school.

TRADING MONEY FOR CONTROL

In addition to owing time, you will also have to give up control of a certain level of freedom. The military will limit or even select where you practice medicine while in service. Permission will need to be granted to go home or fly somewhere with family or friends. You cannot simply just purchase a plane ticket while you are in service.

DEPLOYMENT

Although you cannot be deployed while in medical school, residency or fellowship, you should expect to be deployed during active duty. Deployment is likely and can include multiple deployments for several months.

ACTIVE SERVICE

Students will be required to serve 45 days of active duty training each year. You will also be required to meet strict physical standards and measures of physical fitness. Diabetes, asthma, arthritis, anxiety, depression, ADHD, and numerous other medical conditions can all be disqualifying.

MILITARY RESIDENCY

Students must apply to both the military and civilian residency match programs. Students that match with a military residency program must accept these positions if they are offered. If you do not match with a military residency program, you are authorized to take part in the civilian match. If you do not match or have chosen a competitive specialty, you may be required to take a transitional/preliminary year and apply the following year.

MILITARY PAY AFTER RESIDENCY

While you are in military service, you get paid at the level of your military rank. Certainly, this would be an advantage during medical school and residency. However, after residency, your pay tends to be considerably less than your civilian counterparts. This can be as much as a third of your non-military counterpart's salary.

Pursuing military medicine should not be a purely financial decision. There are some terrific benefits, but there is a hefty commitment and sacrifice associated with them. If you are interested in serving your country, there are some great opportunities through the military. Find additional information on military medicine opportunities at these websites:

www.goarmy.com/amedd/
education/hpsp.html

www.airforce.com/careers/specialty-
careers/healthcare/careers/doctor

www.navy.com/what-to-expect/
education-opportunities

MEDICINE AND THE MILITARY

✓ Graduating with little to no student debt, receiving a monthly stipend while in school, and considerable healthcare and retirement benefits are a few of the advantages to practicing medicine in the military.

✓ For these benefits, you will owe time in service to the military. You will give up control on some decisions, such as where you will practice. Expect to be deployed.

✓ Speak with a colleague or peer that has first-hand experience practicing medicine in the military. If you do not know anyone directly, LinkedIn is full of military physicians happy to answer your questions.

✓ If you are interested in learning more about practicing medicine in the military, you can get started by going to the websites for the U.S. Army, U.S. Air Force, and U.S. Navy.

Scan for a full list of the links and tools listed.

Chapter 5
WORKING THROUGH SCHOOL

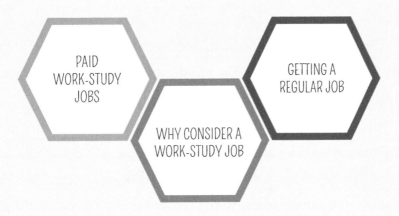

Eight to ten years can pass between the time you initially take out undergraduate loans and the time you start to pay back those loans. The interest on these loans can easily add thousands of dollars to your original loan amount. That makes this period particularly valuable to your future financial picture. Working through school can be an opportunity to gain valuable work experience while significantly reducing your burden of debt.

Paid Work–Study Jobs

(AMANDA) I took advantage of a paid work-study program as an undergraduate. I found the flexibility to work on campus in a position that worked around my studies to be a great fit for me at the time. You may also find a work-study opportunity to be a great fit to reduce your student debt while focusing on your studies.

Paid work-study jobs are offered through the federal government for both graduate and undergraduate students. Your paycheck is subsidized by the federal government, meaning they pay for a portion of your work-study income, and your employer pays the remainder.

There is a section in the FAFSA that asks whether you want to be considered for work-study programs. Always select yes; this doesn't mean you have to accept a position, but it will give you the option to apply for positions during the school year.

The work-study program is based on financial need, and funds are limited. This program is often on a first-come, first-served basis for both the funds and the positions available at the school.

If you are successful in qualifying, you will earn at least the federal minimum wage. The school you are attending will determine how much you will make and how many hours per week you work. If you do qualify for work-study, that doesn't guarantee a position. You will still need to find an employer and go through a normal process of interviewing and hiring as you would for any other job.

Why Consider a Work-Study Job

- If you are enrolled in 6 or more credit hours and do work-study on campus, your income is taxable, but you are exempt from Social Security and Medicare taxes, which make up 7.3% of your earnings. If you're making $300 a week, that is an extra $22 in your pocket every week.
- The money you earn from work-study programs is not included in your financial aid calculation for the FAFSA.
- When the school goes on break, so does your work-study program.
- Work-study jobs are more likely to be understanding of your academic responsibilities and give you time to study.

- These jobs can be both on-campus or off-campus.
- If you are awarded work-study funds, you do not have to accept the award. If you find a better alternative, you can reject the award.

Getting a Regular Job

There are on- and off-campus jobs that are not part of the work-study program. Your financial aid office will let you know what options are out there for on-campus employment. Unlike a work-study job, you are not limited by how much you can make in a year or how many hours you can work.

Remember that earning money can affect your financial aid. Students can earn up to $6,970 for the 2021-2022 school year before their financial aid will be affected. Half of every dollar after the $6,970 mark will be counted towards your expected family contribution.

For example, let's say as a student, you made $20,000 in a year. If you subtract the $6,970 of income that will not affect your FAFSA, then you are left with $13,030. Since student income affects your FAFSA by 50%, your financial aid would be reduced by $6,515 in this case. (Our table in Chapter 1 breaks down the effect different income will have on the FAFSA.)

When choosing a work-through-college job, flipping burgers or mowing lawns is fine. (Money is money, right?) But if you can, choose a job that gives you insight into the medical industry. Many require certification of some type. However, many of these programs may be low to no-cost if you go through your local community college. These are positions at hospitals, outpatient clinics, medical research centers, and universities, and many may offer tuition assistance.

- Transcriptionist (requires knowledge of medical terminology)
- Pharmacy Technician
- Emergency Medical Technician (EMT)
- Medical Scribe
- Medical Assistant
- Certified Nursing Assistant (CNA)

If you don't get into the medical field right away, other off-campus jobs can offer tuition assistance, which is another perk worth pursuing. We've put together a list of general employers that offer competitive tuition reimbursement programs to help pay for college.

EMPLOYERS WITH TUITION ASSISTANCE[7]

01 STARBUCKS
100% tuition paid for bachelor's degree through Arizona State University's online program

02 AT&T
$5,250 per calendar year after 6 months of employment

03 VERIZON
Full-time employees receive up $8,000 per year (part-time employees receive $4,000) for associate, bachelor's, or MBA programs; eligible on day one of employment

04 UPS
$5,250k per calendar year for tuition; eligible on day one

05 AMAZON
Pre-pays 95% of tuition and textbooks for associates degrees in high-demand occupations like nursing, medical lab tech, physician assistants, and physical therapist assistants; eligible after 1 year of employment

06 TARGET
$3000 to $5000, depending the type of program (undergrad, grad, or MBA)

07 HOME DEPOT
$1,500 to $5,000 per year for part-time to salaried employees on first day of employment

08 CHICK-FIL-A
5 to 20% off tuition and books at over 100 universities

09 CHIPOTLE
$5,250 per year for undergraduate and graduate degrees

10 ANTHEM
Up to $5,000 for full-time and $2,500 for part-time employees after 6 months of employment

Some hospitals in smaller towns will help pay for undergrad and medical school if you agree to come back and work once you finish residency.

Whether you work on or off-campus, part-time or full-time, the goal is to reduce the amount of money you have to borrow. Borrowing the maximum amount of student loans available in the hopes that everything will work out is not a healthy financial strategy. These decisions around income and debt will be with you for years to come.

Chapter 5 Recap

WORKING THROUGH SCHOOL

✓ Check the work-study option on your FAFSA if you'd like to be considered for these jobs.

✓ Work-study jobs are not included in your financial aid calculation, and they are exempt from Social Security and Medicare taxes, which add up to 7.3%.

✓ Getting a job while in school is a great way to reduce your student debt.

✓ For 2021, students can earn up to $6,970 before student income affects their financial aid calculation. Additional student income will reduce aid by 50% of every dollar earned.

✓ Consider employers that offer tuition reimbursement to reduce your college expenses.

Scan for a full list of the links and tools listed.

Chapter 6
APPLICATION & INTERVIEW COSTS

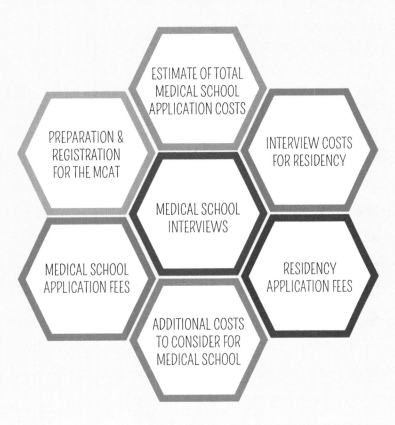

The cost of applying to medical school can come as a shock. The expenses of travel, lodging, and test preparation add up for college students. Many students apply to fewer medical schools than anticipated, while others find themselves in stressful financial situations due to these unexpected costs. We hope the information below will encourage you to begin planning early so that you can remain focused on preparing for the MCAT and interviews rather than on how to pay for flights to medical school interviews.

Due to the COVID-19 pandemic, the AAMC recommended that all medical school and residency interviews be conducted virtually in 2020. It is difficult to imagine returning to in-person interviews in the coming years considering the financial benefits to both the students and the institutions. At this point, you may only need to purchase a suit from the waist up! However, if institutions resume in-person interviews, this guide will help provide the breakdown of costs.

Preparation & Registration for the MCAT[8]

The registration fee for the MCAT is $320 (or $375 for late registration). The tools and services available for preparation can be expensive. The costs incurred will depend on what company you choose and whether you are purchasing materials online or attending an in-person prep course. Using Kaplan as an example, the self-paced online course is offered for $1,599, while both their live online and in-person courses are available for $2,299.

There are hundreds of MCAT testing locations to choose from (**students-residents.aamc.org/register-mcat-exam/register-mcat-exam**). If there is no one in your area, stay at a nearby hotel the night before the test. Ensure you are well-rested and not stressed over the uncertainty of traffic delays on the day of testing.

You may incur the following expenses if you have to travel for testing:

- Fill up your gas tank: $40

- Stay the night in a hotel: $120

- A couple of meals on the road: $60

You can reduce these costs by staying with a friend or family member or packing your own food.

Medical School Application Fees

Most people in the US will apply to at least 15-20 medical schools. Application fees will begin with access to the Medical School Admission Requirements (MSAR), which is $28 for a one-year subscription. The MSAR provides up-to-date profiles on every MD and LCME accredited medical school in the U.S. and Canada.

Most students will apply to medical schools through the American Medical College Application Service (AMCAS). The processing fee for 2020 is $170 for your first medical school selection and $40 for each additional medical school application.

Once you submit your first round of applications, the schools may ask you to submit a secondary application. These secondary application fees can range from $50 to $100, depending on the school.

For students applying to osteopathic medical schools, applications can be filed through the American Association of Colleges of Osteopathic Medicine Application Service (AACOMAS). The fee is $197 for the first application and $48 for every additional application.[9]

Medical schools require an official transcript from your undergraduate college/university. The fees for transcripts normally range from $10 to $20 for each copy.

Medical School Interviews

The icing on this terribly expensive cake is the medical school interview. These are often the most expensive part of the process because of the travel costs involved. There are too many variables to create a meaningful average for the number of interviews you can expect, so we'll assume three interviews on average. Travel and hotel expenses can be anywhere between $300 to $1000 per school, depending on whether you are flying or driving to interviews.

Additional Costs to Consider for Medical School

INTERVIEW APPAREL. If you do not already own a suit, you will need to purchase one. A suit can cost between $200 to $500. Remember, you can use the same suit for multiple interviews—also, there is no shame in borrowing a suit from a friend, as long as it fits well.

DEPOSIT. Once you have been accepted, medical schools usually require a deposit to hold your spot. The deposit can range from $100 to $500.

Estimate of Total Medical School Application Costs

We have compiled the costs in the table below. We are assuming the student will apply to 15 programs, interview at 3 schools, and put down an acceptance deposit at 2 locations while making their final decision.

	COST
MCAT REGISTRATION	$320
MCAT PREP COURSE	$2,000
ACCESS TO MSAR	$28
AMCAS APPLICATION FEES	$730
SUIT FOR INTERVIEW	$300
TRAVEL EXPENSES ($500/SCHOOL)	$1,500
ACCEPTANCE DEPOSIT	$100
	$4,978

Sadly, the estimated total of $4,978 is on the low end. The total increases to $10,000 if you choose to take the in-person MCAT prep course ($2,299), and you fly to several of your interviews. Adjustments like these can easily double your medical school application expenses.

AAMC'S FEE ASSISTANCE PROGRAM

AAMC offers a fee assistance program[10] to help pay the application costs. If you qualify for the fee assistance program, it comes with some nice perks, such as official MCAT prep products (a $268 value). It also waives the application fees for AMCAS, which is $730 if you apply to 15 programs.

In order to qualify, you will need to put down your parent's financial information regardless of whether you are financially independent. In 2020, you will qualify if your 2019 total family income is 400% or less than the 2019 national poverty level. The table below will help you determine whether you qualify for assistance.

2020 POVERTY GUIDELINES FOR THE 48 CONTIGUOUS UNITED STATES AND THE DISTRICT OF COLUMBIA

PERSONS IN FAMILY/HOUSEHOLD	POVERTY GUIDELINE	Family Income Not To Exceed for Fee Assistance
1	$12,760	$51,040
2	$17,240	$68,960
3	$21,720	$86,880
4	$26,200	$104,800
5	$30,680	$122,720
6	$35,160	$140,640
7	$39,640	$158,560
8	$44,120	$176,480

*For families/households with more than 8 persons, add $4,480 for each additional person.

Interview Costs for Residency

Once you have completed medical school, you need to dust off that suit, put on that smile, and prepare for residency interviews.

According to the 2014 AMA national survey[11] of 1,000 fourth-year medical students, on average, the students applied to 36 programs and ended up interviewing at 12 locations. The survey shows some interesting differences between costs depending on the specialty chosen. For example, nearly 75% of family resident applicants spent less than $3,000, while nearly 50% of applicants for surgery residencies spent $4,000 or more, with close to 20% of that group spending more than $7,000!

Residency Application Fees

Applications for residencies are submitted through the Electronic Residency Application Service (ERAS: apps.aamc.org/myeras-web). The fees follow the stair-step cost structure shown below.

PROGRAMS PER SPECIALTY	APPLICATION FEES
Up to 10	$99
11 to 20	$15 each
21 to 30	$19 each
31 or more	$26 each

So, if we are still assuming an average of 36 applications from earlier, here is the breakdown.

THE FIRST 10 PROGRAMS = $99 +
                        +$15 EACH FOR THE NEXT 10 PROGRAMS
                        +$19 EACH FOR THE NEXT 10 PROGRAMS
                        +$26 EACH FOR THE NEXT 6 PROGRAMS
                        = $595

For each application, you'll need to send a copy of your MCAT score. There is a one-time fee for exam score reporting of $80 for your USMLE or COMLEX-USA transcript.

Your travel costs will depend on how many programs you apply to and how close they are to home. If you assume a combination of both flying and driving to interviews, estimate around $300 in travel and accommodation expenses per interview.

You could dust off that suit from your medical school interviews or estimate $200-$500 for a new one.

In February, once you are done with interviews, you will rank the programs through the National Resident Matching Program for most specialties. The standard registration fee is $85 to rank up to 20 programs (www.nrmp.org/match-fees). In the unlikely situation, you chose to interview at more than 20 programs, it is an additional $30 per program for ranking.[12]

Neurosurgery, ophthalmology, and plastic surgery students will use the San Francisco Residency and Fellowship Match Services for ranking their residency programs. The fee is a straightforward $100.

For urology, program matching services will be completed through the American Urological Association (AUA) and will cost you $75 for registration.

Military residencies are managed through the Joint Service Graduate Medical Education Selection Board (JSGMESB). Students in the Health Professions Scholarship Program and at the Uniformed Services University of Health Sciences will use this. Applicants still use ERAS for civilian programs.

Here is a summary of the costs to expect for residency applications and interviews. We are assuming that the student is applying to 36 programs and interviewing at 12 schools.

ITEM	COST
Electronic Residency Application Service (ERAS)	$595
USMLE/COMLEX-USA Transcript	$80
Suit for interview	$300
Travel expenses for interview ($500/school)	$3,600
National Resident Matching Program (NRMP)	$80
ESTIMATED TOTAL	$4,655

Like medical school interviews, your travel costs could be significantly higher if you fly to most of your interviews. Some students get through residency interviews on a smaller budget, but we want to emphasize the importance of preparing for the expenses beforehand so they don't sneak up on you or cause you more financial pain.

REDUCING RESIDENCY INTERVIEW COSTS

01 START SAVING

Open a high-interest savings account for the sole purpose of interview costs. You can add a separate account to your existing online bank account or utilize a savings app and create a bucket specifically for this purpose. Saving up early will allow you to focus on the interview rather than how you pay for interviewing expenses.

02 LOGISTICS

Driving rather than flying (when possible) will save you quite a bit of money. If you're driving a junker and unsure if your car can manage the trip, renting a car may still be cheaper than flying. Reduce your travel costs by staying with friends or family during interviews. Try to organize the interviews to group them geographically and around the same time; aim to makeone long trip instead of several.

03 IT NEVER HURTS TO ASK

Some programs offer opportunities to stay with residents. Ask what options the program offers to reduce cost during interviews; the answer may pleasantly surprise you. Because ofthe recent pandemic, schools are becoming more open to video conferencing. Don't be afraid to ask if that is an option at the school you are applying to.

04 USING A CREDIT CARD

Consider taking advantage of credit card rewards, which can provide cash back or travel points. Make sure you know what the interest rate is after the grace period is over.

Chapter 6 Recap

APPLICATION & INTERVIEW COSTS

✓ In 2020, most interviews went remote due to COVID. Expect this to become more common. Ask if this is an option at the schools you apply to.

✓ Traditionally, you can expect registration and application fees, travel, and interview costs of $500 to $1500 per medical school.

✓ AAMC offers a fee assistance program if your family's income meets their requirements.

✓ Traditionally, you can expect total costs of $2,000 to $8,000 for residency interviews, with travel being your largest expense.

✓ Start now by opening up a savings account specifically for the purpose of saving for interview costs.

✓ Do not place interview costs on a credit card with a hefty interest rate of 20% or more if you cannot pay the balance off within one payment cycle.

Scan for a full list of the links and tools listed.

Chapter 7

QUESTIONS TO CONSIDER WHEN GOING INTO DEBT

DEBT-TO-INCOME RATIO

CALCULATING DEBT IN THE EQUATION

CALCULATING INCOME IN THE EQUATION

There's student debt, and then there's medical student debt. According to educationdata.org, the average amount of student loan debt was $32,731 in 2020.[13] Compare that with AAMC's 2020 medical student debt, which averaged at around $200,000 per student.[14] The costs of a medical education today is staggering. Many of us fall into the trap of believing that our debt is not much of a concern since a considerable income awaits us after residency. That kind of thinking can be costly. It can result in students making poor decisions around their debt early in their career that they will come to regret. Understanding your debt-to-income ratio will help you in formulating an acceptable debt strategy.

Debt-to-Income Ratio

It's important to ensure that you are striking a good balance between your debt and income. Even physicians can live paycheck to paycheck if their debt is poorly managed. Your debt-to-income ratio will help you understand your ability to manage debt payments in the future. Lenders use this ratio to help determine your eligibility for home, auto, and personal loans.

Your debt-to-income ratio is the total amount of debt divided by your income. For those still in school, you will estimate the amount of debt you are likely to incur through undergrad and medical school divided by your expected income after residency. For budgeting purposes, it's more helpful to look at this ratio on a monthly basis. The lower the number, the better.

For example, for someone with an annual income of $200,000, this would equate to a monthly income of $16,667. Let us also assume monthly student debt payments of $3,452. The debt-to-income ratio in this example would be .207, or 20.7%. That means the 20.7% of your income would need to go towards paying back your student debt. For an accurate picture, you should include all your debt obligations, such as a mortgage or other loans.

As that percentage increases, your financial burden becomes heavier, and a larger portion of your salary will need to go to paying off your debt. In this chapter, we'll give you the tools to help you calculate your own expected debt-to-income ratio.

Calculating Debt in the Equation

The first step is to understand and appreciate how much debt you will have after residency. The AAMC's most recent Tuition and Student Fees Report[15] does a wonderful job of breaking down tuition, fees, and health insurance cost for each medical program. The spreadsheet not only provides the fee breakdown for over 150 medical programs, but also provides the difference in cost at public and private institutions for both residents and non-residents. Here is a summary of the data for the 2019-2020 school year for first-year medical students.

TUITION AND STUDENT FEES FOR FIRST-YEAR STUDENTS
Summary Statistics for Academic Years 2012-2013 through 2019-2020
AAMC Tuition and Student Fees Questionnaire
Data as of February 2020

ACADEMIC YEAR	COST TYPE	OWNERSHIP TYPE	RESIDENCE STATUS	MINIMUM COST	MEDIAN COST	MAXIMUM COST	AVERAGE COST
2019-2020	Tuition, Fees, and Health Insurance	Public	Resident	$0	$39,149	$56,522	$37,556
2019-2020	Tuition, Fees, and Health Insurance	Private	Resident	$27,633	$62,948	$71,042	$60,665
2019-2020	Tuition, Fees, and Health Insurance	Public	Nonresident	$0	$64,765	$99,622	$61,858
2019-2020	Tuition, Fees, and Health Insurance	Private	Nonresident	$37,165	$63,088	$71,042	$62,230

At most schools, you are looking at approximately $60,000/year in tuition, fees, and health insurance unless you attend a public institution as an in-state resident, which can save you around $20,000/year. Choosing an in-state medical school to reduce your student debt is definitely something to consider. If you are already in medical school or have been accepted to a program, you can use the link above to look up your specific program to get a more detailed estimate.

> ### KEEP IN MIND:
> *Your student debt does not fluctuate based on specialty.*

Your debt is primarily incurred in undergrad and medical school before your residency. A general rule of thumb is to keep your student loan debt below your expected annual salary after you complete your residency. So, if you have $240,000 in student debt, ideally, you want to make the equivalent in annual compensation.

Many experts suggest limiting your student loan payments to 8-10% of your monthly income to break this down for your monthly budget. So, if your annual salary as an attending is $240,000, this equates to $20,000 per month, you want to limit your student loan payments to $2,000 per month. We go into a lot more detail on repayment plans in our chapter on STUDENT DEBT REPAYMENT OPTIONS, but for illustrative purposes, we went with the 10-year standard repayment plan to show what you can expect to pay monthly on your student debt.

EXPECTED MONTHLY PAYMENTS ON A STANDARD 10-YEAR LOAN WITH A FIXED INTEREST RATE OF 6.8%

STUDENT DEBT OWED	MONTHLY DEBT PAYMENT
$50,000	$575
$100,000	$1,152
$200,000	$2,302
$300,000	$3,452
$400,000	$4,604
$500,000	$5,754

Do the monthly payment amounts make your jaw drop? It did for us. The amount we would be paying every month on our loans as an attending was more than we both made in an entire month during residency!

Note that the interest rate shown above (6.8%) is more relevant for those that have accumulated student debt pre-pandemic. There has been a substantial reduction in interest rates for those taking out student debt for the 2020-2021 school year. As of the beginning of 2021, the Federal Stafford loans now have a fixed interest rate of 2.75%, Perkins loans have a fixed interest rate of 5%, and Federal PLUS loans have a fixed rate of 5.3%.

For a quick standard loan repayment calculation, you can use the finaid.org calculator.[16] For more information on repayment plans and more advanced repayment calculators, you can jump to our section on STUDENT DEBT REPAYMENT OPTIONS. Calculating how much we would have to fork over to our student loan payments each month really drove the point home for us—make sure the debt you take on is worth the income you expect to make.

Calculating Income in the Equation

A good place to start is the Medscape Physician Compensation Report,[17] which provides data on expected income based on the physician's specialty. This data is collected from physicians voluntarily answering questions and completing surveys. Compensation will vary depending on different factors such as location, years in practice, and the type of group you're in, but this provides a good starting point.

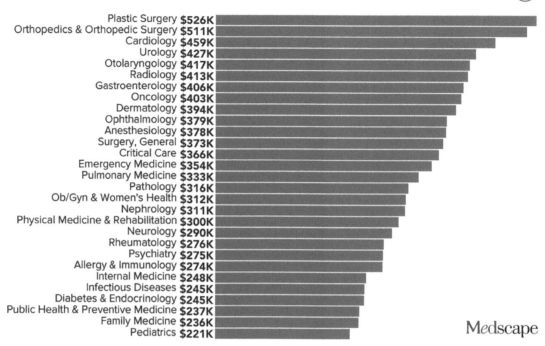

Specialty	Compensation
Plastic Surgery	$526K
Orthopedics & Orthopedic Surgery	$511K
Cardiology	$459K
Urology	$427K
Otolaryngology	$417K
Radiology	$413K
Gastroenterology	$406K
Oncology	$403K
Dermatology	$394K
Ophthalmology	$379K
Anesthesiology	$378K
Surgery, General	$373K
Critical Care	$366K
Emergency Medicine	$354K
Pulmonary Medicine	$333K
Pathology	$316K
Ob/Gyn & Women's Health	$312K
Nephrology	$311K
Physical Medicine & Rehabilitation	$300K
Neurology	$290K
Rheumatology	$276K
Psychiatry	$275K
Allergy & Immunology	$274K
Internal Medicine	$248K
Infectious Diseases	$245K
Diabetes & Endocrinology	$245K
Public Health & Preventive Medicine	$237K
Family Medicine	$236K
Pediatrics	$221K

Medscape

Lenders tend to use your *gross income* for the calculation when assessing your ability to make payments on a loan. Using gross income will paint a rosier picture of your financial situation than reality permits. When calculating your own debt-to-income ratio, I would suggest using *net income* since it is a much more accurate picture of how much income is available to service your debt.

Gross income: the amount of money earned before taxes or other deductions are taken out.

Net income: your take-home pay. This is your income after federal, state, Social Security, and Medicare taxes are withdrawn. Additional payroll deductions for health insurance, 401(k) plans, and flexible spending accounts can also lower your net income.

In the same report, physicians were asked whether they would choose the same specialty if they could go back and do it again. The results were interesting and worth considering. The data shows that 29-32% of internal and family medicine physicians would choose another specialty, while those working in the highest-compensated specialties (such as orthopedics and oncology) were much happier with the choices they made.

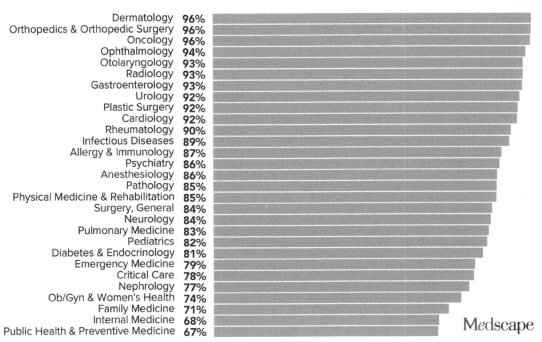

I WOULD CHOOSE THE SAME SPECIALTY

Specialty	%
Dermatology	96%
Orthopedics & Orthopedic Surgery	96%
Oncology	96%
Ophthalmology	94%
Otolaryngology	93%
Radiology	93%
Gastroenterology	93%
Urology	92%
Plastic Surgery	92%
Cardiology	92%
Rheumatology	90%
Infectious Diseases	89%
Allergy & Immunology	87%
Psychiatry	86%
Anesthesiology	86%
Pathology	85%
Physical Medicine & Rehabilitation	85%
Surgery, General	84%
Neurology	84%
Pulmonary Medicine	83%
Pediatrics	82%
Diabetes & Endocrinology	81%
Emergency Medicine	79%
Critical Care	78%
Nephrology	77%
Ob/Gyn & Women's Health	74%
Family Medicine	71%
Internal Medicine	68%
Public Health & Preventive Medicine	67%

Medscape

There are many factors that contribute to overall job satisfaction. Work-life balance, call, compensation, malpractice insurance, patient population, and work environment are all pieces to the puzzle.

Is it because some primary care physicians took on so much debt, after so many years of education and training, they feel their income and lifestyle do not meet their expectations? The report doesn't detail the reasoning for their decision, but from the two charts, one would assume that compensation was a factor.

As I'm writing this, we are still going through the COVID pandemic, and according to the same report, practices are reporting a 55% decrease in revenue and a 60% decrease in patient volume. We are uncertain what effect this will have moving forward; it is worth considering the current climate among the many other factors when considering your specialty.

Calculating Your Debt-to-Income

So now it's time to do your own debt-to-income calculation. Try to include all your debt (not just your medical school debt) and divide it by your expected compensation for the specialty you are pursuing.

What percentage of your income will go towards paying off your debt? Did you include your expected mortgage payment? While there is no specific cutoff and the choice of specialty is yours alone, be aware that the higher the percentage, the larger the toll your student loan payments will have on your income.

As a comparison, mortgage lenders like to see a ratio of 36% or less of debt to income, which includes the mortgage payment. A high debt-to-income ratio will also translate to less discretionary spending while you pay back your loans.

(AMANDA) I want to acknowledge that compensation and debt do not have to be at the top of your priority list when choosing a medical specialty, but they should at least be somewhere on that list. Acknowledge that you are making an investment in yourself and for your future, but know the terms of that investment before you dive in.

My choice to become an OB/GYN was not based on the highest compensation and surely not the most beneficial work/life balance. I went into this field because I was passionate about women's health, wanted to work in a surgical specialty, and wanted the continuity of care that an OB/GYN practice provided. Also, the blend of clinic work, hospital rotations, and procedures was attractive. Additionally, compensation was directly tied to production and, depending on the contract, could be easily scaled up or down as desired. You want to find a specialty that makes you enjoy getting up to go to work every day and will provide the type of lifestyle that you want.

Chapter 7 Recap
QUESTIONS TO CONSIDER WHEN GOING INTO DEBT

✓ Debt-to-income ratio is the total amount of your debt divided by your income. This can be calculated monthly or annually.

✓ When calculating your debt-to-income ratio, use your total debt and expected annual income after residency to help you understand how much of your income will go towards servicing your debt.

✓ To calculate future debt not yet incurred, you can use AAMC's most recent Tuition and Student Fees Report.

✓ To calculate income after residency, you can use the Medscape Physician Compensation Report.

Scan for a full list of the links and tools listed.

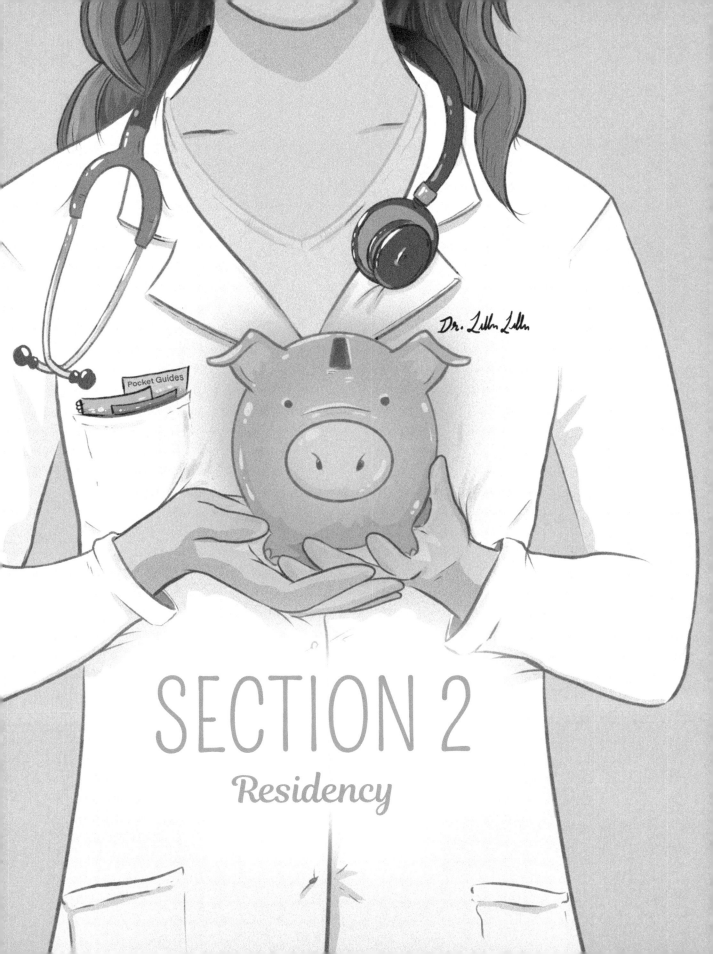

SECTION 2

Residency

Residency puts you in a state of survival mode. In no period of your career will your profession demand so much of your time and effort. You will barely have enough time to sneak in a couple of hours of sleep, let alone dedicate brain cells to your financial future. The earlier in your residency you tackle money issues, the better. This section will help guide you through the maze of creating a student loan repayment strategy and financial decisions for life after residency.

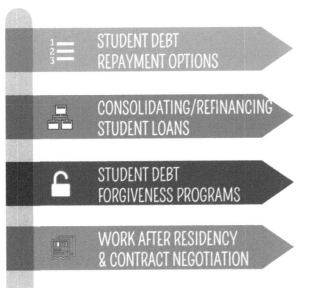

STUDENT DEBT
REPAYMENT OPTIONS

CONSOLIDATING/REFINANCING
STUDENT LOANS

STUDENT DEBT
FORGIVENESS PROGRAMS

WORK AFTER RESIDENCY
& CONTRACT NEGOTIATION

YOUR FIRST PAYCHECK
AFTER RESIDENCY

Chapter 8
STUDENT DEBT REPAYMENT OPTIONS

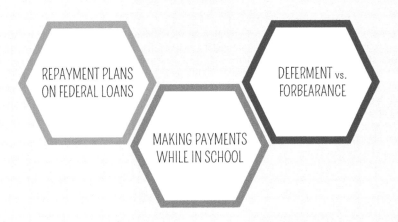

REPAYMENT PLANS ON FEDERAL LOANS

MAKING PAYMENTS WHILE IN SCHOOL

DEFERMENT vs. FORBEARANCE

Repayment Plans on Federal Loans

Taking out student loans is much easier than paying them off. The good news for some is that federal loans have decreased by 1.78% for the 2020-2021 school year. That adds up to significant savings over time. The not-so-good news is that despite the high salaries, most physicians take 15 to 20 years to pay off their student loans.[18] But their story doesn't have to be yours.

Take the time to consider your student loan repayment plan. Sit down and calculate the interest your loans will accrue and take action to reduce your debt. There are several student loan repayment plans to choose from, each with their own advantages and disadvantages. Here are the highlights for each of the options currently available.

NON-INCOME-BASED REPAYMENT PLANS ON FEDERAL LOANS

	STANDARD REPAYMENT	GRADUATED REPAYMENT	EXTENDED REPAYMENT
ELIGIBLE LOANS	All federal loans	All federal loans	Direct Subsidized and Unsubsidized loans, Direct PLUS loans made to students, Direct Consolidation Loans (that are not Parent PLUS loans)
REPAYMENT PERIOD	Non-consolidated loans are 10 years; consolidated loans are 10-30 years	Non-consolidated loans are 10 years; consolidated loans are 10-30 years	Up to 25 years
HIGHLIGHTS	• When you graduate, you're automatically enrolled in a 10-year standard repayment plan. • Monthly payments are high, but you will pay less over time than most other plans. • Monthly payments are fixed amount for the life of the loan. Does NOT qualify for PSLF	• This plan starts off with lower monthly payments, with payments, increasing every 2 years. • Income will need to grow as payments increase. • This plan is like the standard plan as it you have the option to pay off the debt in a shorter amount of time. Does NOT quaify for PSLF	• This is like the standard plan, but with longer pay-off period (10-30 years depending on the amount borrowed). • You must have more than $30,000 in loans. Does NOT qualify for PSLF

©2020 MoneyOverMilkshakes.com

The remaining repayment plans are based on your income; the monthly payments increase as you earn more and decrease if you have a salary reduction. Your family size also affects the calculation. These plans usually result in lower monthly payments, but you end up paying more interest over the life of the loan. Although these plans are based on your income, plans differ in:

- who qualifies
- monthly payment amounts
- the time it takes to pay off the loan
- which loans are eligible for each plan

Although you can defer payments if you are unemployed, the interest normally doesn't stop accumulating on your balance during times of financial hardship. The COVID-19 pandemic was an exception—all interest on federal student loans was deferred during this time.

INCOME-BASED REPAYMENT PLANS ON FEDERAL LOANS

	REVISED PAY AS YOU EARN (REPAYE)	PAY AS YOU EARN (PAYE)	INCOME BASED REPAYMENT (IBR)	INCOME-CONTINGENT REPAYMENT (ICR)
ELIGIBLE LOANS	• All Direct Loans • Direct Subsidized and Unsubsidized Loans • Direct PLUS loans made to students • Direct Consolidation Loans (that do not include PLUS loans)	• All Direct Loans • Direct Subsidized and Unsubsidized Loans • Direct PLUS loans made to students • Direct Consolidation Loans (that do not include PLUS loans)	• All Direct Loans • Subsidized and Unsubsidized federal Stafford Loans • All PLUS loans made to students • Consolidation Loans (Direct or FFEL) that do not include Direct or FFEL PLUS loans made to parents	• Direct Subsidized and Unsubsidized Loans • Direct PLUS Loans made to students, Direct Consolidation Loans
REPAYMENT PERIOD	• Undergraduate loans: up to 20 years • Graduate loans: up to 25 years	Loan forgiven after 20 years of qualifying payments	20 years if you're a new borrower on or after July 1, 2014. 25 years if you're not a new borrower on or after July 1, 2014	25 years
HIGHLIGHTS	• You'll pay no more than 10% of your discretionary income. • If your payments do not cover interest, the government pays the interest for up to three years. After that, they will pay 50% of outstanding interest. • REPAYE has a lower interest rate than PAYE. • Your spouse's income will also be factored in when determining monthly payments. • This plan does not require financial hardship requirements.	• You'll pay no more than 10% of your discretionary income • Unpaid interest is only capitalized until the principal amount on the loan increases by 10% • This plan has a higher interest rate than REPAYE • If you file taxes separately from your spouse, spouse's income will not be counted towards your monthly payment calculation, unlike REPAYE • Loans had to be taken out after Oct 1, 2011 • Requires proof of financial hardship.	• For new borrowers after July 1, 2014 you will not pay more than 10% of your discretionary income and never more than the 10-year Standard Repayment Plan. Borrowers before July 1, 2014: 15% of your discretionary income but never more than the 10-year Standard Repayment Plan amount • This is the only income driven repayment option for students with FFEL Program loans • Requires proof of financial hardship	• Monthly payments are based on the lesser of 20% of your discretionary income or what you'd pay under a repayment plan with a fixed payment over 12 years • Only available to those with FFEL loans • Spouses income will be counted if you file your taxes jointly • This is the only income driven repayment option for Parent PLUS loans • Does not require financial hardship
	This plan does qualify for PSLF	This plan does qualify for PSLF	This plan does qualify for PSLF	Does NOT qualify for PSLF

If a portion of your student loans are forgiven through one of the federal plans mentioned above, you must pay income taxes on the amount that is forgiven. This can turn out to be a substantial tax bill.

We've covered the primary payment plans available, but there are a few additional options that aren't as popular. There is a helpful student loan simulator that can be found on the studentaid.gov website (studentaid.gov/loan-simulator). It will provide an estimate of your monthly payments under different plans and guide you in selecting a repayment plan that best fits your individual needs. You can find it here.

Making Payments While You're in School

Most of us have little discretionary income while attending school or during residency. But making small payments before you're done with medical school can save you thousands of dollars on student loans in the future.

Remember that with subsidized loans, the government pays the interest on the loan while you are in school, so all your payments eat away at the principal. Unsubsidized loans continue to accrue interest, even if you are in school or under deferred status.

NO PAYMENTS IN SCHOOL

You borrow $50,000 per year in medical school for 4 years at 5% interest. You make no payments until 6 months after you graduate.

Original Loan Amount	$200,000
Monthly Payments in School	$0
Interest on Loan While in School	$30,020
Loan Amount When Payments Start	$230,020

SCENARIO #2
MAKING PAYMENTS IN SCHOOL

Same scenario, except that you make $200/month payments on your loans while in school.

Original Loan Amount	$200,000
Monthly Payments in School	$200
Interest on Loan While in School	$1,200
Loan Amount When Payments Start	$201,200

> You've paid $10,800 in monthly payments but you saved $28,820 in interest in 4½ years!

you can place the money you have designated for loan payments in an account until the end of the semester. Once you receive your loan disbursement for the following semester, you can then make a lump sum payment back on your student loans. This way, you pay down your loans with any additional funds left over at the end of the semester.

Also, if you are considering the Public Service Loan Forgiveness (PSLF) program, you will need 10 years of qualifying payments to be considered for debt forgiveness. If you start those payments while in residency, as an attending, you will only have 5 or 6 years of payments left. Shaving off 4 to 5 years of monthly payments as an attending is the key to maximizing your debt forgiveness because your income-based repayment is so much lower as a resident. You can expect your monthly payments to increase by a factor of 10 after residency. (More on the student debt forgiveness program in CHAPTER 10.)

Deferment vs. Forbearance

Deferment and forbearance are both options for postponing your student loan payments. The difference between the two is that your debt will continue to grow in forbearance because your interest still accrues, regardless of the type of loan.

With deferment, interest will not accrue on subsidized loans and Perkins loans. Other types of loans, such as unsubsidized loans, will continue to accrue interest during deferment. The length of deferment on loans can vary but typically does not exceed a total of three years. You'll need to qualify for deferment through your student loan servicer. Some qualifying events are becoming unemployed, serving in active military duty or in the Peace Corps, or undergoing medical treatment.

Forbearance, as we mentioned, will pause student loan payments; however, your interest and therefore your balance will continue to grow during this period. The pause in payments normally does not exceed 12 months at a time and tends to be less difficult to qualify for compared to a deferment. The decision is at the discretion of your student loan servicer.

If you have to choose between the two, deferment is your better option especially if you have subsidized or Perkins loans. Another option is to consider an income-based repayment plan. If you are making little to no money, you may qualify for monthly payments as low as $0 a month. This can go towards student debt forgiveness if you are pursuing that option.

STUDENT DEBT REPAYMENT OPTIONS

✓ Every dollar you borrow now will cost you 1.5 to 2 times the original amount in the future.

✓ Always explore your federal loan options before considering private loans. The benefit of deferring your federal loan payment during financial hardship is invaluable.

✓ Interest rates on federal loans have decreased by 1.78% for the 2020-2021 school year.

✓ Utilize the student loan simulator to explore repayment plans.

✓ Making small payments toward your loans in residency can save you tens of thousands of dollars in interest.

Scan for a full list of the links and tools listed.

Chapter 9

CONSOLIDATING/REFINANCING YOUR STUDENT LOANS

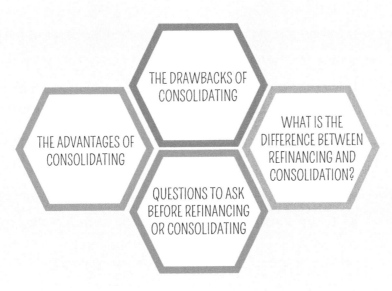

In this chapter, we'll discuss why you might want to consider consolidating your loans or whether refinancing through a private bank may be your preferred option. Timing is also important, as we discuss when you should be reviewing these options.

The Advantages of Consolidating

Consolidating your federal loans is simply combining all the individual loans you have into one federal loan with a single monthly payment and a fixed interest rate. Almost any loan can be consolidated as long as it is federally guaranteed and not a private loan.

MINIMIZE STRESS

It can be stressful to manage multiple loans and keep track of each loan's interest rate, terms, payment amount, and due date. If you have five separate loans by the time you graduate, you will have to make five separate payments monthly to keep current—on top of your normal bills.

Consolidating to one loan gives you one fixed interest rate and one monthly payment to keep track of, freeing up brain space for other things in your life. With just one loan payment to worry about, you're also less likely to forget a payment and wind up with late fees or penalties.

ACCESS TO INCOME-DRIVEN REPAYMENT PLANS AND DEFERMENT DUE TO FINANCIAL HARDSHIP

Consolidating to a single federal loan gives you access to income-driven repayment plans. The monthly amount due on your loans is adjusted based on your income.

Contact your loan servicer about deferment options. When you consolidate your loans, a new loan is created, so the three-year duration on how long you can defer your student loans due to financial hardship restarts.

LOWER MONTHLY PAYMENTS

Lower monthly payments result from extending your loan term. The traditional repayment period is between 10 and 30 years; if you owe $60,000 or more, you qualify for a 30-year repayment plan.

By extending your loan term, you'll decrease the amount of money devoted to repaying your loans every month, freeing up cash flow for the rest of your budget. This can be particularly useful if you are using the money saved to pay off debt at higher interest levels.

When you consolidate your student loans, the new interest rate will be the weighted average of the current rates of your loans, rounded up to the nearest one-eighth of a percent.

NO ORIGINATION FEE

Unlike private loans, there is no origination fee for consolidating to a single federal loan.

ELIGIBLE FOR PUBLIC STUDENT LOAN FORGIVENESS PROGRAM

You are also still eligible for the Public Student Loan Forgiveness Program. (More on this in the next chapter.)

The Drawbacks of Consolidating

END UP PAYING MORE OVER TIME

Extending your loan term is a double-edged sword. Extending the loan repayment time will lower your monthly payments, but you will end up paying more in interest over the life of the loan.

MAY LOSE CERTAIN BENEFITS

You can lose important perks after you consolidate, such as interest rate discounts for automatic payments. Depending on your lender, you may also lose your 6-month grace period after graduation.

RESTART ON LOAN FORGIVENESS PROGRAMS

Loan forgiveness programs require you to make payments on your student loans for 10 years prior to receiving forgiveness. If you are part of any loan forgiveness program, the clock will restart when you consolidate your loans since consolidation creates a new loan.

So if you have been making payments towards a student debt forgiveness program for two years and then decide to consolidate your loans, you will lose two years of qualifying payments. Because of this stipulation, the best time to consolidate is at the beginning of residency, when you should start making small payments.

What is the Difference Between Refinancing and Consolidation?

The consolidation we have been discussing up to now is with a federal loan servicer. However, you also have the option to refinance your loan with a private bank. Refinancing is also combining several loans into one using a private bank rather than a federal loan servicer.

This might be worth considering if you have good credit (or a cosigner with good credit) and you are planning on paying off your loans quickly. A private loan may offer lower interest rates, but this will depend on current market conditions and varying rates with each bank.

On the other hand, refinancing eliminates any loan forgiveness options you had with your federal loans. You will also give up the option of deferment for financial hardship afforded by federal loans.

Questions to Ask Before Refinancing or Consolidating

You will only be able to consolidate your loans once, and there is no option to reverse that decision. If you refinance with a private bank, find out their policy for financial hardship and ask for the language in the agreement. You should also ask about what happens to your loans upon your death. You might be surprised to know that some private lenders will try and collect the money after you die.

An online loan consolidation calculator will help you compare your current loan situation to what your new loan will look like after consolidation. The calculator we like is from finaid.org.[19]

Make sure you have reviewed all the pros and cons before and reached out to your loan servicer to understand your loan agreement's specific terms before deciding to refinance or consolidate. To ask questions about consolidating your loans, contact the Student Loan Support Center at 1-800-557-7394.

CONSOLIDATING/ REFINANCING YOUR STUDENT LOANS

✓ Consolidation can lower monthly payments by extending your payback period. However, this will also increase the total payback amount.

✓ If you plan to apply for student loan forgiveness, make sure you know how consolidating will affect your eligibility.

✓ Explore consolidating your loans with a federal loan servicer before refinancing your student debt with a private bank.

✓ Refinancing with a private bank may lower your interest rate. However, be aware of the downsides to losing your federal loan status.

✓ If you are exploring private loans, make sure to read through the loan agreement for policies on financial hardship and loan forgiveness if you die.

Scan for a full list of the links and tools listed.

Chapter 10
STUDENT DEBT FORGIVENESS PROGRAMS

Understanding whether the Public Service Loan Forgiveness Program is a good fit for you is essential in developing the best repayment strategy. Whether you participate in the program or not, exploring your options will guarantee that you have taken the least costly approach to the most significant debt of your career.

What is the Public Service Loan Forgiveness (PSLF) Program?

Physicians, nurses, dentists, pharmacists, and veterinarians whose work qualifies as public service can qualify for the Public Service Loan Forgiveness (PSLF) Program. Public service requires full-time employment by a 501(c)(3) tax-exempt nonprofit or public institution. Many hospitals qualify, but you should not assume your residency program or employer qualifies without verifying their status for yourself.

Reasons to Consider PSLF

This program may be a good fit if you have high loan balances relative to your salary (high debt-to-income ratio). We discussed this in Chapter 5, but let's get a refresher on calculating this number. Let's say you owe $300,000, and as an attending, you will make $250,000 in annual salary. Your debt-to-income ratio is $300,000 / $250,000 = 1.2. The higher your debt-to-income ratio, the more seriously you should consider PSLF, since you are likely to need more time to pay off your debt

A good way to know whether this program is a good fit for you is to use an online PSLF calculator that compares different repayment plans. It will also show you how much of your loan you will still have left after 120 payments.

We like the calculator from Student Loan Hero[20] as it clearly shows the estimated amounts that are eligible for forgiveness. Also, keep in mind that debt forgiveness under this program is tax-free, which is not the case under the standard and income-based federal repayment plans. Instead, those plans offer forgiveness after 20 to 25 years, and currently, you will have to pay taxes on the amount forgiven.

If, after exploring your options, you have chosen to pursue PSLF, try to begin payments during residency. If you're able to make qualifying payments during a 4-year residency, you will only have 6 years as an attending before you qualify for loan forgiveness.

Your loan payments in residency on an income-based repayment plan might be $200 or $300 per month. This is a lot of money in residency, but your loan payments will be closer to $2,000 to $3,000 per month as an attending. Yes, you are making more money as an attending, but if you defer your loans until after residency, you'll be looking at the full 10 years of elevated monthly payments before you can be considered for loan forgiveness.

How Do You Qualify?

Borrowers must make 120 payments of their own while working for a qualified employer. This translates into 10 years of monthly payments. If 120 qualified payments are made, your remaining debt will be forgiven.

Although this sounds simple enough, there are plenty of horror stories from people who were under the impression they were making qualified payments but found out years later that they were not.

Here are five steps to review to ensure your employment qualifies:

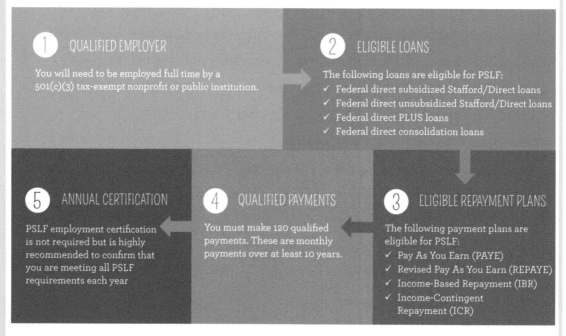

Important to note that only payments made after October 1, 2007, will qualify. Perkins loans and Federal Family Education Loans (FFEL) are not eligible for forgiveness.

What Options Do I Have if My Loans are Ineligible?

If you find out your loans are ineligible, you may be able to consolidate your loans into a single direct consolidation loan. Direct consolidation loans are eligible for PSLF.

Be mindful of the fact that once your loans are consolidated, your required 10 years of qualified payments will reset to zero, so you will lose out on any qualified payments you've already made.

If you have not made payments on your loans, the best way to take advantage of a loan forgiveness program is to consolidate into a single direct consolidation loan and start making qualifying payments as early as possible during your residency.

Do Payments Have to Be Made Consecutively?

No. You must make 120 qualified payments for PSLF to apply, but they do not have to be made consecutively. For that reason, it will take at least 10 years to qualify for PSLF, but it could take longer.

You also don't need to work for the same employer during the entire 120-month period. However, you must work an average of at least 30 hours per week each year or the number of hours that your employer considers to be full-time work.

Are Qualifying Payments Retroactive?

Yes. If you meet all the criteria of PSLF and have been making qualifying payments for 10 years, you could qualify for loan forgiveness right now.

There is no requirement to sign up for or register for the PSLF program; you apply at the end of your ten years of qualifying payments with the correct loan types. However, that isn't a gamble you want to take. You can remove this stress and uncertainty by certifying your payments every year.

What is PSLF Annual Recertification?

This allows you to certify that the payments you make meet all the necessary requirements for PSLF. You and your employer will submit a form, and you will receive confirmation of your qualified payments. This way, after 10 years of payments, there shouldn't be any big surprises regarding qualifications or eligibility.

At the end of the program, when you have reached 120 qualified payments, you submit your application for loan forgiveness, which will include your full 10-year employment history. If you submit annual certifications, the process for approval from the Department of Education will move considerably faster.

Student Loan Payments During the COVID Pandemic

Due to the 2020 coronavirus pandemic, your direct federal loan payments were suspended from March 20, 2020, through September 2021.[21]

Additionally, the interest on qualified loans was suspended during the same period. So if you were fortunate enough to qualify for loan forgiveness criteria during this period, you would have received credit for up to 19 months of payments without having to pay a dime.

How to Apply for PSLF Annual Certification

We found the easiest way to complete the annual certification for PSLF online is to create an account on myfedloan.org and upload the form there. You can also apply online if your student loans are with FedLoan Servicing by submitting your application online through their portal.

If you send a paper application, mail this application to:

U.S. Department of Education

FedLoan Servicing

P.O. Box 69184

Harrisburg, PA 17106-9184

Additional Forgiveness Programs[22]

Many people have heard of the federal debt forgiveness program but are not aware that there are also state-specific forgiveness programs. Many states offer repayment on loans for service in underserved areas. TheCollegeInvestor.com has done a great job gathering all the student loan forgiveness programs and organizing them by state.

Other programs to consider are:

- The National Health Service Corp (Military)
- Faculty Loan Repayment Program
- NIH Loan Repayment Program for those pursuing careers in biomedical research

Hospitals across the country are willing to provide loan assistance for working in rural or underserved communities. These loan assistance programs can be substantial and help you eliminate your student debt in a short amount of time. If you're open to working in smaller towns, a recruiter can help you explore your loan assistance options. We discuss utilizing a recruiter in our next chapter.

STUDENT DEBT FORGIVENESS PROGRAMS

✓ The Public Service Loan Forgiveness Program (PSLF) can help physicians, nurses, dentists, pharmacists, and veterinarians who meet program qualifications by forgiving their student loans after 120 qualifying payments.

✓ Annual certification will help avoid any confusion over whether you have made qualified payments and worked for qualified employers.

✓ Suspension of student loan payments and interest during the COVID pandemic count towards PSLF-qualified monthly payments.

✓ Use a PSLF calculator to see if you are a good candidate for the program.

✓ Making payments in residency towards PSLF can save you tens of thousands of dollars in repayment.

✓ Research student loan forgiveness programs in your state.

Scan for a full list of the links and tools listed.

Chapter 11

WORK AFTER RESIDENCY & CONTRACT NEGOTIATION

FINDING A JOB

CONTRACT NEGOTIATION

HAVING A LAWYER REVIEW YOUR CONTRACT

CONTRACT TERMS YOU SHOULD BE FAMILIAR WITH

BILLING AND CODING

If you are finishing up residency, we want to extend a heartfelt congratulations! We've been there, and this is a big deal—the end of an arduous journey. I like to joke that medical school and residency are comparable to raising a one-month-old baby for almost a decade. The lack of sleep, the strain on relationships, and the overall stress can be intense. But you've made it! Your hard work will start paying off soon enough.

In the chaos of your last year of residency, spend some time thinking about your long-term goals and what you want in life after residency. Salary, work-life balance, location, and type of employer are all things to consider. What is important to you and why?

If your residency leads directly to full-time employment afterward, congratulations! If not, your job hunt is about to begin. Here are some things to consider when looking for your first job as a licensed physician.

Finding A Job

CLEANING UP YOUR RESUME

Polish up your resume and add your most recent experience, publications, awards, and board certifications. Don't be intimidated to ask a friend, colleague, or mentor to review your resume and provide their feedback. Also, more and more companies are using algorithms to filter through resumes for employers. Consider adding in keywords from the job posting and placing them in your resume to avoid getting filtered out when applying for a position.

TIMING IS IMPORTANT

It's ideal to begin searching for employment 6 to 12 months before you complete residency. This should give you enough time to explore your options, interview for multiple positions, and negotiate the best contract.

USING YOUR NETWORK

A great way to learn about job vacancies is to reach out to previous graduates from both your medical school and residency programs. If there are open positions available, your peers can speak to your professionalism, work ethic, demeanor, and other characteristics.

This can really make a difference when competing against other applicants for a job opportunity. Use whatever tools are available to you: social media, email, phone calls, or in-person meet-ups. A personal favorite is LinkedIn, which is a professional networking site that will allow you to quickly connect with recruiters, HR Managers, and other physicians. You can target your search by location, company, and job title.

UTILIZING RECRUITERS

A physician recruiter's job is to help you find employment. An experienced recruiter will have a much larger network to help expose you to opportunities that would be difficult to find on your own. This is particularly helpful when coming out of residency when your professional network can be somewhat limited.

As far as the recruiter fee, you do not pay the recruiter; your employer will pay that fee if you are hired through a position that the recruiter has found for you. A recruiter's fee for finding a position can range between 15–25% of your first year's salary. Although many recruiters will claim their fee has no consequence in your salary negotiations, it is impossible to deny that not using a recruiter will save the employer money. If you're fortunate enough to find a position without a recruiter, those savings might be discussed during your negotiations.

If you have a particular position, group, or hospital in mind, reach out to their HR/recruiting office directly before reaching out to a recruiter. Make sure to let the recruiter you work with know which hospitals/practices you will be reaching out to directly. (Get this in writing to avoid any confusion.)

While it is a great strategy to reach out to specific hospitals yourself, recruiters play an important role in discovering opportunities that you will not have the time or network to find on your own.

Remember that you are not obliged to accept any given offer, and there are no out-of-pocket costs to have a recruiter search on your behalf. If you accept a position that a recruiter has found, they will receive a fee from the hospital. Try not to get hung up on their fee, but rather, consider the opportunities they can provide that you wouldn't have found on your own.

Contract Negotiation

You may not feel comfortable negotiating a contract, but after years of hard work and preparation, it would be a shame to leave available money and other perks on the table.

Every employer has a salary range that they are authorized to offer you. And here's a little-known secret: they never start with their best offer. It is *your* job to negotiate.

OUR CONTRACT NEGOTIATION STORY

(AMANDA) When I completed residency, I knew the state I wanted to live in but was open to opportunities in several cities. It is important to pick a state because you will need to obtain a medical license in this state you'll be practicing in, which can take a while. I narrowed it down to two positions, one opportunity in an urban area and another in a more rural area. Nick and I felt we could make either location work.

After receiving an initial offer from the urban hospital, I politely and professionally informed the rural hospital that I had a competitive offer. The rural hospital suggested we continue with their interview. Surprisingly, the rural hospital came back with a significantly better offer than the urban one, which also included student loan forgiveness. (Loan forgiveness is typically an added benefit of working in rural areas.)

We informed the urban hospital of the offer we received and gave them an opportunity for a final counteroffer if they were interested. The urban hospital came back with a final offer, which we decided to take.

The difference between the first offer received and the final offer accepted was a 20% increase in annual salary, a doubling of the sign-on bonus, and an additional 6.5% per *RVU*.

THE DIFFERENCE ALONE WAS MORE THAN OUR COMBINED ANNUAL SALARIES DURING RESIDENCY!

Relative Value Unit (RVU): the methodology used to determine reimbursement rates for physician services. These units define the value of a service or procedure.

Although it may seem like we went through a lot of negotiating, we simply gave each employer one opportunity to improve their offer. While a prolonged back-and-forth may result in an employer getting frustrated, you should always feel comfortable asking for a more competitive offer at least once, even if you do not have multiple offers. If you are satisfied with the terms, you can rest assured you did not leave any money on the table.

It is also important not to take offense if the employer does not increase their offer.

Communication needs to be professional and sensitive to the fact that both you and the employer have other opportunities. Negotiations will often boil down to your likeability and professionalism toward the person you are negotiating with.

Having A Lawyer Review Your Contract

Once you agree to basic terms, you can expect your employer to send over a long and comprehensive contract filled with legal jargon that you are expected to sign. This is your second round of negotiations.

Do not assume that the contract is standard and written equitably; contracts are written to be advantageous to the person who created them. Understanding the terms of the agreement and having a contract lawyer review it can save you significant headaches down the road.

There are plenty of horror stories of physicians wanting to leave a job, but because they didn't fully understand the contract, they ended up stuck in an unpleasant situation or had to pay back a substantial sum of money to get out of a contract.

Use a contract lawyer that specializes in physician contracts. One good way to find one is to ask graduates of your residency program for recommendations. Contract lawyers may charge by the hour or a flat fee. The costs are typically between $300 to $1,000 for a contract review.

Our personal preference is the flat fee so you can avoid a run-up in hours and costs.

Expect the charges to be on the higher end of that range if you have the lawyer negotiate on your behalf. We chose to have the lawyer review the contract and make his suggested amendments, and we took it from there. We sent the amendments to the employer and directly discussed any changes. If you are not comfortable negotiating yourself, explore having the lawyer assist you with the negotiations.

Contract Terms You Should Be Familiar With

Here are some contract terms that are negotiable and should be reviewed with your lawyer:

BASE PAY

- Base Pay is the initial salary before any benefits, bonuses, or overtime.
- What kind of compensation model is this—fixed or base plus a percent of revenue or base plus performance factors?
- Is there an income guarantee?
- Is there a limit to how far income can decrease?

RVUs and BONUSES

- Relative Value Unit (RVU) is the metric commonly used to evaluate performance. You receive a standard number of RVUs for specific services/procedures. Your employer then pays you on either a set or graduated rate per RVU.
- Is there a bonus? What are the incentive variables?
- Is bonusing attainable? How many physicians in your group received a bonus last year?
- You may be able to ask the hospital for data around RVUs and bonus payouts for the group, although not all hospitals provide this information.

SIGN-ON BONUS

- This is a one-time, lump sum, cash payment normally given upon hiring.
- When does this payout? Some hospitals will allow you to negotiate to receive half of the bonus when you sign the contract and the other half when you start work.

RELOCATION ASSISTANCE

- These are your moving expenses incurred in moving to a new area for a new position.
- Relocating can cost thousands of dollars. If the employer doesn't offer this initially, use a relocation package as a negotiating tool if they are not meeting your expectations elsewhere in the contract. Relocation packages can also include home sale assistance and temporary housing.

STUDENT LOAN REPAYMENT ASSISTANCE

- Do they offer student loan forgiveness?
- Is there a cap? Some hospitals will offer to help pay your student loans. This should be added to your calculation when looking at compensation packages and comparing offers. You may feel your salary is below what you expected, but the student loan support could make up the difference.

MATERNITY LEAVE/VACATION

- Find out if paid leave is offered and whether it comes with a minimum number of days worked to qualify. An employer may mention Family Medical Leave Act (FMLA) as a response, but that is unpaid leave.

OUTSIDE ACTIVITIES

- Are there circumstances in which you are allowed to work outside the practice?

DUTIES AND REQUIREMENTS

- Is the employment full-time or part-time?
- Does the position include administrative duties?
- What is the on-call Schedule? Is there after-hours call?
- To whom does the physician report?
- How many patients are physicians expected to see in a day?
- Can you take calls from home?
- How many surgeries are you able to secure in a week?
- What procedures are physicians expected to perform?
- Is there a performance evaluation process?

NON-COMPETE CLAUSES

- What does the non-compete clause prohibit? How long does it last? These clauses are intended to prohibit you from practicing medicine in a specific geography or for a particular period of time after your employment ends.

GAP/TAIL INSURANCE

- Is this offered? This is professional liability coverage after the employee has left the employer. The policy should cover claims during the period you worked for the employer.

ASSIGNABILITY CLAUSE

- In the event the group or practice is acquired, does your contract continue, or will a new contract need to be negotiated?

END OF CONTRACT

- Consider adding a clause that states the employer must present you with a new contract 6 months prior to the contract expiring. This will give you time to negotiate or work on your exit strategy.

Billing and Coding

Over the years, physicians have gone from primarily practicing medicine to acting as their own scribe, their own defense attorney in medical documentation, and their own biller/coder. In order to succeed in medicine, you need to be able to quickly and appropriately document your patient encounters in order to:

1 Communicate with other physicians

2 Avoid being sued

3 Get paid by insurance companies

New expansions in electronic medical records have turned the physician's note into a legal document, an insurance document, and more recently, patient education material as some patients now have access to their complete medical records.

This topic may seem out of place, but it can directly affect your income. This is typically not taught in residency. It is something that you can learn on your own the hard way, or you can spend a little time and money and hit the ground running after residency.

Studies have shown that a billing/coding course will pay for itself after only a few weeks. Also, keep in mind that state-administered Medicaid coding/billing rules may change depending on where you practice. Look into your specialty's offerings and consider completing a billing course after an ICD update or after moving to a different state.

Chapter 11 Recap

WORK AFTER RESIDENCY AND CONTRACT NEGOTIATION

✓ Utilizing your connections from medical school and residency, in addition to a recruiter, is a well-rounded approach to finding a job.

✓ Your employer expects you to negotiate the terms of your contract. First, negotiate the basic salary and benefits. A second negotiation takes place once you receive your contract and review all the terms.

✓ You should counter with increased salary and/or benefits at least once during the initial negotiation. Use multiple offers to your advantage.

✓ Have a contract lawyer who specializes in physician contracts review your contract before accepting a position.

✓ Familiarize yourself with the 13 contract terms in the chapter, and be aware that these are all negotiable.

Scan for a full list of the links and tools listed.

Chapter 12

YOUR FIRST PAYCHECK AFTER RESIDENCY

That first paycheck after residency is a special moment—one you will never forget. Your first paycheck is likely a great deal more than you've ever made. We felt like we had just won the lottery, but this payout didn't just happen by chance. It came with a sense of accomplishment for so many years of hard work.

Part of you will want to buy all the things you could never afford: a large new house, a fancy new car, and all the new toys. If you are not prepared for it, that first paycheck out of residency can be too much of a good thing. For many of us, the increase in income is 5 to 10 fold. If you haven't experienced this for yourself, believe us when we tell you that you'll feel like Scrooge McDuck swimming in a giant pool of money. This false sense of invulnerability can lead to decisions to take on substantial debt.

It is truly scary how quickly you get used to that extra discretionary income. No matter how much money you make, it's easy to find ways to spend it. Sadly, there are plenty of people making six figures that still live paycheck to paycheck.

When you see a colleague recently out of residency with a fancy sports car and a large mansion living lavishly, don't look at them in admiration. If they haven't inherited the money, they are either in debt or spending most of their paycheck to keep up with their new lifestyle.

We'll be the first to admit that we got caught up in the euphoria brought on by a huge, sudden influx of cash. We bought a large house with a pool, along with new furniture. We started eating out at fancy restaurants, and we made what seemed like hourly purchases on Amazon. (I mean, everyone needs disco lights on their toilet seat in the middle of the night, right?)

After the initial shock wore off, we opened up our checking account and were shocked to see what little money we had left. It was a profound wake-up call. We stopped what we were doing and spent time discussing how we had let the situation get away from us.

Setting Goals

(AMANDA) One of the most valuable takeaways from our conversation that night was not when we discussed our outlandish purchases, although that was helpful. Instead, it was discussing what we were working towards. The single most significant goal in my life had just been achieved. I had become a physician. Now what? We had to create new goals.

Here's what we came up with.

We knew we had a lot of work to do on refining our goals but, we had a start. Whatever your list of goals looks like, odds are the majority will revolve around possessing the financial freedom to accomplish them.

Overcoming False Expectations

(NICK) Another question we asked ourselves that night was, "Did spending all this money make us happier?" To be honest, the short answer was yes. Spending money on items that we could never afford undeniably felt good, but that good feeling was fleeting. The novelty eventually wore off.

What money *can* offer is peace of mind through financial security. You sleep a little better at night, knowing that if life throws a few curveballs, you have set your family up to weather the storm. That's only possible with financial planning through budgeting, saving, and investing.

In our money wake-up conversation, we talked about what life was like for us during the last few years. Despite the demands of medical school and residency, we agreed that we were relatively happy. We were not making six figures, but we had our little family of four, and we had created some amazing memories.

After our discussion, we concluded that there was no good reason we couldn't cut back significantly while still enjoying the good life.

After implementing these changes over time, we came to realize that working towards financial freedom offers a much deeper satisfaction than buying a new toy to play with.

Have Your Cake and Eat It Too

There is a common misconception that being financially responsible means you have to suck all the fun out of life. For physicians, this is not remotely the case. With the large increase in income after residency, you can have your cake and eat it too.

Going from a resident salary to an attending, you can triple what you spend on necessities such as housing, food, insurance, utilities, and transportation, as well as double what you were spending on your wants like travel and entertainment—all while still saving for retirement and paying off debt.

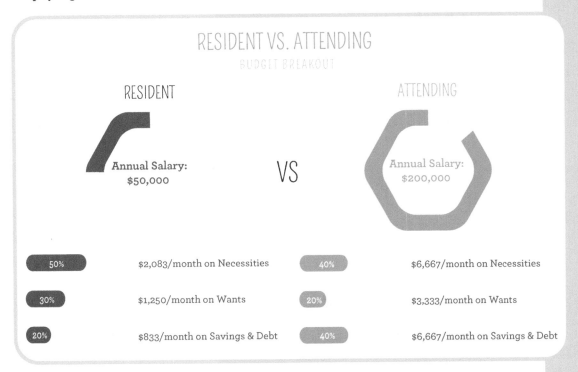

RESIDENT VS. ATTENDING
BUDGET BREAKOUT

RESIDENT

Annual Salary:
$50,000

VS

ATTENDING

Annual Salary:
$200,000

50%	$2,083/month on Necessities	40%	$6,667/month on Necessities
30%	$1,250/month on Wants	20%	$3,333/month on Wants
20%	$833/month on Savings & Debt	40%	$6,667/month on Savings & Debt

You might even feel that doubling your wants and tripling your needs is too generous. If you think you can do better, challenge yourself to do so. If you speak with friends or family members who excel at saving, many of them will tell you that saving has become a game for them. They take pride in limiting their spending and achieving their budgeting goals.

If you wait to do this until after you've been living high, spending most of your post-residency income, those habits will be much more difficult (though not impossible) to break. The first year after residency is crucial in developing decisive habits towards saving money and living below your means.

YOUR FIRST PAYCHECK AFTER RESIDENCY

✓ The first paycheck out of residency is a pivotal moment in creating healthy spending and saving habits.

✓ Setting specific goals and creating a budget will help you avoid spending money carelessly.

✓ The joy of spending your newfound wealth is fleeting. The novelty eventually wears off.

✓ Physicians can save for retirement while enjoying a substantial increase in living standards after residency.

Scan for a full list of the links and tools listed.

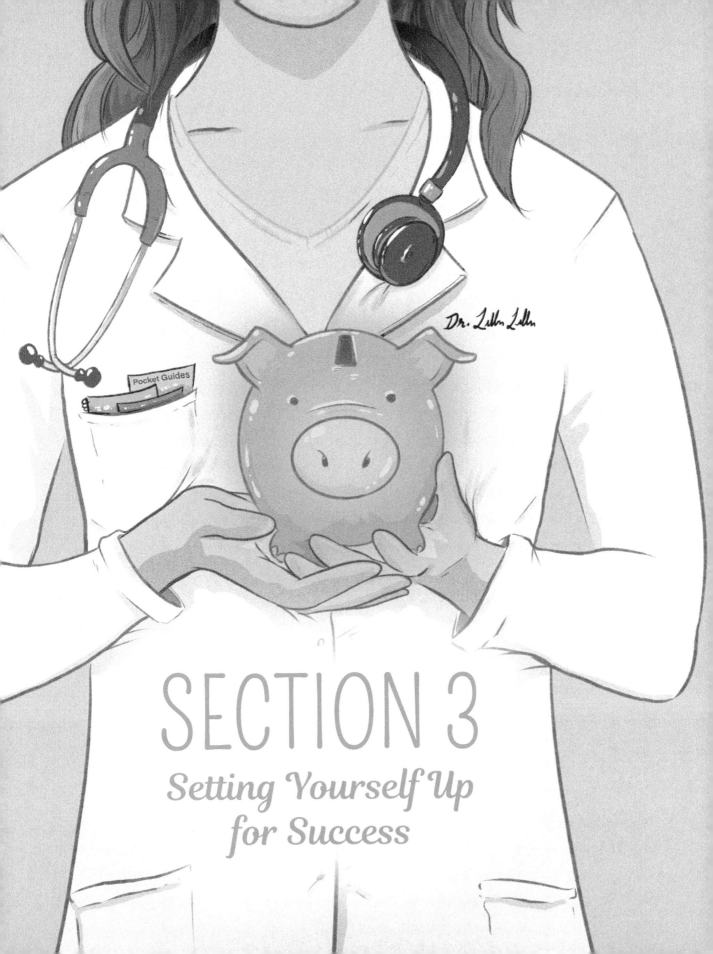

SECTION 3

*Setting Yourself Up
for Success*

We cover a lot of different topics in this section—everything from budgeting, banking, and credit cards to financial advisors, savings accounts, and mortgages. Basically, if it affected us financially over the last decade, we've included guidance on it in this section.

These topics are unattractive for most financial advisors—topics that are unrelated to investing or estate planning, with no opportunity to make a commission or referral fee. The chapters in this section are about building a foundation of good financial habits and educating yourself on common pitfalls, both of which can save you money and time.

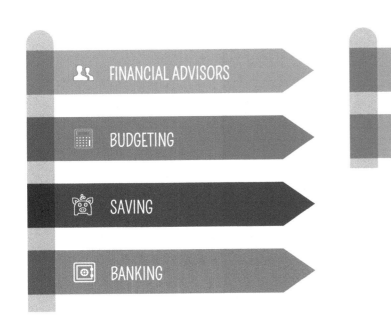

FINANCIAL ADVISORS

BUDGETING

SAVING

BANKING

CREDIT CARDS

BUYING, RENTING, & HOME LOANS

Chapter 13

FINANCIAL ADVISORS

WHAT FINANCIAL ADVISORS DO & WHEN TO USE THEM

HOW DO FINANCIAL ADVISORS MAKE MONEY?

WHAT TO BE WARY OF WITH FINANCIAL ADVISORS

QUESTIONS TO ASK A FINANCIAL ADVISOR

HOW DO I FIND A FINANCIAL ADVISOR?

If you read our section on WHY WE WROTE THE BOOK, you might think we have a negative view of financial advisors. Although our initial experience was disappointing, that is not the case. A financial advisor is an important tool you can use to assist you in your financial goals.

Ideally, everyone would have access to a trusted financial advisor that they could call regularly, but there are a few practical limitations here. The first is that advisory fees can be cost-prohibitive. Another (which we experienced in medical school) is that many advisors have little interest in taking you on as a client unless you have a few hundred thousand dollars for them to manage.

If you are reading this book, you're looking to further educate yourself on personal finance matters to make smarter decisions for you and your family. The majority of people who walk into a financial advisor's office have done little to no financial planning on their own. And the less you know, the more money the financial advice will cost you. Taking the time to educate yourself can save you thousands of dollars in advisor fees. This chapter focuses on the when, why, and how to best work with a financial advisor.

What Financial Advisors Do and When to Use Them

In this next section, we discuss the primary services financial advisors offer. We share how the material provided in the book can help you accomplish these tasks for each of these services. We will also share with you which services we personally seek the advice of a professional for. Important disclaimer here. This is our family's personal approach to utilizing a financial advisor. You may find that you require a more customized approach for your particular situation.

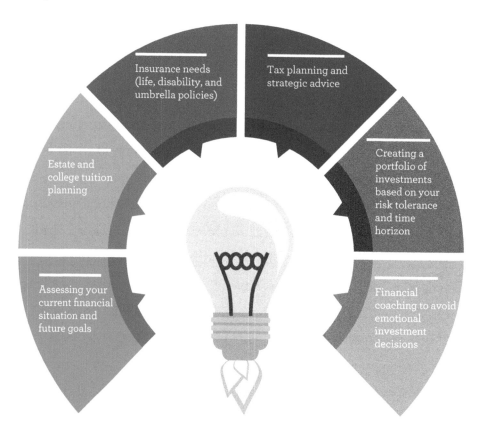

Let's take each of the 6 areas that a financial advisor can help you with and discuss which of these areas you can educate yourself on using this book and other sources to save you thousands in fees.

1. HELP ASSESS YOUR CURRENT FINANCIAL SITUATION AND FUTURE GOALS

A financial advisor can be helpful here to get you to dedicate time to look at your financial situation. The accountability can be nice, but it may not be worth the fee. If you're reading this, you have already decided to take on some of that responsibility yourself.

Regardless of whether you get financial advice from books (like this one) or an advisor, *you* are the one who must do the work on assessing your current financial situation.

Once you gather all the necessary data, an advisor puts that information into a program, which spits out charts and graphs that summarize where you currently stand financially and highlights potential improvement areas. This assessment is often the first step in financial planning for financial advisors, and this step alone may cost you $1,000 or more.

We suggest using a more cost-effective alternative, which (in our experience) provides a more detailed analysis—a budgeting app. Both Mint and Personal Capital are free apps that do a great job providing a snapshot of your current financial situation. We discuss these apps in much more detail in our next chapter.

2. ESTATE AND COLLEGE TUITION PLANNING

Estate planning is simply passing your assets and investments down to your spouse or children in the most tax-effective way. Financial advisors are a great resource for recommendations around complicated estate planning, such as trusts. Suppose you want your child to meet certain criteria (such as maintaining a certain GPA, reaching a certain age, or running a gauntlet full of fire and blades) before they inherit your fortune. In that case, you'll want to speak with an estate or trust attorney. Financial advisors will ultimately recommend an attorney in these situations.

However, if you're situation is uncomplicated, and you want to make sure your assets are protected, and your family inherits your investments without getting stuck in the court system, check out our section 5, PROTECTING WHAT YOU'VE EARNED, to help get you started and save you a few thousand dollars in fees.

As far as planning for college tuition, our chapter SAVING FOR YOUR CHILDREN will help you better understand your options.

3. INSURANCE NEEDS—LIFE, DISABILITY, AND UMBRELLA POLICIES

Many financial advisors receive a commission for pointing you in the direction of a particular insurance provider. We recommend using a third party that will provide you with options from multiple companies. We have separate chapters on LIFE INSURANCE, DISABILITY INSURANCE, and other forms of insurance dedicated to helping you navigate the terrain.

4. TAX PLANNING AND ADVICE

A tax specialist is one of the most valuable professionals to add to your team of advsiors. We discuss our taxes with a professional twice a year to ensure we are staying up to date with the ever-evolving tax code. We recommend utilizing a tax accountant or certified public accountant (CPA) for tax-related services.

The more assets and investments you have, the more complicated your tax situation becomes. We discuss tax consequences throughout the book to help you better understand the implications of those choices. We have also created our INTRODUCTION TO TAXES chapter to help summarize the tax-related advice throughout the book.

5. CREATE A PORTFOLIO OF INVESTMENTS

This is a financial advisor's bread and butter. Their primary responsibility is to offer clients a *portfolio* of investments tailored to their needs. In order to customize a portfolio for you, an assessment of your *risk tolerance* and your financial goals for retirement must be completed.

Our section, INVESTING FOR YOUR FUTURE, has ten chapters related to investing that cover everything from stock market basics to assessing your risk tolerance and the type of investment we select for our own portfolio. We present options to keep your investment strategy simple while historically outperforming most investment advisors on Wall Street. Whether you're new to investing or have been trading for years, we hope to challenge some of the common preconceived notions out there.

A good financial advisor can tweak your portfolio and make suggestions to improve your strategy. Arming yourself with the knowledge to challenge the investment strategy suggested by an advisor is the goal when these conversations take place. The information we provide in section four will help you do that.

> *Portfolio:* a collection of investments owned by an individual, and managed as a collective whole with specific investment goals in mind.
>
> *Risk tolerance:* the amount of loss and uncertainty an investor is comfortable taking with their investments.

6. FINANCIAL COACHING TO HELP AVOID EMOTIONAL INVESTMENT DECISIONS DURING UNCERTAIN TIMES

Coaching through uncertain economic times is valuable and another reason to check in with a financial advisor you trust from time to time. It is all too common to panic when the economy experiences a downturn and sell investments to limit your exposure. On the flip side, when the market is doing well, naturally, it feels like a good time to get into the market.

This is emotionally based trading and can result in a 'buying high and selling low' strategy. A financial advisor can help you to avoid those mistakes. We really like the infographic from the BhFS Behavioural Finance Solutions GmbH white paper below titled "Behavioral Finance: The Psychology of Investing"[23] that illustrates what emotional investing often looks like.

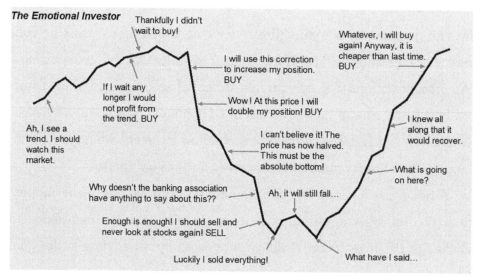

The Emotional Investor

Thankfully I didn't wait to buy!

If I wait any longer I would not profit from the trend. BUY

Ah, I see a trend. I should watch this market.

I will use this correction to increase my position. BUY

Wow! At this price I will double my position! BUY

Whatever, I will buy again! Anyway, it is cheaper than last time. BUY

I can't believe it! The price has now halved. This must be the absolute bottom!

I knew all along that it would recover.

What is going on here?

Why doesn't the banking association have anything to say about this??

Ah, it will still fall...

Enough is enough! I should sell and never look at stocks again! SELL

Luckily I sold everything!

What have I said...

Credit Suisse White Paper: Behavioral Finance: The Psychology of Investing

Anyone with experience investing in the market will be guilty of making similar emotional decisions at one time or another. A good financial advisor will talk you out of making investment decisions when panicked.

In the book, we discuss circumventing emotional investment decisions by having a *long-term investment* strategy in place. If you are well diversified, with many years before retirement, it is about weathering the storm. You need to accept that a *bear market* is inevitable, and watching the value of your retirement shrink at times can be extremely difficult. If you are nearing retirement, a good financial advisor can go a long way in helping you exit some of your investments for safer alternatives.

Long-term investment: stocks, bonds, or funds that are held for more than a year.

Bear market: a period when stocks are declining. Normally, a stock market decrease of 20% from recent highs is considered a bear market.

Our hope for you and your family is that you are the master of your own financial plan and that an advisor is there to do what they do best—give advice on tweaking that plan from time to time. Setting up the necessary investments is truly not that difficult. With this strategy, you can limit your advisory costs to one or two visits a year once you have your strategy in place.

How Do Financial Advisors Make Money?

There are four main cost structures that financial advisors will use to charge you for their services.

01. ANNUAL/MONTHLY RETAINER

A retainer is a set annual (or monthly) amount that provides you with full access to the advisor's services when needed. Expect to pay $2,000 to $10,000 for an annual retainer, depending on your assets and income.

02. % OF ASSETS UNDER MANAGEMENT

An advisor will charge a percentage of the value of the investments being managed. For example, if your advisor manages $500,000 for you and their fee is 1% of managed assets, you will pay the advisor $5,000 per year.

03. HOURLY RATE

An hourly rate may vary between $100 to $400 per hour, depending on the advisor and location.

04. FLAT FEE PER SERVICE

Advisors may charge flat fees for certain services. For example, an initial assessment of your current financial picture may cost $1,000. Different packages may be offered at a flat fee.

Let's talk about the percentage fee for assets under management (AUM). 1% doesn't sound like a lot of money when you are thinking about 100% of your assets, but that is not the comparison you need to make. What you really have to compare is the return on your investments every year. If you consider the average market return, you are looking at making 5 to 7% per year on your investments. So, if you're making a 5% a year and you are paying a 1% fee, that means you are LOSING 20% OF YOUR RETURN PER YEAR TO ADVISORY FEES.

NerdWallet's analysis on fees[24] does a great job of illustrating how much a 1% fee will cost you over time. In their example, they assume you have $25,000 in a retirement account, and you add $10,000 a year to the account and earn an average 7% annual return. They show that a 1% fee charged on your investments over 20 years would have cost you almost $62,000.

The cost of fees continues to accelerate, and that 1% fee over 30 years would have cost you approximately $210,000 in fees. If you are a millennial and you held your investments for 40 years with a 1% fee, you would be looking at having paid over $592,000 IN FEES ALONE. So the next time someone tells you a 1% fee is a small price to pay for financial advice, remember that you are actually paying 15 to 20% on your average return every year. Whether they are financial advisor fees or mutual fund fees, avoiding needless fees is one of the most important decisions we make as insightful investors.

What to Be Wary of with Financial Advisors

To start with, you will want to avoid advisors that talk over you. They will have done their introductory spiel many times, which can result in an advisor babbling on a complicated subject. Interrupt them. Ask them questions. Find someone who will spend the time to make sure you are comfortable and that you understand what is going on. Professionals in finance, medicine, and other fields tend to use industry jargon that is not common outside of their fields. Please make sure you stop them when you do not understand a term or phrase. If you do not leave the meeting with a strong understanding of what was discussed, find another advisor.

Furthermore, you'll want to avoid advisors that are being paid to recommend financial products and services to you. These products may not always be in your best interest. Whichever way you slice it, this is a potential conflict of interest. If you ask your financial advisor for advice on their recommended mutual fund, and they are paid if you select a particular package, that is likely not the best choice for you. In our experience, the products that graciously compensate advisors and are pushed to clients are often not the most attractive or competitive.

What is surprising to us is how many websites and organizations will tell you to stay away from advisors that are paid a commission when recommending products and then turn around and have their websites riddled with advertisements for financial services. Actually, we were unable to find any personal finance-related websites that did not receive commission for recommending or advertising financial institutions. We think this is hypocritical, and that is why you will not find financial services advertisements on MoneyOverMilkshakes.com.

Some advisors are also paid based on the number of trades you make. This can incentivize advisors to buy and sell frequently for a commission or put you in investments that may not be the best option for you. That is why we recommend fee-only *fiduciary* advisors—more on that below.

Fiduciary: a person legally required to place their clients interest ahead of their own.

Questions to Ask a Financial Advisor

When you're ready for a financial advisor's help, arrive at their office having done your homework. Come with a solid foundation and a plan in hand.

Here is a list of questions to help you gauge whether an advisor is a good fit for you.

01 QUALIFICATIONS
What are your qualifications?
Are you a fiduciary?

02 EXPERIENCE
What is your experience working with physicians? What is your experience in general?

03 COMPENSATION
How do you get paid: percentage of assets? Retainer? Hourly rate? Flat fee? What extra costs should I be aware of?

04 SERVICES
What services do you offer?

05 COMMUNICATION
How often will we communicate? How can I contact you?

06 INVESTMENT PHILOSOPHY
What does a moderate portfolio look like? What types of investments do you offer? What does their performance look like over the last 10 years?

07 DISCIPLINARY ACTIONS
Advisors must disclose any past regulatory, criminal, or disciplinary actions for themselves and their organization.

08 REFERENCES
Advisors should be able to provide references from individuals or online testimonials.

How Do I Find a Financial Advisor?

There are many different types of advisors, but we recommend focusing on a FEE-ONLY FIDUCIARY ADVISOR to cut through the maze. A fiduciary is legally obligated to act in your best interest rather than their own. Like most people, you might assume that all advisors would be obligated to act in your best interest, but unfortunately, that is not the case. The "fee-only" designation means that an advisor is only paid by you, the client, and not through commissions for selling their investment products to you.

What seems to be an intentionally confusing title is another type of advisor referred to as fee-based advisors. These advisors are paid commission to sell you financial products such as investments or insurance policies. There can be a conflict of interest here since they naturally tend to offer you the products with the highest commissions, which may not be in your best interest. Not to say that there aren't fee-based advisors with the best of intentions, but the conflict of interest is a concern. I prefer not to question whether an advisor is recommending a product to me because it offers them a financial incentive once I purchase it.

Certified Financial Planners (CFPs) are among the most common certifications that fee-only fiduciary advisors hold. CFPs require demanding training and exams to acquire that accreditation. The National Association of Personal Financial Advisors website[25] is a good place to find local advisors near you.

Chapter 13 Recap

FINANCIAL ADVISORS

✓ Financial advisors should be an important part of your financial strategy, but over-reliance on advisors can cost you considerably in fees.

✓ Understand how your advisor is being paid. Avoid advisors that push products and services they receive a commission for.

✓ Use this book and its resources to create your own financial plan before having an advisor fine-tune your strategy.

✓ Look for a fee-only fiduciary advisor.

✓ Arrange interviews with multiple advisors to see who would be the best fit for you and your family.

Scan for a full list of the links and tools listed.

Chapter 14
BUDGETING

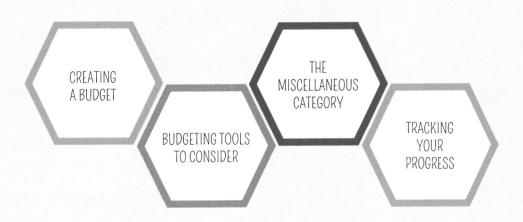

CREATING A BUDGET

BUDGETING TOOLS TO CONSIDER

THE MISCELLANEOUS CATEGORY

TRACKING YOUR PROGRESS

If you're still in medical school, you may not be able to imagine even needing a budget after the post-residency income hike. As an attending, you'll be rolling in the dough, right? Well, let me ask you this:

What do 50 cent, Nicolas Cage, Dennis Rodman, and Mike Tyson all have in common?

For one, they all made considerably more money than you could ever hope to make as a physician. Secondly, despite their wealth, they all declared bankruptcy with millions of dollars in debt. Whether you're Nicolas Cage or a physician, we all realize we need a budget sooner or later.

Creating a Budget

If you would rather stare at a wall than create a budget, you're in good company. Budgeting might not be the most thrilling task, but it's essential to meeting your financial goals. Not only is budgeting a vital step to regularly saving money, but the process of creating or updating a budget can be highly motivating in and of itself—I promise.

The most challenging part of consistently saving money is forming the habit to begin with. Like all habits, saving gets easier with time and eventually becomes second nature. Many people live paycheck to paycheck, regardless of their income. Without a budget and a savings plan, it is disturbing how quickly you can get comfortable making bad financial decisions, even after residency. We've made our own mistakes and have dedicated a chapter to your first paycheck after residency to discuss those mistakes in more detail.

Budgeting Tools to Consider[26]

We'll be the first to admit that keeping a detailed budget can be challenging, but the apps and software available today make budgeting considerably more manageable and less time-consuming than it has been previously.

Below is a brief overview of some of the most popular budgeting tools out there.

	MINT	YOU NEED A BUDGET	POCKETGUARD	EVERYDOLLAR
TAGLINE	See Everything in One Place	Give Every Dollar a Job	Money Simplified	Show Your Money Who's In Charge
HIGHLIGHTS	❖ Simple setup ❖ Highly automated ❖ Syncs to banks, credit cards, and investment accounts ❖ Overbudget alerts ❖ Free credit score	❖ Zero-based budgeting ❖ Hands-on approach ❖ Syncs to your banks, credit cards, and investment accounts ❖ In-depth education and support material ❖ 34-day free trial (free for students for 1 year)	❖ Clean user Interface ❖ Syncs to banks, credit cards, and investment accounts ❖ "In My Pocket" feature helps you answer, "Can I afford this?" ❖ Free version available with limited features	❖ Zero-based budgeting ❖ Easy to setup and use ❖ Created by Dave Ramsey ❖ Ad-free service (with the exception of Dave Ramsey products) ❖ 15-day free trial ❖ Free version available with limited features
WHAT WE DON'T LIKE	❖ Many targeted ads ❖ Synchronization issues with bank logins at times	❖ Requires time and commitment to use effectively ❖ Expensive compared to other options	❖ Only paid version allows tracking of cash transactions ❖ Not suited for complicated financial situations	❖ Cannot sync up banks or credit cards with free version ❖ Extremely expensive
PRICING	**Free**	$11.99/MO Or $84/YR	$3.99/MO Or $34.99/YR	$129.99/YR

Mint, You Need a Budget (YNAB), PocketGuard, and EveryDollar are all impressive budgeting tools that make budgeting, dare I say, almost fun. These apps will save you hours of combing through bank statements and recording transactions. Each of these apps can link to your bank accounts and credit cards and will help categorize your expenses. They will help keep you on track with reminders and alerts if you overspend on a particular category. Getting a big picture of how much you are actually spending on Amazon or Starbucks can be a real eye-opener.

Any of these apps will help you tremendously if you are not currently maintaining a regular budget, but each one has unique strengths and weaknesses. If you are looking for a more hands-off, automated budgeting tool, Mint is a good option.

We also very much enjoyed the You Need a Budget (YNAB) app. This app is more hands-on, as you'll need to assign a category for every dollar. That is not necessarily a bad thing since it will keep you more engaged in the budgeting process. This may be a good fit for those that are willing to dedicate regular time weekly to budgeting. To help you better understand the app, YNAB offers a one-on-one conversation with a coach for 15 minutes to answer any questions you might have.

The only app we have trouble recommending is EveryDollar. If you are a Dave Ramsey fan, this app follows his Baby Steps program. The app is well made, but we can't recommend an app that costs you $130 a year to help you budget when there are free or inexpensive options available that offer more features. EveryDollar does offer a free version, but you have to manually track all of your transactions, and you cannot auto-sync your bank and credit card accounts with the free version.

All of the paid apps offer free trials, so feel free to experiment with the different options and pick the one that works best for you.

We personally use the Mint app. It is hard to beat free, especially when the features are comparable to other paid-for budgeting apps. You can link your bank account and credit cards to your Mint account, and it will automatically categorize your expenses, so you know how much you are spending on shopping, travel, entertainment, and any other categories you create. (This automation has been a great fit for our budgeting style.)

It's also nice to see all of your accounts in one place; you can get a true sense of your overall financial picture that way. The app will provide you with a single net worth number. Mint will also alert you if you spend considerably more on a particular expense compared to your normal spending patterns.

At first, you will need to help the system categorize expenses to help guide the app's algorithms. Once an expense has been categorized, the app will remember what you have selected, and you shouldn't have to categorize the costs from that vendor again. Vendors like Amazon and Walmart are the exception since you can buy items in multiple budgeting categories from these stores.

After getting everything set up, the only time you'll spend budgeting is checking in for a few minutes every month to look at your budget and clean up uncategorized expenses. Mint has the added bonus of providing you with your Equifax credit score for free.

If you're not comfortable linking all your accounts in one place or do not want to use an online budgeting tool, you can enter your budget into a spreadsheet or create a pen-and-paper version. The principle in any version of a budget is the same—track your income, categorize your expenses, and see where you can trim unnecessary spending

Now that we've explored budget-tracking tools, let's take a look at the two most popular philosophies of budgeting: envelope budgeting and zero-based budgeting.

ENVELOPE BUDGETING

The concept here is to identify different categories for your expenses and assign a set amount of money towards each expense category. Some people physically separate out their income into cash envelopes and label those envelopes with different expense categories.

Since cash in hand is not as common today, the envelope system can be done digitally, either on a spreadsheet or through a budgeting app. To make an envelope budget, start by listing out expense categories.

As shown in the image below, you can take a broad approach to your categories or a more detailed approach. Over time, you'll add or subtract categories that fit your personal needs.

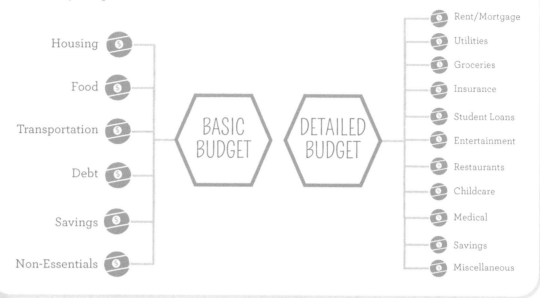

Next, you'll want to create buckets with the amount of money you assign to each expense category. This is where apps really come in handy and save you considerable time by analyzing all your transactions from bank and credit card accounts. If you prefer, you can also do this manually and go through bank and credit card statements to see how much you are spending each month.

Whether you are using an app or not, it will take some time to fine-tune your expense categories and how much you want to earmark for each expense. Essentially, the whole point of the envelope method is that there is no more spending in that category unless you borrow from another category when the money is gone.

ZERO-BASED BUDGETING

The idea here to assign every dollar you make to a category. Your income minus your expenses should equal zero. This doesn't mean you will have zero dollars in your bank account at the end of the month; it means that every dollar has a purpose.

This is the methodology used for the YNAB and EveryDollar apps. You'll create expense categories similar to what we discussed earlier. With this system, every dollar must be accounted for. If you have "extra" dollars left in your budget, you need to assign them to a category.

Regardless of the budgeting style you use, it's important to prioritize your spending categories. As a complement to the systems above, you can keep in mind the reverse budgeting concept. The Reverse Budgeting concept is creating a budget by first prioritizing your savings goals and building the rest of your expenses around those goals. The one modification we personally make is to prioritize high-interest debt first, which is closely followed by our savings goals. After that, our expenses are related to our needs and essentials such as food, utilities, housing. Finally, we spend on our wants, like entertainment, travel, etc.

The Miscellaneous Category

Almost everyone has a category in their budget labeled "miscellaneous." Even if you're using zero-based budgeting, you will need a category like this to account for the unexpected items you've forgotten to budget for, like a friend's birthday present or a random lunch date.

This category has been a black hole for us in the past, so be wary of it if you are just starting your budgeting journey. The miscellaneous monster seems to continuously grow and can take on a life of its own. If you are not careful, you can end up just tossing in all of your excessive spending into this category. For us, this category became the most important to analyze when reviewing our budget. If your budget has very broad categories, you're more likely to have a larger miscellaneous category.

We personally decided never to have more than a couple of hundred dollars in this category. If you see considerably more spending in this category, consider creating a new expense category by breaking out the recurring expense on its own. For example, if you're paying for afterschool activities for the kids and it is a considerable and reoccurring expense, you can create a new category labeled "child-related expenses."

Tracking Your Progress

Creating your budget is half the battle. (Actually, it's more like three-quarters of the battle.) Once you have a solid budget, you get to move on to the easy part—maintaining it. It usually takes 30 minutes to an hour a month to review your expenses, celebrate your wins, and identify areas for improvement.

Developing good habits takes regular practice, whether the habit is exercising regularly, focusing on a good night's sleep, or setting up a time to review your budget. It is often difficult at first, but it does become easier over time—one might even say it becomes enjoyable.

Another significant advantage of utilizing a budgeting app is the reminders it provides. If you are spending too much on restaurants one month, it's very helpful to receive a reminder that you have reached your budget limit for that category before you blow through your allotted amount. As you budget from month to month, you can expect to tweak your expense categories and the amounts you allocate to each bucket.

Here are a few mistakes to avoid when creating and maintaining your budget:

- BASE YOUR BUDGET ON YOUR INCOME AFTER TAXES. The difference between before and after taxes is enormous. If your taxes have already been taken out, you won't need to adjust your income to accommodate taxes.

- HAVE REALISTIC EXPECTATIONS. Making unattainable goals is the quickest way to lose motivation for maintaining a budget.

- START SMALL WITH YOUR SAVINGS. Get a few wins under your belt and gradually increase your savings over time.

Chapter 14 Recap
BUDGETING

✓ Start a free trial of Mint, YNAB, or another budgeting tool of your choice.

✓ Connect your accounts to help the system categorize your spending.

✓ Calculate your financial net worth.

✓ Create a recurring calendar reminder to open up your budgeting app and review your expenses.

✓ Keep an eye on your miscellaneous expenses and set a limit on them.

Scan for a full list of the
links and tools listed.

Chapter 15

SAVING

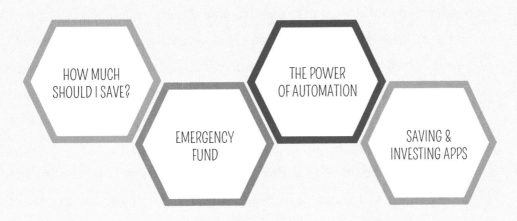

> "If we never save money or invest, we will always be poor,
> no matter how much we earn."
> —UNKNOWN

Saving is arguably the most crucial step to financial freedom. It's also one of the hardest. According to Bankrate's March Financial Security Index Survey, 21% of working Americans aren't saving any money at all. But there are ways to make saving for your future easier, even effortless. This chapter will review some options for automating your savings and explore different tools to help you track your progress toward your savings goals.

How Much Should I Save?

There are several schools of thought to help you decide how much money to allocate to different expense categories. One of the most popular is the 50/30/20 budget, which suggests you should spend around 50% on necessities, 30% on wants, and 20% towards savings and debt repayments.

The 50/30/20 budget is a good place to start early in your career. After residency, you will want to tweak this plan due to student loan payments and your increase in income. When that salary increase occurs, you will have a critical time-sensitive opportunity. You will not have become accustomed to spending the additional income yet, so you can increase your savings and debt payments a great deal while still enjoying an increase in your discretionary spending.

Your goal should be to shrink both the 50% bucket of necessities and the 30% bucket of wants. As a financially mindful physician, you might allot 40% of your budget to necessities, 20% to wants, and 40% to debt and savings.

HERE IS AN EXAMPLE TO ILLUSTRATE THE POINT: If you were making $50,000 after taxes in residency and spending 30% of your salary on wants such as entertainment, vacations, eating out, and other discretionary items, that would equate to $15,000 a year or $1,250 per month.

Say you lavishly double that amount after residency to $2,500 per month. If you are making $200,000 a year after taxes, that equates to just 15% of your budget. Even if you double the dollar amount you were spending on necessities ($25,000 to $50,000) as well, that leaves you with a whopping $120,000 or 60% of your salary to demolish your student debt and beef up your savings account. On a budget like this, the average physician could eliminate their $200,000 of student debt in less than two years.

This is not a penny-pinching plan. You'll be able to double your spending on necessities, double your discretionary spending, all while building a financially secure future for yourself and your family through your savings and investments.

RESIDENT VS. ATTENDING

BUDGET BREAKOUT

RESIDENT

Annual Salary:
$50,000

VS

ATTENDING

Annual Salary:
$200,000

50% $2,083/month on Necessities
30% $1,250/month on Wants
20% $833/month on Savings & Debt

40% $6,667/month on Necessities
20% $3,333/month on Wants
40% $6,667/month on Savings & Debt

Emergency Fund

Before you begin investing, you'll want to build a financial cushion for the unexpected. We all need this safety net, regardless of income level. There are black swan events in everyone's life—car accidents, medical bills, job losses, flooding basements, and a hundred other curveballs. When these catastrophes happen, you will dip into this fund for emergencies. Having it will insulate the rest of your finances from the devastating effects of these disasters.

Emergencies comprise a very narrow category. They are unforeseen and unpreventable. Home repairs and car maintenance are usually not emergencies—you know that you'll need a new roof every 20 years and new brakes every 50,000 miles. A vacation is not considered an emergency, no matter how stressed out you're feeling. All of these things can and should have a distinct place in your budget. Reserve your emergency fund for true emergencies.

Setting a goal of three months' worth of income in your emergency fund is a good place to start. Once you have achieved that, slowly increase the fund from 3 to 6 months' worth of salary. These aren't arbitrary numbers; most long-term disability policies don't kick in for 90 days, so if you have an unforeseen health emergency, you'll be waiting 3 months before you are eligible for payments.

Another reason for having 3 to 6 months of expenses on hand is to cover an extended period of unemployment. When determining how much to allot for emergencies, check your deductible on your insurance policies (home, car, and medical) to make sure you can cover the out-of-pocket amounts on these policies.

What happens when you don't have an emergency fund in place? Unfortunately, most of us know all too well. Your car is in bad shape. The mechanic says you need a new transmission. You're looking at a couple of thousand dollars to fix it. You don't have enough cash to cover it, so you pull out your credit card—problem solved.

It feels like magic, but in reality, you've only put a Band-Aid on a much bigger issue. The emergency fund is there to prevent you from going into debt when these situations arise. It can be difficult to dig yourself out of debt if credit cards are often used for emergencies.

Keep your emergency fund out of sight. If you don't look at your emergency fund every time you access your checking account, it will be considerably less tempting to dip into that account. Out of sight, out of mind goes a long way to keeping you on track. There are many ways to generate interest from your emergency fund. The money can be placed in a savings account, money market account, or a taxable investment account in very low-risk assets. All of these accounts can be accessed quickly.

The Power of Automation

You can set your bank or employer to deposit a certain amount to savings each paycheck, putting your savings plan on autopilot. The power of automating your savings is that it removes the decision fatigue we all experience from having endless choices followed by constant decisions. It's done—the decision has already been made. Regularly saving money without having to think about it is key to building wealth.

Automating your savings allows you to focus on your career rather than dedicating time to depositing savings, or worse—waiting till the end of the month to put aside what's left over in your account. (Spoiler alert: most of the time, there's not much left over.)

Automation also helps with budgeting. If you are like most people, your main budgeting strategy consists of looking at your checking account periodically to see how much money you have left until your next paycheck. Depositing savings right after you get paid will remove the temptation to spend your savings since it's already gone. The quicker you transfer your allocated savings away from your checking account, the better.

Our self-control is not what we would like to believe it to be. In a 1996 study,[27] Roy Baumeister conducted an experiment to test the willpower of 67 participants. In the first part of his experiment, he placed them in a room that smelled of freshly baked cookies. The participants could see the yummy treats lined up as they entered the room, but they were told they could not eat them. Instead, he had them eat radishes. To put it simply, they were not happy at this point.

The second part of the experiment was to give the participants a puzzle that took patience and persistence to solve. The results were clear in that those who were denied chocolate and had to eat radishes made far less effort than a separate group of participants who were able to enjoy the chocolate. This relatively simple experiment was considered a breakthrough in psychology. The authors of the study concluded that "these results point to a potentially serious constraint on the human capacity for control and deliberate decision making." In other words, the study identified that responsible decision-making is a finite resource that can be easily depleted.

That is why automating your savings can be such a powerful tool. Here are some easy ways to automate your savings:

THE POWER OF AUTOMATION

SPLITTING YOUR DIRECT DEPOSIT THROUGH YOUR EMPLOYER
Ask your employer to split your paycheck between multiple accounts. Your HR department can set this up for you. The advantage here is that the money you save never goes into your checking account. By doing this, you use the "out of sight, out mind" principle to minimize the likelihood of spending your savings.

AUTOMATIC BANK TRANSFERS
Use automatic transfers to routinely move money from your main checking account to a savings or investment account. This takes just a few minutes and can usually be done in the transfer section on your bank's website. You can also set it up as a bill pay and send a check to a savings account. If you are unsure of how to do this online, call your bank's customer service and they will guide you through the setup.

With either option, you set up your savings deposit once, and it remains in place until you decide otherwise.

Savings & Investing Apps[28]

A great way to start saving is to download a savings apps on your smartphone. These are easy to set up and provide the critical advantage of a set-it-and-forget-it approach. These apps are known as micro-investing apps since they allow you to invest your savings with as little as $5.

All of these apps are straightforward regarding their fees, depending on the features you are interested in. Several of the plans start at $1 per month. It might sound counterintuitive to pay for an app that helps you save your own money, but the automation and ease that savings apps provide can be well worth it if you struggle to save money. We personally found these apps to be highly effective when we were struggling to save money on a regular basis. You can always give one a try, then cancel after a month or two if the app isn't worth it to you.

There are dozens of micro-investing apps to choose from, but here are a few of our favorites. We've personally used each one and have found that they've added value to our finances.

ACORNS

The app's goal is to help you invest your spare change automatically. When you purchase an item with a linked card, the app will round the purchase up to the nearest dollar, then save and invest the difference. You can connect as many credit cards and debit cards as you like to link to the service to round up your spare change.

Here's an example of the app in action. If you purchase a bottle of water for $1.45, the app will round up to the nearest dollar and transfer $0.55 to your Acorns account, which will invest it in the stock market in a diversified portfolio. You also have the option to set up recurring deposits from your bank account to be invested.

Acorn simplifies your investment strategy down to five investment options that gauge your appetite for risk. These range from conservative to aggressive.

Here is the pricing and highlights for each type of plan Acorns offers:

ACORNS
PRICING PLANS

LITE	PERSONAL	FAMILY
$1 /month	**$3** /month	**$5** /month
• Investment account with five investment funds to choose from	• Everything included in the $1/month plan	• Everything included in the $3/month plan
• Subscription to investment publication	• Individual Retirement Account (IRA)	• Investment account for children (UGMA)
• Earn bonus money shopping with their affiliates	• Checking account	• Education resources for families
LITE	PERSONAL	FAMILY

Researched as of April 15th, 2021. The fees and services reviewed will surely change over time.
Please call or visit individual company websites for most up to date information on services offered.

© 2020 by Money Over Milkshakes LLC

DIGIT

This app focuses on saving money for you, but it doesn't offer the investment options you receive from Acorn. Digit uses an algorithm to identify your spending patterns, then regularly withdraws a few dollars from your checking account and transfers the money to a Digit savings account.

When we signed up for Digit, we found the algorithm quite effective and were surprised at how much we saved. The account will also pay you 1% per year in interest, paid out quarterly. Digit also promises to reimburse you if your account becomes overdrawn. We enjoyed using Digit, but the monthly fee has now gone up to $5/month and (in our opinion) has become too pricey for what it offers.

ALTERNATIVE OPTIONS

With these apps, what you are really paying for is the automation of saving and investing without much time or effort. If you struggle to put away money each month, an app is a good way to get started with saving and investing. The biggest obstacle to saving money for most is just getting started, and these apps can do that for you.

SAVING

✓ Use your budget plan to establish how much to save each month.

✓ Build a 3 to 6 month emergency fund. You will need it.

✓ Emergency funds and savings accounts are best kept out of sight to reduce the temptation to spend that money.

✓ Automate your savings by contacting your HR department and having a percentage of your paycheck go directly to your savings account.

✓ If you are having trouble saving regularly, consider a savings app such as Acorns to help automate your savings.

Scan for a full list of the links and tools listed.

Chapter 16
BANKING

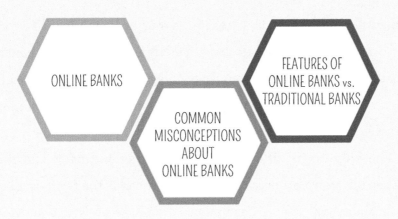

ONLINE BANKS

COMMON MISCONCEPTIONS ABOUT ONLINE BANKS

FEATURES OF ONLINE BANKS vs. TRADITIONAL BANKS

Back in the early 2000s, as a college student, I was always strapped for cash. My paycheck seemed to disappear as soon as it hit my bank account. There were days I would run a few errands, fill up the tank, pick up some food at a drive-through, and then on my last purchase, my card would be declined. I would hop online to find out that not only did I not have any money in my account, but that I'd been hit with multiple overdraft fees.

At times, these overdraft fees would add up to more than $100. And to make matters worse, they were often for small purchases like buying a bottle of water at a gas station or a burger at a fast-food place. Talk about feeling kicked when you're down.

Online Banks

Thankfully, today there is no reason to ever deal with fees like that again. You can avoid almost all of these fees by using an online bank. Online banks, also known as online-only or internet banks, are financial institutions that have few or no physical branches and allow customers to do virtually all of their transactions online.

The only major difference between an online bank and the banks you see on every corner is overhead. Overhead is the term used for ongoing business expenses. These physical branches cost money. Rent, staff, equipment, utilities, and other expenses at these branches are all types of overhead. Large traditional banks like Chase or Bank of America have physical branches across the nation. These physical branches cost money—and a lot of it. The customer ends up having to pay for these expenses one way or another.

On the other hand, online banks have no physical branches, which significantly reduces their overhead cost. Those savings can then be passed on to the customer.

Common Misconceptions about Online Banks

Let's touch on some common misconceptions and put them to rest.

CAN ONLINE BANKS BE TRUSTED?

In my younger years, people believed that a bank with a trustworthy reputation must have physical locations as a sign of stability. You can walk through the doors, see a teller take your cash, and get a deposit slip you can feel and put in your wallet—all things that denote the legitimacy of the institution.

Today, that way of thinking is outdated. Most physical banks have online portals and transactions anyway, plus online banks operate with significantly less overhead and offer the same services as a traditional bank. Many online banks offer customers more competitive rates since they do not have the burden of physical location expenses.

IS MY MONEY SAFE?

Online banks have the same insurance that traditional banks possess, so your money is as safe in an online bank as it is in a traditional one. The Federal Deposit Insurance Corporation (FDIC) ensures that if there is a bank failure, the federal government will step in and protect your checking, savings, and CDs up to $250,000 per individual.

If you're shopping around for a different bank, verify that they are FDIC insured. The FDIC covers all banks that we discuss in this book.

DO ONLINE BANKS HAVE LIMITATIONS ON CUSTOMER SERVICES COMPARED TO TRADITIONAL BANKS?

If you do not have a smartphone and need to make regular cash deposits, I will admit that an online bank is probably not for you. However, that's about the extent of the limitations of online banks. Aside from not making cash deposits or discussing your banking needs face-to-face, online banks offer all the other services you are accustomed to with a traditional bank.

If you have a smartphone, you can make electronic deposits on the checks you receive. We have also found the customer service with online banks to be considerably better than that of local banks. So, if you're not making regular cash deposits, there's no need to get in your car, drive to a branch, and wait in line—ever again!

I HAVE CONSIDERED THE BENEFITS OF AN ONLINE BANK, BUT ISN'T IT TOO TROUBLESOME TO SWITCH BANKS?

It took us 5 minutes to set up a checking and savings account with our online bank. It took another 20 minutes to transfer all our bill pay contact information.

We've also found wait times to be substantially better with online banks. At the time of this writing, our personal average wait time is 20 minutes with Bank of America, while Ally averages a 1- to 2-minute wait time. Ally also publishes their current wait times on the top right corner of their webpage once you log in, so you can wait to call until the queue is less full.

Features of Online Banks vs. Traditional Banks[29]

In the next section, we provide side-by-side comparisons of checking accounts, savings accounts, and CDs between a few of the larger traditional banks and online banks.

CHECKING ACCOUNTS

Let's start with a side-by-side comparison of checking accounts at some popular banks. The first three on the left are online banks, while the remaining three banks are traditional, large banks with branches across the U.S.

I did come across checking accounts and savings accounts with slightly more competitive offers than the ones we discuss; however, these were stand-alone accounts that tended to offer limited services. Our approach focused on banks that provide a full package of options on the accounts mentioned to reduce the time and complexity for those considering a new bank.

CHECKING ACCOUNTS SIDE BY SIDE

	ALLY BANK (INTEREST CHECKING ACCOUNT)	DISCOVER BANK (CASHBACK DEBIT ACCOUNT)	CAPITAL ONE (360 ACCOUNT)	CITI BANK (SIMPLE CHECKING ACCOUNT)	BANK OF AMERICA (ADVANTAGE PLUS ACCOUNT)	CHASE BANK (BASIC CHECKING ACCOUNT)
MONTHLY MAINTENANCE FEE	$0	$0	$0	$12	$12	$12
MINIMUM BALANCE REQUIRED TO WAIVE MONTHLY FEE	$0	$0	$0	$1500 minimum daily balance	$1500 minimum daily balance	$1500 minimum daily balance
YOUR % RATE ON SAVINGS (APR)	.10%	0% (but cashback on 1% for every physical swipe up to $3000 per month	0.02%	0%	0%	0.01%
YOUR SAVINGS INTEREST ON $10,000	$10	$30 for every $3000 spent	$2	$1	$0	$1
ORDERING CHECKS	Free for the life of the account	Free for the life of the account	1st order is free. After that $50 for every 50 checks	1st 10 are free; $20 to $25 for 100 checks	Start at around $28 for every 100 checks	1st 3 are free; $20 to $25 for 100 checks
STOP PAYMENT FEE	$15	$0	$35	$30	$30	$30
OVERDRAFT FEE	$25; no fee if linked to savings account	No fee if pay back within 75 days	No fee if pay back within 24 hours; $35	$34	$35: if linked to savings there is a $12 fee	$34
INCOMING WIRES (DOMESTIC)	No fees	No Fees	No Fees	$15	$15	$15
OUTGOING WIRES (DOMESTIC)	$20	$30	Up to $30; Cannot send to individuals	$35	$30	$35
ATM FEES (NO FEE FOR IN NETWORK)	No fee from Ally but may incur fee from ATM Operator	No fee from Discover but may incur fee from ATM Operator	$2 from Capital One plus fee charged by ATM Operator	$2.50 from Chase plus charge by ATM Operator	$2.50 from Chase plus charge by ATM Operator	$2.50 from Chase plus charge by ATM Operator
CARD REPLACEMENT	Free for replacements	Free for replacements; No fee for rush delivery	Free for replacements	Free for replacements; $6 for rush delivery	$5 per card; $15 for rush delivery	Free for replacements; $5 for rush delivery

Researched as of December 15th,2020. The fees and services reviewed will change over time.
Please call or visit individual bank websites for most up-to-date information on services offered.

© 2020 by Money Over Milkshakes LLC

It's worth mentioning that the three banks in the table that charge monthly maintenance fees do provide ways to avoid the monthly fee. For example, in the table above, if you can maintain the $1,500 daily average, you won't have to pay the fee, but if your account drops below that amount for any 24-hour period, you can expect to pay the fee for that month. There are other ways to avoid the fee, but in our opinion, the whole premise is unnecessarily complicated. There are banks that don't charge a fee, and you won't have to worry about slipping up on one of their requirements.

In our opinion, if you are depositing money with a bank, you should receive some interest on that money since the bank uses your money to make a profit. To compare the checking accounts in the table above, Ally offers 10 times the interest that Chase, Bank of America, and Citi Bank do.

LASTLY, A NOTE ON EXCESSIVE FEES: Large banks have preyed on the financially vulnerable with fees for too long. Peter Smith, a Senior Researcher at the Center for Responsible Lending, co-wrote a report on overdraft fees,[30] which reviewed fees of the 10 largest banks in the United States. The report shows that these banks collected over $11 billion in overdraft fees every year between 2015 and 2019—that's billion with a "B." According to the World Bank, that's more money than the entire annual GDP of 45 different countries.

The banks that collected the highest income from overdraft fees were Chase, Wells Fargo, and Bank of America. Each of these banks can charge you up to $100 a day for overdraft fees. And these aren't the only fees—banks charge maintenance fees, monthly service fees, account closure fees, ATM fees, check ordering fees, paper statement fees, and the list goes on.

SAVINGS ACCOUNTS

The main difference between a checking account and a savings account is that you are limited by federal law to 6 withdrawals/transfers a month with a savings account. Your checking account allows you to withdraw funds as often as you'd like and is better suited for everyday use.

Here is another side-by-side comparison of the same institutions we looked at earlier, but this time we're looking at the savings account options.

	Online Banks			Traditional Banks		
	ALLY BANK (SAVINGS ACCOUNT)	DISCOVER BANK (SAVINGS ACCOUNT)	CAPITAL ONE (360 SAVINGS ACCOUNT)	CITI BANK (BASIC SAVINGS ACCOUNT)	BANK OF AMERICA (ADVANTAGE SAVINGS)	CHASE BANK (REGULAR SAVINGS ACCOUNT)
MONTHLY MAINTENANCE FEE	$0	$0	$0	$4.50	$8	$5
MINIMUM BALANCE REQUIRED TO WAIVE MONTHLY FEE	$0	$0	$0	$500	$500	$300
INTEREST RATE ON SAVINGS (APR)	0.50%	0.40%	0.40%	0.50%	0.01%	0.01%
YOUR INTEREST SAVINGS ON $10,000	$50	$40	$40	$50	$1	$1

Researched as of April 15th,2021. The fees and services reviewed will change over time.
Please call or visit individual bank websites for most up-to-date information on services offered.

© 2020 by Money Over Milkshakes LLC

As shown in the table, there are substantial differences in the savings account interest rates. The savings rates with the online banks listed are 14 to 15 times greater than a regular Chase Savings account.

CERTIFICATES OF DEPOSIT (CD)

While we're discussing what services banks can offer, we need to touch on certificates of deposit, better known as CDs. CDs are simply another option to place your money in an account that will pay you interest for the deposit. The rates on the savings accounts we've been discussing up to now are variable—banks can change the rates at any time.

During the COVID pandemic, rates decreased quite dramatically. When I first started putting this book together in early 2020, Ally was offering 1.50%, but as of April 2021, that rate has been reduced to 0.55%. The interest rates are fixed with CDs, meaning they are locked in for a specific period of time—anywhere from 3 months to 5 years, depending on which one you choose.

Here is a list of CDs offered by the same banks we have discussed thus far.

	Online Banks				Traditional Banks	
	ALLY BANK (NO PENALTY CD)	DISCOVER BANK (12 MONTH CD)	CAPITAL ONE 360 (12 MONTH CD)	CITI BANK (NO PENALTY CD)	BANK OF AMERICA (12 MONTH CD LESS THAN $10K)	CHASE BANK (12 MONTH CD LESS THAN $10K)
TERM	11 Months	12 Months	12 Months	12 Months	12 Months	12 Months
EARLY WITHDRAWAL PENALTY	No penalty	6 months interest on amount withdrawn	3 months interest on amount withdrawn	No penalty	3 months interest on amount withdrawn	6 months interest on amount withdrawn
INTEREST RATE ON SAVINGS (APR)	0.50%	0.50%	0.20%	0.30%	0.03%	0.02%
YOUR SAVINGS INTEREST ON $10,000	$50	$50	$20	$25	$3	$2
MINIMUM BALANCE REQUIRED	No Minimum	$2500	No Minimum	$500	$1000	$1000

Researched as of April 15th,2020. The fees and services reviewed will surely change over time. Please call or visit individual bank websites for most up to date information on services offered.

© 2020 by Money Over Milkshakes LLC

Once again, there is a significant difference between the offerings of online banks and larger, traditional banks for the interest rate on CDs. For instance, the Discover Bank CD rate is 25 times greater than the Chase Bank CD. That is not a typo—you give the bank $10,000 to hold for 12 months, and in return, Chase will provide you with a grand total of $2 at the end of 12 months. They say thanks for profiting off your thousands with the equivalent of a cup of coffee. All interest rates on CDs are low right now, but at least the interest on an online CD will buy you coffee for a few months.

Typically, CDs charge a penalty if you withdraw your funds before the predetermined time period; however, some institutions offer no-penalty CDs. Although CDs are not as popular as they have been in the past (primarily due to the low interest rates), there is a place for CDs in your savings plan.

For example, during the COVID pandemic, your emergency fund would have been much better served in a no-penalty CD with a fixed interest rate than in a checking or savings account with a variable rate that has gone down to essentially 0%. A no-penalty CD offers significantly higher rates than many checking or saving accounts and doesn't charge a penalty to withdraw the funds; your deposits are available to you as they would be in a checking or savings account.

All of the rates mentioned above are current as of April 2021. The rates and conditions for the checking, savings, and CDs mentioned are constantly changing. We've provided a snapshot in time to help you make some comparisons. Through your own research, you may find more competitive rates or incentives.

Chapter 16 Recap
BANKING

- ✓ Consider switching to an online bank. You will save money on monthly maintenance fees, overdraft fees, incoming wire fees, check ordering fees, and card replacement fees.

- ✓ Online banks pay up to 25 times as much interest as their traditional counterparts do.

- ✓ Large banks like Bank of America and Chase collected over $11 billion a year in overdraft fees between 2015 and 2019.

- ✓ A no-penalty CD with a fixed interest rate is a reasonable way to lock in savings during uncertain times.

Scan for a full list of the links and tools listed.

Chapter 17
CREDIT CARDS

The Double-Edged Sword

Credit cards are most definitely a double-edged sword. Using credit cards to pay monthly bills can earn you free cash back, gift cards, or travel rewards. There is really only one question to ask yourself before deciding whether to use credit cards to pay bills:

CAN YOU PAY OFF YOUR BALANCE EVERY MONTH?

If you find your balance growing over time, stop using your card to pay your monthly bills.

Using credit cards to pay bills takes an incredible amount of financial discipline. Credit card debt can get away from you very quickly—car repairs one month, travel expenses on top of that, and a vacation for the family. Then the bill arrives, and like a cartoon, your eyes pop out of your head. You might look at the minimum due and say to yourself, "I can at least pay that" while the debt continues to grow. A GOOD RULE OF THUMB: Before using your credit card each time, ask yourself if you can pay cash for it. If the answer is no, don't swipe the card.

Predatory Interest Rates

Interest rates on credit cards range from around 15% up to 25% or more. This is the annual interest that accrues on your outstanding debt. In our opinion, this is predatory lending, plain and simple. Compare this to the 1-2% you receive if you lend your money to a bank through a savings account. Home loan interest rates with good credit scores are at 3-4% in 2021, while personal loans are closer to 9-10%. Nothing comes close to the exorbitant interest rates on credit cards. The staggering interest rate is often why many cannot keep up with credit card payments and are forced into bankruptcy.

Credit Cards and Your Credit Score

Credit cards can help build your credit score or destroy it. Your credit score is one of the largest determining factors for your interest rate on loans throughout your life. The two most impactful actions that influence your credit score are paying your bills on time and the amount of debt to available credit you have. Your payment history (or, in other words, making payments on time) is the largest determining factor in your credit score. Your credit utilization ratio is the second most important influence on your credit score. This ratio represents the amount of debt you owe compared to the amount of credit available to you. If you owe $1,000 across multiple credit cards and your available credit to spend on those cards total $5,000, then your credit utilization ratio is 20%. The credit reporting agencies recommend keeping your debt under 30% of your available credit. Paying off your debt in full every month is one of the most impactful steps you can take to improving your credit score.

An option to decrease your credit utilization ratio is to request an increase in available credit from your credit card company. In doing this, you'll want to avoid what is referred to as a "hard" pull. This is when the credit card company requires a copy of your credit score. This normally lowers your score by a few points. Request a "soft" pull, which is a limited-access credit pull and does not show up on your credit report.

Credit Card Rewards

There are lots of different rewards offered for using credit cards—free travel, gift cards, discounts, and more. The truth is credit card companies offer these rewards since they are paid for by the people that get stuck paying high interest rates on their debt. Lets' call this what it is—a rat trap. But you can game the system by paying off your debt every month in full, never paying a cent in interest while reaping the credit card rewards.

Credit card rewards usually come in the form of cashback, points, or miles when purchases are made with a credit card. Cashback is pretty straightforward. For example, you might get $0.01 back for every dollar you spend, or you might receive 1-2% cash back on purchases made. If your reward comes in the form of points and miles, you'll need to research what their true value is.

You might assume that one point or one mile would be equivalent to one dollar. From what we've seen that is far from accurate. One point is closer to a penny. When comparing card rewards systems, make sure you are comparing apples to apples.

If you use a credit card to earn rewards, just make sure you are selective on what card you pick and only spend money you were planning on spending anyway. We like The Points Guy's website as a good resource for comparing rewards on credit cards. Again, if you give this a shot and find that after a few months that your credit card bill keeps growing, then using only cash is the way to go.

Chapter 17 Recap
CREDIT CARDS

✓ Credit cards should not be used to gain rewards if you cannot pay off the total outstanding balance each month. You will lose more in interest than you gain in points.

✓ Annual interest rates on credit cards can be up to 25%. For every $100 you spend, you will have to pay an additional $25 in interest if you carry the balance for a year.

✓ Using credit cards responsibly can improve your credit score—the largest determining factor of your interest rate on future loans, such as mortgages. However, the opposite is true if you use credit cards irresponsibly.

✓ Consider The Points Guy as a good resource for comparing rewards on credit cards.

Scan for a full list of the links and tools listed.

Chapter 18

BUYING, RENTING, & HOME LOANS

TO BUY OR TO RENT A HOUSE

DOWN PAYMENT ON A MORTGAGE

REVIEWING YOUR CREDIT SCORE BEFORE PURCHASING A HOME

PREQUALIFICATION & PREAPPROVAL

WALKING THROUGH THE LOAN ESTIMATE DOCUMENT

BEFORE YOU GET A MORTGAGE

TYPES OF LOANS

WHAT DOES IT MEAN TO BUY POINTS?

HOW MUCH SHOULD MY MONTHLY MORTGAGE PAYMENTS BE?

RATE SHOPPING WITH DIFFERENT MORTGAGE COMPANIES

(AMANDA) On Match Day, we were having a fancy lunch at the top of an impressive building downtown. A speaker was sharing with the room their own journey through medical school, but I couldn't hear a thing. The sounds around me felt muted. My thoughts were consumed by the little envelope in front of me. In a few minutes, we would be asked to open our envelope and find out where we would spend the next several years of residency.

We were really hoping to stay where we were at, close to family. We could use the help, as we'd just had twins three months prior. My husband, Nick, had a good job in town, and picking up and leaving all that behind would be difficult.

Well, the moment came, the envelope was opened, and we were not staying put. We were going to have to pack our bags and start fresh in a new town and a new state.

It was a hectic few months trying to get settled into a new place. We had to quickly make the decision whether we were going to buy or rent a home in this new town. We decided to buy a home for a few reasons. We were moving to a smaller town in the Midwest, with property values increasing at around 5% a year. Interest rates were low, and housing prices were very affordable.

Buying a home turned out to be a good decision for us, but it was not an easy one to make. Residency is just enough time to make that decision difficult. You are often right around the break-even point between renting or buying.

In this chapter, we provide some questions to ask yourself before making that decision and questions to consider after you've decided to buy a home.

To Buy or To Rent a House

Deciding whether you should buy or rent a house is a highly personal decision based on many factors. There are many pros and cons to each choice.

Here are some good questions to ask yourself to get you started in making that decision.

HOW LONG WILL YOU BE IN THE HOUSE?

As a medical student or resident, you may only be living in that area for three to five years. It takes time for the decision to own a home to be financially advantageous compared to renting because of the additional costs that come with buying a home. Below, we discuss calculating the breakeven point.

DO YOU HAVE AN EMERGENCY FUND? AND CAN YOU PAY FOR UNEXPECTED REPAIRS?

If a pipe bursts, your water heater dies, or an air-conditioning unit breaks, it will be your responsibility to pay for it. These are repairs you don't have to worry about with renting. Repairs can cost several thousand dollars and might be devastating to a homeowner without a large enough emergency fund.

WHAT IS THE COST OF RENTING A SIMILAR HOME? ARE YOU COMPARING APPLES TO APPLES?

When you're looking at comparing the costs of renting or buying a home, make sure to include property taxes, closing costs, and maintenance fees.

When opting to rent or buy, there are some great calculators online[31] that will do the heavy lifting for you and help you decide. Two of the calculators we like are those built by Zillow and the New York Times.

In the example below using the Zillow calculator, if you were moving to Oklahoma City for medical school or residency and buy a home for $150,000, after 2 years and 1 month it would be cheaper to buy a house than to rent one with a similar value.

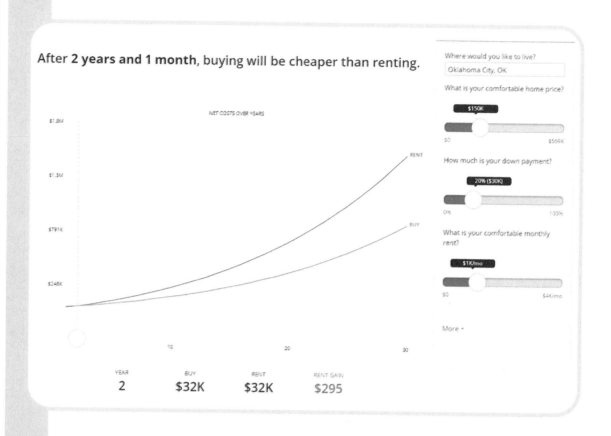

An important note on using these calculators is that they assume that you are investing rather than spending the money you would have used on a down payment if you choose to rent. If you spend that money, that will push the result more in favor of purchasing a property.

Keep in mind that the calculators are only a guide, and there are factors outside the control of any calculation, such as significant changes in the housing market. Your location also has a lot to do with determining whether buying a house might be a good decision. The cost of living and the local housing market dynamics are different from place to place.

Before You Get a Mortgage

A mortgage is the single largest personal expense for most of us, perhaps aside from student debt. It's a financial decision that involves hundreds of thousands of dollars with 15-30 years of payments. Purchasing a property will have a substantial impact on your month-to-month finances and can be an essential part of your investment portfolio and retirement.

Throughout the country, real estate markets and related opportunities vary drastically depending on many different factors. Your geography and timing will play a big part in what the supply and demand of homes look like in your area. In larger metro area markets, home prices can be volatile, as these areas quickly gain or lose their appeal.

We live in the Midwest, where property tends to be more affordable and prices more stable. Property values do not drastically increase or decrease around here. In comparison to other parts of the country, prices did not drop severely during the housing crisis. Property values in our area tend to take a slow but gradual increase over time with less risk than larger markets, reducing some of the uncertainty when purchasing a home. With these factors in mind, we decided to purchase a home in residency and another after getting settled as an attending.

Before you go house-hunting or get a pre-approval for a mortgage, you should know how much you can afford and what kind of down payment you can make. If you haven't updated your budget in a while, now is a good time to dust off the cobwebs and update it with current income and expenses. If you are transitioning to a different stage in your career and your income is changing, make sure you are using your after-tax income since there is a 20-40% difference between pre-tax and after-tax income depending on your tax bracket. (In case you missed it, our section dedicated to helping create a budget can be found on page 127.)

Down Payment on a Mortgage

There are arguments for both a large and small down payment on a house. The benefits to a larger down payment tend to outweigh the alternatives, but we'll discuss these nonetheless. Choosing the down payment amount for your home loan is not an exact science, but here are some things to consider when making that decision.

BENEFITS TO A LARGE DOWN PAYMENT

01 LOWER INTEREST RATE

02 NO PRIVATE MORTGAGE INSURANCE (PMI)

03 LOWER MONTHLY PAYMENTS WITH LESS INTEREST OVER THE LIFE OF THE LOAN

04 MORE EQUITY IN THE HOME

1. LOWER INTEREST RATE

The more money you put down, the less of a risk the bank will consider you as far as *defaulting* on your loan. Many banks will lower your interest rate with a down payment of 20% or more. A quarter- or half-percent reduction may not sound like much, but converting that percentage into actual dollars saved will highlight its true value.

> *Defaulting:* the failure to repay a debt. Lenders will label a loan in default when the minimum required payments have not been made for a certain number of months, specified in the loan contract

The infographic below demonstrates that even a half of a percent reduction on your interest rate can save you around $70 per month, translating into a savings of almost $25,000 by the end of the loan term.

MORTGAGE INTEREST RATE REDUCTION

$300,000 FIXED LOAN OVER 30 YEARS WITH A 20% ($60,000) DOWN PAYMENT

	4% INTEREST RATE	3.75% INTEREST RATE	3.5% INTEREST RATE
MONTHLY PAYMENT (PRINCIPAL + INTEREST)	$1,145 per month	$1,111 per month	$1,077 per month
TOTAL INTEREST PAID (THIS IS IN ADDITION TO THE $300,000 PRINCIPAL)	$172,753	$160,277	$148,169

2. NO PRIVATE MORTGAGE INSURANCE (PMI)

If you're putting down less than a 20% down payment on a home, you will pay private mortgage insurance (PMI). This is not the regular homeowner's insurance that protects you from damages. PMI protects the lender if you, as the borrower, stop making payments on your mortgage. This applies to most loans (except for Veteran Affairs (VA) loans, USDA loans, and a few other specific types).

This is an additional 0.5% to 1.5% on top of your existing interest rate. Using the previous example, if you pay $300k on a home, you will end up paying an extra $120 to $360 per month for PMI until you have paid off 20% of the home's purchase price. At that point, you will no longer need to pay PMI on your loan. It may not seem like that big a deal since the additional interest does not last for the life of the loan. However, in this example, you'll end up paying an additional $12,000 to $35,000 on your loan—just for the PMI.

Don't hold your breath waiting for the mortgage company to remove the PMI once you have paid 20% of the home's purchase price; they will usually need reminding. Get the details from the mortgage company of the exact amount that will need to be paid for the PMI to drop off your loan. Figure out how many months it will take to get there. Once you know that, you can set your own calendar reminder to contact your mortgage company to remove it from your loan.

3. LOWER MONTHLY PAYMENTS WITH LESS INTEREST OVER THE LIFE OF THE LOAN

A large down payment means you will be borrowing less money. Therefore, your monthly payments will end up being less. You also end up paying less interest over the life of the loan.

SMALL VS. LARGE DOWN PAYMENT ON A MORTGAGE

ASSUMPTIONS
Purchase price: $250,000, Loan term: 30 years, Interest rate: fixed 4%

DOWN PAYMENT OF $50,000	VS	DOWN PAYMENT OF $10,000

NEW LOAN BALANCE		NEW LOAN BALANCE
$50,000 down payment would reduce your loan to $200,000		$10,000 down payment would reduce your loan to $240,000

MONTHLY PAYMENTS		MONTHLY PAYMENTS
$1,357 per month with no Private Mortgage Insurance (PMI) to be paid		$1,648 per month including $100 of Private Mortgage Insurance (PMI)

INTEREST PAID		INTEREST PAID
Over the life of the loan you would pay $143,739 in addition to the original loan of $200,000		Over the life of the loan you would pay $172,487 in addition to the original loan of $200,000

4. MORE EQUITY IN THE HOME

The difference between the value of the home and the outstanding balance on your loan is your equity. Building up equity increases your net worth and can be part of your investment strategy to building wealth. You can also use the equity in your home to borrow against. You do not need to sell your home in order to take out a home equity loan.

AN ARGUMENT FOR A SMALLER DOWN PAYMENT: Although larger down payments are generally a good thing, you also do not want to empty your savings or retirement accounts to beef up your down payment. One argument for putting down less is that for some people, it might take years to save up a 20% down payment. Putting down less than 20% to purchase a home might be preferred over renting, especially if you plan on keeping the home for many years. That way, at least some of your house payments will go to equity instead of paying a landlord's equity while you save for your own.

You may also decide to place some of that money into another investment or retirement account. The decision will be based on your personal circumstances. Whatever decision you make, you'll want to make sure you still have an emergency fund as well as some money for the inevitable home improvements.

How Much Should My Monthly Mortgage Payments Be?

How much of your income should go towards a mortgage payment? After the national mortgage crisis, many banks have limited mortgages to 28% of your *gross income*. Even these lender approval amounts can be overly generous.

When we were buying our first home and going through the pre-approval process, we were surprised at how much we had been approved for. It's easy to look at that number and say to yourself, "Well if the bank thinks I can do it, maybe I have more room in my budget than I thought."

DO NOT FALL INTO THAT TRAP! Overspending on a house is a mistake, and you should stick with your original budget. Everyone's circumstances are different, but we do NOT recommend taking out the maximum amount offered on a home loan, or any other loan for that matter.

In most cases, loan officers receive a commission on the total value of the loan. The bigger the loan, the more they profit. That means it is up to you to decide how much you can truly afford. Aim for a smaller percentage than the 28% of your monthly gross income that many banks suggest.

Repairs and maintenance costs can come as a surprise for first-time homeowners. Fixing fences, replacing water heaters, and repairing A/C units can add up, and you'll want to make sure to have money set aside for the unexpected.

> Many people are not aware that first-time homebuyers are eligible to take out up to $10,000 from their IRA or 401(k) without penalty for a down payment on their first home.

Gross income: the amount of money earned before taxes or other deductions are taken out.

Reviewing Your Credit Score
Before Purchasing a Home

An important item to review before applying for a mortgage is your credit score. Your credit score has a massive impact on your interest rate, *points*, PMI, required down payment, and the approved amount on the loan. The table below from myfico.com[32] illustrates how your score can affect your *annual percentage rate (APR)*.

Home Purchase Center

Mortgage rates as of May 20, 2021

30-year fixed	15-year fixed	7/1 ARM	3/1 ARM	1/1 ARM

FICO® score	APR [?]	Monthly payment
760-850	2.633%	$1,206
700-759	2.855%	$1,241
680-699	3.032%	$1,270
660-679	3.246%	$1,305
640-659	3.676%	$1,377
620-639	4.222%	$1,471

Location: National Avg.   Loan amount: $300,000   **RECALCULATE**

Source: Informa Research Services

On a loan of $300,000, the difference in monthly payments for someone with a credit score of 620 and someone with a score of 760 is $269 a month. Multiply that difference over 30 years, and the person with the 620 credit score will pay an additional $95,000 on the exact same loan.

Points: in this context means paying money upfront for the option to lower your interest rate. Normally 1 point is equal to 1% of the amount you're borrowing.

Annual percentage rate (APR): the annual rate charged for borrowing expressed as a percentage.

It's in your best interest to keep your credit score as high as you can. If your credit is less than perfect, here are some suggestions on how to improve it:

- Resolve any accounts in collections
- Reduce your debt, especially high-interest debt in accounts that are close to the credit limit
- Remove any errors on your report
- Make payments on time
- Avoid closing the accounts you've had for a long time

WHERE TO FIND A FREE CREDIT REPORT[33]

You should never pay for your credit report. By law, each of the three credit reporting companies (Equifax, Transunion, and Experian) are legally obligated to provide you with a free copy of your credit report once every 12 months. To access the reports, go to annualcreditreport.com or call them at 1-877-322-8228.

There are other untrustworthy websites with similar-sounding names that will try to get you to pay for a credit report. Steer clear of other sites and go specifically to the website mentioned above.

Once you order your report, the reporting agencies try to get you to pay to see your credit score. The credit report and the credit score are considered two separate items. In our opinion, this is a sleazy business practice. It's like ordering a dessert at a restaurant, and the waiter brings you the ingredients and tells you it will cost you extra for them to put all the ingredients together and make your dessert for you.

Luckily, you can get your credit score for free from several places. Many credit cards such as Discover, Citi, Chase, and Capital One now offer customers access to their credit scores through their online portals.

Here are some additional sites that will offer you an estimated credit score for free. These sites may not provide the exact number the reporting agency would, but they will give you a close enough understanding of where your credit score stands. Again, these are free and a great resource for estimating your credit score.

Types of Loans

There are different types of loans available with different features to consider. Here are the more common loans to consider:

FEDERAL HOUSING ADMINISTRATION (FHA) LOANS: These are backed by the government and require a minimum of 3.5% down payment with a credit score of 580 or higher. These loans tend to be easier to qualify for since they are backed by the Federal Housing Administration. It's worth noting that is if you put less than 20% down, you may be required to pay mortgage insurance for the life of the loan.

CONVENTIONAL LOANS: These are not backed by the government and tend to require higher credit scores. These loans will require PMI if the down payment is less than 20% of the purchase price.

JUMBO MORTGAGE: This is exactly what it sounds like—an extra-large loan. For 2021, if the loan is more than $548,250, it will require a jumbo loan. Considering the amount of the loan, the bank's requirements for credit score and qualifications are much more stringent than those for other loans. Jumbo loans can be difficult to qualify for.

VA LOANS: These are for veterans or active-duty military. VA Loans do not require a down payment, and there is no PMI.

Prequalification & Preapproval

There is a difference between prequalification and preapproval for a mortgage. Prequalification is asking a bank to estimate how much you *may* qualify for. You provide the bank information regarding your income, debt, and estimated credit score, and they will provide you with an estimated approved amount for a loan.

Preapproval, on the other hand, is more than an estimate. It is an offer from a lending institution that they agree to lend you the funds if certain requirements are met. They will require proof of your financial situation and may request follow-up documentation. To finalize your loan, you will go through what is referred to as underwriting. This is the process in which they verify your income and debt to evaluate your financial picture.

There are advantages to getting pre-approved before you begin looking at houses. Once pre-approved, you tend to move to the top of the list over other prospective buyers if there are multiple bids on a home. Pre-approvals are generally good for 90 days.

ASIDE FROM YOUR CREDIT SCORE, LENDERS WILL BE LOOKING AT:

- Your credit report
- Total debt
- Savings
- Total assets
- Current income

Rate Shopping with
Different Mortgage Companies

Reaching out to multiple mortgage companies and having them bid for your business is not only prudent, but it can save you tens of thousands of dollars. Homebuyers are generally discouraged from shopping around since you are told your credit score can be negatively impacted. Although a hard pull of your credit can negatively impact your credit score, the consequence is normally quite small. The general discouragement to shop around for multiple loans is a failure to the public by the three credit reporting agencies.

You can avoid any negative ramifications by exploring your options within a short period, typically less than 30 days. You can play it even safer if you choose to compare rates within a two-week period. Multiple hard pulls within a short timeframe only count as one since the credit reporting agencies assume you are shopping around. Don't let the fear of lowering your credit score stop you from shopping around for the best deal.

On two separate occasions, our lenders made last-minute changes and increased our interest rate when purchasing a home. We can't be certain, but we felt that the bank assumed we would simply accept the increased rate since we were in the middle of the approval process, and looking elsewhere would involve too much effort. On both occasions, we told those lenders to kick rocks and went with other lenders that provided better rates.

Because of this experience, we always negotiate with at least two lenders up until the rate is locked and the underwriting process has been completed. Whether we are shopping for cars, insurance, or mortgages, our personal approach is to always reach out to two or three companies and have them bid for our business. Each mortgage company will provide you with a loan estimate like the one shown below. This is an important document to review. These loan estimates are three pages long and are required by the Consumer Finance Protection Bureau to be in the same format. This makes loans easy to compare. It is important to get familiar with the information in the loan estimate to compare one offer with another accurately.

Walking Through the Loan Estimate Document

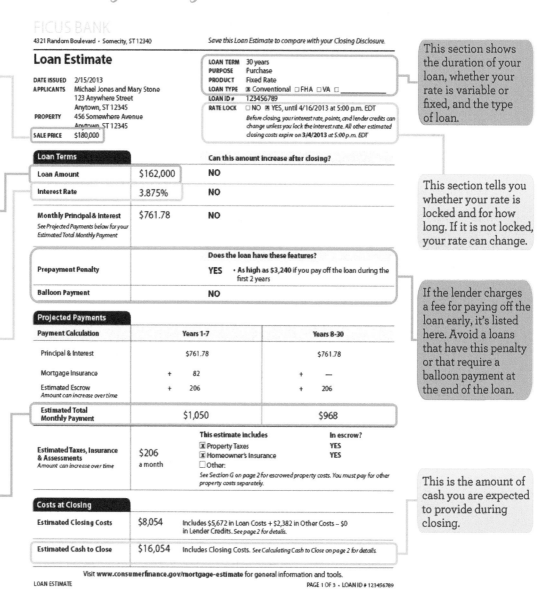

This shows the full purchase price of the home. The down payment plus the loan amount should equal the sales price.

This is the amount you will need to borrow. (Sales price of $180,000 minus a down payment of $18,000 = loan amount of $162,000)

This is the rate you will pay on the outstanding loan balance every year before mortgage fees and other charges.

This is what you can expect your monthly payments to look like (keep in mind these are estimates).

This section shows the duration of your loan, whether your rate is variable or fixed, and the type of loan.

This section tells you whether your rate is locked and for how long. If it is not locked, your rate can change.

If the lender charges a fee for paying off the loan early, it's listed here. Avoid a loans that have this penalty or that require a balloon payment at the end of the loan.

This is the amount of cash you are expected to provide during closing.

Closing Cost Details

Loan Costs

A. Origination Charges	$1,802
.25 % of Loan Amount (Points)	$405
Application Fee	$300
Underwriting Fee	$1,097

These are the costs the mortgage company is charging for the loan. Compare the costs here with other lenders. No matter what they say, these costs ARE negotiable.

B. Services You Cannot Shop For	$672
Appraisal Fee	$405
Credit Report Fee	$30
Flood Determination Fee	$20
Flood Monitoring Fee	$32
Tax Monitoring Fee	$75
Tax Status Research Fee	$110

Although these fees are required, compare the overall costs of the fees with those of other lenders.

C. Services You Can Shop For	$3,198
Pest Inspection Fee	$135
Survey Fee	$65
Title – Insurance Binder	$700
Title – Lender's Title Policy	$535
Title – Settlement Agent Fee	$502
Title – Title Search	$1,261

These fees are required, but you can shop around for different prices. The lender should provide a list of approved companies.

D. TOTAL LOAN COSTS (A + B + C)	$5,672

Other Costs

E. Taxes and Other Government Fees	$85
Recording Fees and Other Taxes	$85
Transfer Taxes	

F. Prepaids	$867
Homeowner's Insurance Premium (6 months)	$605
Mortgage Insurance Premium (months)	
Prepaid Interest ($17.44 per day for 15 days @ 3.875%)	$262
Property Taxes (months)	

Shop around for homeowners' insurance. The lender will provide an estimate, but it is up to you to find and select an insurance company.

G. Initial Escrow Payment at Closing			$413
Homeowner's Insurance	$100.83 per month for	2 mo.	$202
Mortgage Insurance	per month for	mo.	
Property Taxes	$105.30 per month for	2 mo.	$211

H. Other	$1,017
Title – Owner's Title Policy (optional)	$1,017

Lender credits lower your closing costs in exchange for a higher interest rate. Make sure this something you negotiated and is in your best interest.

I. TOTAL OTHER COSTS (E + F + G + H)	$2,382

J. TOTAL CLOSING COSTS	$8,054
D + I	$8,054
Lender Credits	

Calculating Cash to Close

Total Closing Costs (J)	$8,054
Closing Costs Financed (Paid from your Loan Amount)	$0
Down Payment/Funds from Borrower	$18,000
Deposit	– $10,000
Funds for Borrower	$0
Seller Credits	$0
Adjustments and Other Credits	$0
Estimated Cash to Close	$16,054

This section shows the amount of cash you will need to bring to closing and how it was calculated. Make sure everything looks in order.

Additional Information About This Loan

Your loan officer should be licensed and registered with NMLS database (nmlsconsumeraccess.org). This database will tell you if the loan officer has any disciplinary actions against them.

LENDER	Ficus Bank
NMLS/__ LICENSE ID	
LOAN OFFICER	Joe Smith
NMLS/__ LICENSE ID	12345
EMAIL	joesmith@ficusbank.com
PHONE	123-456-7890

MORTGAGE BROKER	
NMLS/__ LICENSE ID	
LOAN OFFICER	
NMLS/__ LICENSE ID	
EMAIL	
PHONE	

These calculations are one of many ways to compare loans from different lenders. Some lenders just focus on the interest rate rather than the APR. The APR is your interest rate plus the bank's fees and is a more accurate representation of the interest rate you'll be paying.

Comparisons

Use these measures to compare this loan with other loans.

In 5 Years	$56,582	Total you will have paid in principal, interest, mortgage insurance, and loan costs.
	$15,773	Principal you will have paid off.
Annual Percentage Rate (APR)	4.274%	Your costs over the loan term expressed as a rate. This is not your interest rate.
Total Interest Percentage (TIP)	69.45%	The total amount of interest that you will pay over the loan term as a percentage of your loan amount.

Other Considerations

Appraisal	We may order an appraisal to determine the property's value and charge you for this appraisal. We will promptly give you a copy of any appraisal, even if your loan does not close. You can pay for an additional appraisal for your own use at your own cost.
Assumption	If you sell or transfer this property to another person, we ☐ will allow, under certain conditions, this person to assume this loan on the original terms. ☒ will not allow assumption of this loan on the original terms.
Homeowner's Insurance	This loan requires homeowner's insurance on the property, which you may obtain from a company of your choice that we find acceptable.
Late Payment	If your payment is more than 15 days late, we will charge a late fee of 5% of the monthly principal and interest payment.
Refinance	Refinancing this loan will depend on your future financial situation, the property value, and market conditions. You may not be able to refinance this loan.
Servicing	We intend ☐ to service your loan. If so, you will make your payments to us. ☒ to transfer servicing of your loan.

The lender must list the fees for making a late mortgage payment. Know what the fees are and whether there is a grace period.

Confirm Receipt

By signing, you are only confirming that you have received this form. You do not have to accept this loan because you have signed or received this form.

_____   _____   _____   _____
Applicant Signature   Date   Co-Applicant Signature   Date

LOAN ESTIMATE

PAGE 3 OF 3 • LOAN ID #123456789

There is an important difference between your interest rate and your annual percentage rate (APR). The interest rate listed on page one of your loan estimate is the interest you will pay on the outstanding amount of the loan each year. This rate does not include bank fees and other charges. Your APR, listed on page three, is your true cost of borrowing. Your APR is your interest rate in addition to the bank fees and other charges listed. This will give you a full picture of the interest you will pay on the loan.

We have been personally disappointed at the number of agents that are very dismissive of the APR and try to get you to focus on the interest rate alone. Of course, that would be ignoring the fees the bank is trying to charge you for the loan.

When speaking with lenders, make sure they provide you a complete picture of your actual monthly mortgage costs. You'll want to make sure the estimate includes homeowner's insurance, property taxes, and private mortgage insurance (PMI) if you are putting down less than 20% down. Trulia has an easy-to-use calculator[34] that will include all the fees you can expect. For an apples-to-apples comparison, make sure the loan amount on the document is the same across all lenders.

What Does It Mean to Buy Points?

You can lower your interest rate by buying points. You essentially are paying money upfront for the option to lower your interest rate. You can find this in the first section on page two of your loan estimate.

Normally a point is equal to 1% of the amount you're borrowing. So, if your home loan is $200,000, a point would cost you $2,000. That $2,000 generally lowers your interest rate on your mortgage by 0.25%. Usually you can purchase up to three points. The discount rate and the number of points available will vary from lender to lender.

You should ask yourself two questions to determine if buying points would be a good idea. The first and most practical question to ask yourself is: "Can you afford to buy points?" Most of us can barely come up with a down payment, so the additional amount of buying down the interest may be difficult for many.

If you find yourself in a position in which you can answer that question affirmatively, your next question should be, "How long do you plan on living in the house?" The longer you plan on living in the home, the more it makes sense to pay for discounted points to lower your interest rate. The benefit of lowering your interest grows with time. If you're planning on selling the house in a few years, the situation changes.

Calculating your breakeven will help you to determine whether you should buy points. Breakeven is the juncture in which buying points to lower your interest becomes cheaper in the long run. NerdWallet has a helpful calculator[35] to help you determine whether buying points is a good idea.

Below is an example that illustrates when buying points can be a good decision.

BUYING POINTS ON A MORTGAGE

ASSUMPTIONS

- Home loan of $200,000
- 30 year term
- 4% fixed interest rate
- 1 discount point costs $2,000 and lowers interest rate by 0.25%

WHAT HAPPENS WHEN 1 POINT IS PURCHASED?

The cost would be $2,000, and the interest rate would lower from 4% to 3.75%. This also reduces the monthly mortgage payment from $955 to $926.

HOW LONG BEFORE IT'S WORTH IT?

You would need to own the house for 5.7 years to break even on the $2,000 you spent to lower your rate. The longer you own the house, the better that decision looks.

WHAT IF YOU ARE NOT PLANNING ON OWNING THE HOME FOR 5.7 YEARS?

Instead, consider using the money for investments, or a larger down payment on your home rather than buying points to lower your interest rate.

Whether you are considering purchasing a home in the next year or several years from now, creating a savings plan for a down payment will go a long way in helping you reach your financial goals. Whether you are using a savings app or a traditional savings account, we suggest renaming the account "Down Payment on a Home" and putting money in regularly. If you do not end up using that money for a down payment, you will have built up savings for other investment opportunities.

BUYING, RENTING, AND HOME LOANS

✓ Calculate how much you can afford on a monthly mortgage payment before shopping for houses.

✓ On most loans, if you put down less then 20% of the home's purchase price, you'll have to pay private mortgage insurance (PMI) in addition to the mortgage. This can cost you 0.5% to 1% a year until you reach 20% equity in your home.

✓ Start improving your credit score several months before applying for a mortgage.

✓ Getting pre-approved on a home loan takes a lot of the hassle and uncertainty out of purchasing a home.

✓ Have multiple lenders compete for your business by asking one lender to beat another lender's loan estimate offer.

✓ Make sure you understand the loan estimate document in order to compare the different offers from lenders.

✓ If you want to buy points to lower your interest rate, use a calculator to determine how many years you'll need to own the house for that choice to be worth it.

Scan for a full list of the links and tools listed.

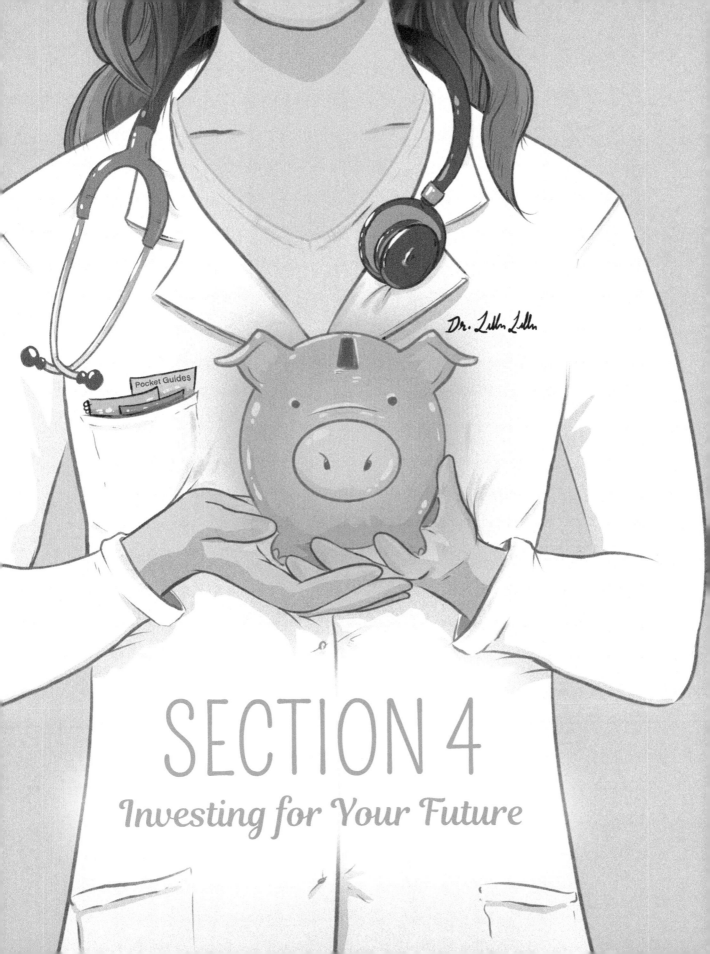

SECTION 4

Investing for Your Future

In this section, we cover stock market basics and investing for retirement. Understanding what investment accounts are available and their advantages is the first step to becoming an informed investor. After that, we'll bring together all the tax-related information we've gone over thus far so you can optimize your taxes as a part of your wealth-building strategy.

If you're new to investing, the following chapters will contain a lot of information for you to digest. Feel free to refer back to these chapters for guidance when needed. Whether you want to better understand your retirement account options or create a personal investment strategy, this section will help demystify and deconstruct the world of investing.

WHAT I'VE LEARNED AFTER 20 YEARS OF INVESTING

STOCKS, BONDS & FUNDS

RETIREMENT ACCOUNTS

ROTH & TRADITIONAL IRAs

INDEX FUND

HEALTH SAVINGS ACCOUNTS (HSAs) & FLEXIBLE SPENDING ACCOUNTS (FSAs)

ASSET ALLOCATION

REBALANCING YOUR PORTFOLIO

SAVING FOR YOUR CHILDREN

INTRODUCTION TO TAXES

Chapter 19

WHAT I'VE LEARNED AFTER 20 YEARS OF INVESTING

Lessons Learned

(NICK) I was seven when I first watched the movie *Wall Street*. I didn't understand most of it, but I did understand that Charlie Sheen's character had very little money to begin with, and by the middle of the movie, he had made a lot of money and was having a lot of fun doing it. My seven-year-old attention span didn't make it to the end of the movie when it all blew up in his face. So as far as I knew, it ended on a high note, and I wanted to be just like that guy.

The summer after graduating high school, I had become fascinated with the stock market. Online brokers had become accessible and affordable by that time. Movies like *Wall Street* and *Boiler Room* had also piqued my interest. The stock market was booming and constantly on the news. New startup internet companies were all the craze. Nowadays, we refer to that period as the Dot-Com Bubble.

I committed to learning as much as I could, and I started with a Google search on the best investment books of all time. I devoured as many books as I could get my hands on. I read books like *The Intelligent Investor* by Benjamin Graham, *A Random Walk Down Wall Street* by Burton Malkiel, *The Little Book of Common Sense Investing* by John Bogle, and many more. I'll admit that I glossed over some of the more boring advice and focused on strategies to beat the market. Of course, what I found to be boring in my early twenties has come full circle and is more or less the advice that I'll be sharing with you.

I'll try and fast forward 20 years of personal investing and condense them into a few paragraphs. I thought if I studied enough and dedicated enough time, I could beat the market with substantial returns. I went through the gamut of trading strategies from penny stocks, swing trading, technical analysis, financial analysis, several combinations of each, and of course, day trading. I was actively trading through the Dot-Com bubble in the early 2000s, the sub-prime mortgage crisis from 2007 to 2009, the U.S. Debt Downgrade in 2011, and more recently, the COVID-19 outbreak. It took far too long to learn what I need to learn about investing, but I finally came away with three key lessons.

LESSON 1: DIVERSIFY YOUR INVESTMENTS

If you start buying investments during a *bull market* (like I did when I started trading stocks in 1999), you will undoubtedly feel like a stock-picking pro, a borderline genius. It's hard not to make money on your investments during those times.

> *Bull market:* signifies that the stock market is increasing in value, normally for a sustained period.

The market will go through periods of growth, called bull markets, and periods of decline or stagnation called *bear markets*. Diversifying offers some protection when the market is not going your way.

Diversification is the concept of not putting all your eggs in one basket. If a sector or market is declining, spreading the risk among different asset classes will help protect your investments.

The idea is that not all asset classes will decline during a downturn, at least not equally. This basically means that you should invest in unrelated opportunities. Investments that have little to do with each other won't sink under the same economic forces, helping spread the risk during volatile times. Diversification isn't a guarantee that your investments won't go down, but spreading the risk through diversification will help you weather the storm.

There is such a thing as over-diversification, where you are invested in so many things that it will minimize your potential returns and be difficult to manage. There are ways to be both diversified while owning a few holdings that are manageable and easy to understand. Later in this section, we present some options that will help accomplish both.

LESSON 2: BUY AND HOLD

If you are not holding onto your investments with a long-term strategy, that means you are trying to constantly predict the future over short periods of time. Learning to give up timing the market over the short term was one of the most difficult lessons for me to learn. For years, I thought, "Surely I can use market data to buy and sell stocks so that I can avoid the downturns and capitalize as the market increases."

Bear market: a period when stocks are declining. Normally, a stock market decrease of 20% from recent highs is considered a bear market.

Some years this worked amazingly well with impressive returns to boast about to family and friends. Then there were the years I was considerably less talkative during holiday dinners. In those years, my short-term stock picking strategies didn't pan out.

Looking back at all the time and effort I put in combing through financial statements and analyst reports for several hours each day, it's difficult to admit, but it was a waste of time. The truth was I was unable to do any better picking stocks than if I had just put my money in a mutual fund that tracked an index such as the S&P 500.

It turns out I am not alone in my disappointment. Not only do most individual, average Joe investors fail to outperform the overall market, but the vast majority of professional investment advisors do not consistently beat the S&P 500 over the long term. In fact, they don't even come close. The SPIVA Institutional Scorecard was created to compare active and passive investing approaches. The SPIVA Scorecard for 2020[36] compared how actively managed *funds* performed against the S&P 500 index. Over a 10-year period, 82% of actively managed large-cap funds underperformed the S&P 500 index. Over a 20-year period, over 94% of actively managed large-cap funds underperformed the S&P 500. That's a shocking statistic.

Fund: comprised of hundreds or even thousands of stocks and/or bonds in a single holding

In Burton Malkiel's book *The Random Walk Guide to Investing: Ten Rules for Financial Success*, he states:

"It's true that when you buy an index fund, you give up the chance to boast at the golf course that you picked the best performing stock or mutual fund. That's why some critics claim that indexing relegates your results to mediocrity. In fact, you are virtually guaranteed to do better than average. It's like going out on the golf course and shooting every round at par. How many golfers can do better than that? Index funds provide a simple, low-cost solution to your investing problems."

As you get closer to retirement, the timing of selling and *rebalancing* your investments becomes more important, as you'll want to take on less risk since you'll need access to that money sooner rather than later. However, if you are in medical school or residency and many years from retirement, the focus should be on building your investments for the future and allowing those investments to grow with *compounding interest*.

Short-term trading is not a good idea for many reasons, including the fact that you will end up paying short-term *capital gains* taxes if you buy and sell an investment within one year. That can result in paying more than double what you'd pay on long-term investments.

Portfolio rebalancing: the process of buying or selling your investments to maintain a desired asset allocation.

Compound interest: the interest earned on both the original principal amount plus the interest already added to the principal amount. The compounding component can be thought of as interest earned on interest over time.

Short-term trading: the buying and selling of an investment over a period of time that can range from seconds to several days. For tax purposes, short-term trading is an investment held for less than one year.

Capital gains: the profits from the sale of property or an investment like stocks, bonds or real estate.

On short-term investments, you are taxed at your ordinary-income tax bracket, which can be up to 37%. For most of us, long-term investments are typically taxed at around 15% if you hold onto that investment for more than a year.

LESSON 3: KEEP IT SIMPLE

It is easy to get overwhelmed in the world of investing. Many advisors and CNBC pundits will use confusing financial terms foreign to those outside the industry. To some degree, I think that's the point. The barrage of unfamiliar terms is intended to make you feel inept and make the experts look impressive. At the end of a Bloomberg article or conversation with a financial advisor, you may develop a severe headache; part of you says, "HERE—TAKE MY MONEY! I DON'T KNOW WHAT YOU'RE TALKING ABOUT. PLEASE HELP ME!"

Investing is unnecessarily complicated, but it doesn't have to be. Many in the investment community will disagree with me on this. They'll protest that to make the most of your investments, you need a complicated strategy that is actively managed by a professional. And this seems to make sense—surely a full-time, dedicated investment professional is the way to go, right?

However, in many cases, investment advisory fees are just not worth it when comparing simpler alternatives. Remember—the professional managing your money has just a 10% chance of doing better than an index fund, and he'll charge you for the privilege of trying.

You might be asking how you can keep your strategy simple while still diversifying. Aren't those two things contradictory? Rest assured that they are not; there are important distinctions between them. A stock portfolio does not have to have 300 individual stocks to be diversified. That is the purpose of a fund. A fund allows you to purchase a large group of companies within a single investment. A single index fund is a perfect example of an investment that can help you purchase hundreds or even thousands of stocks while minimizing the number of holdings in your portfolio.

I'll end this section on keeping it simple with a quote from one of the most well-respected and successful investors of our generation, Warren Buffet. In 2014, Warren Buffet wrote a letter to his shareholders sharing what was in his will and how he would like the money he was leaving his heirs invested when he passed away.

> "My advice to the trustee could not be more simple: put 10% of the cash in short-term government bonds and 90% in a very low-cost *S&P 500* index fund. I suggest Vanguard's. I believe the trust's long-term results from this policy will be superior to those attained by most investors—whether pension funds, institutions, or individuals—who employ high-fee managers."

Well, there it is—that's my investment advice in a nutshell. I know this feels anticlimactic and may seem like little more than common sense, but I managed to ignore it for years, despite having heard and read it many times. The fact is that short-term stock trading is the most respected form of gambling in our society. It provides a similar level of fun and excitement that roulette or horse races offer.

If you are going to participate in short-term trading, accept that *volatility* and excessive risk are part of the package and that you are statistically very unlikely to outperform the market over the long term. Like gambling, this should be viewed as entertainment and not a long-term strategy for building wealth.

> *S&P 500 (Standard & Poor's 500 Index):* includes the largest, globally diversified American companies across every industry, making it as low-risk as stock investing gets.
>
> *Volatility:* in the market this is normally represented by large increases and decreases in stock prices over a short period time.

Before we dive into investing topics for the following several chapters, I want to underscore what we mentioned in the disclaimer at the start of the book. The information provided in the book has been created to help readers improve their knowledge of personal finance. This information is intended to be educational and is not intended as legal, accounting, financial, or other professional advice. We are emphasizing this because we will provide you with our personal philosophy to investing. However, it is ultimately up to you to make informed decisions that best suit your unique situation.

Why Should You Consider Investing in the Stock Market?

Despite all the ups and downs in the stock market over the last 100 years, one truth remains. Over time the stock market as a whole has always gone up. Individual companies will go bankrupt, different sectors of the economy will go boom and bust, stock market crashes and recessions are inevitable, but it continues to be an essential component in building wealth over time.

You also have the advantage of endless choices of investments. You can choose investments at a risk level that you feel comfortable with, whether that is low or high-risk.

Another reason it is important to grow your investments continually is to outpace inflation. Inflation is the decreased purchasing value of money over time. When your grandparents tell you it used to cost a nickel to watch a movie when they were young, and it is inflation that has increased the price of movie tickets (along with everything else) over time. Inflation fluctuates year to year but averages around 2 to 3% per year. That means that for your money to retain the same value in the future that it has today, you will need to invest that money at a rate that at least equals the inflation rate. The stock market over the last 100 years has averaged about 10% a year before inflation.

The Time Value of Money

No amount of savings is too small to begin with. It's getting started; that's the hard part. The most underappreciated factor of growth for investments is compound interest over time. Compound interest is the interest earned on both the original principal amount plus the interest already added to the principal amount. The compounding component can be thought of as interest earned on interest over time. Continuing to reinvest any earnings allows you to earn interest on interest. It's a beautiful snowball effect with surprising results from simple beginnings.

Similar to the analogy of planting a seed that grows into an impressive oak tree, here is an example of how powerful compound interest can be:

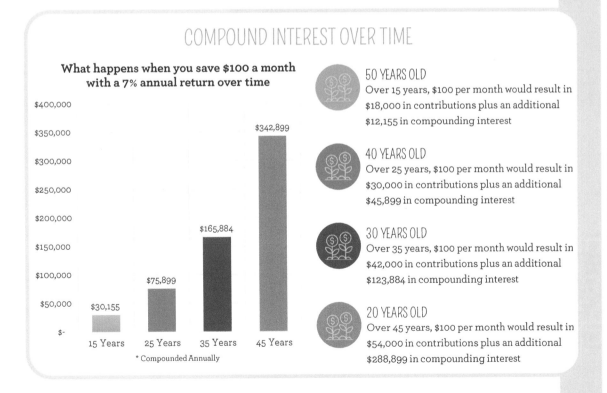

COMPOUND INTEREST OVER TIME

What happens when you save $100 a month with a 7% annual return over time

$400,000

$350,000 $342,899

$300,000

$250,000

$200,000

$150,000 $165,884

$100,000

$50,000 $30,155 $75,899

$-

15 Years   25 Years   35 Years   45 Years

* Compounded Annually

50 YEARS OLD
Over 15 years, $100 per month would result in $18,000 in contributions plus an additional $12,155 in compounding interest

40 YEARS OLD
Over 25 years, $100 per month would result in $30,000 in contributions plus an additional $45,899 in compounding interest

30 YEARS OLD
Over 35 years, $100 per month would result in $42,000 in contributions plus an additional $123,884 in compounding interest

20 YEARS OLD
Over 45 years, $100 per month would result in $54,000 in contributions plus an additional $288,899 in compounding interest

Chapter 19 Recap

WHAT I'VE LEARNED AFTER 20 YEARS OF INVESTING

✓ Diversify your investments in order to limit your risk in any one sector or asset class.

✓ Buy and hold your investments with a long-term strategy. Not only are there significant tax advantages to this, but trying to time the market in the short term is an unnecessary gamble.

✓ The majority of actively managed funds do not perform as well as a passive S&P 500 index fund over time.

✓ Maintaining a straightforward and simple investing strategy will reduce fund and portfolio manager fees. This allows you to enjoy good market returns without being a professional investor.

✓ Remember what Warren Buffet—one of the most successful investors of our time—shared about the handling of his fortune after he dies: "Put 10% of the cash in short-term government bonds and 90% in a very low-cost S&P 500 index fund . . ."

Scan for a full list of the links and tools listed.

Chapter 20
STOCKS, BONDS, & FUNDS

STOCK MARKET BASICS

BONDS

STOCKS

BEAR & BULL MARKETS

EXCHANGE TRADED FUNDS (ETFs) TO STAY AWAY FROM

MUTUAL FUNDS, INDEX FUNDS, & EXCHANGE TRADED FUNDS (ETFs)

Stock Market Basics

If you are new to the stock market world, it can be an intimidating subject. Like medicine, it is constantly evolving, and you are always learning. The good news is that you do not have to spend 8 to 12 hours a day on the subject in order to be a successful investor. This chapter will introduce you to some basic stock market concepts and provide a basic foundation to build from.

Bear & Bull Markets

A bull market represents a period when the market is doing well, and stocks are generally increasing in value. The technical indicators recognizing a bull market can vary. The important thing to remember is that the market is experiencing a sustained increase for a period of time. A bear market describes a period when stocks are declining. Normally, a market decrease of 20% from recent highs is considered a bear market.

If you have not been through large swings in the market, it can be an emotional rollercoaster. We have personally been through four major bear markets over the last 20 years. Bull and bear markets are regularly occurring cycles. It's important not to panic and sell during these times.

NerdWallet has created a great visual calculator[37] that illustrates, that although you may feel like the market will never recover during the most painful periods, the fact is that it always has. They show that had you invested in the S&P 500 at the worst possible time—right before the worst bear market in recent memory—you would have fully recovered your losses within seven and a half years.

Let's take a look at some additional bear market scenarios. In the 2015 market sell-off, you would have fully recovered your investment within 13 months. For the Black Monday crash in 1987, it would have taken 1 year to recover your investment. With the recession in the early 1980s, you would have fully recovered your investment within 1 year and 11 months. This demonstrates that even during some of the worst bear markets in recent history, the market recovers and continually reaches new highs.

Stocks

So, what exactly is a stock? It is a slice of ownership in a company. If you own a share of Wal-Mart's stock, then you are a part-owner of that company. If a company issues a total of 10,000 shares of stock and you own 500 shares, you have 5% ownership of that company.

The stock exchanges are the forums in which investors buy and sell stocks. In the U.S., the two major exchanges are the New York Stock Exchange (NYSE) and the Nasdaq. The New York Stock Exchange is the original platform developed for trading. In 1971, the Nasdaq became the second exchange in the U.S.

On the exchanges are indexes that represent the largest publicly traded companies. For example, the S&P 500 represents 500 of some of the largest publicly traded companies in the U.S. market. The Dow Jones Industrial Average is another index that represents the 30 largest publicly traded *blue-chip* companies. These indexes are often used as benchmarks to gauge how investors and fund managers are performing.

Before the internet, investing in the markets was limited by access to up-to-date information and prohibitive trading costs. Online brokers really changed the investing game, and the information available on publicly traded companies is now extensive. In the late 1990s, when I began trading, it cost $7-$10 every time you wanted to buy or sell stock. Today, most brokers no longer charge any transaction costs to buy and sell stock. With the numerous brokerage apps and account options available, such as Ally and Fidelity, you should not be paying transaction costs to buy and sell stocks.

Blue-chip: a term that refers to well established companies with large valuations that have performed well over time.

Bonds

Bonds are a type of investment in which you lend money to the bond issuer in exchange for interest payments; you're essentially extending a loan to the bond issuer. This is a way for companies, local municipalities, and the federal government to raise money.

Compared to stocks, bonds are generally considered a safer investment, but they tend to produce lower returns. Many investment professionals believe bonds act as a counter to the stock market and will advise those close to retirement to shift many of their investments from stocks to bonds.

There are many bond options to choose from when investing:

- CORPORATE BONDS: These are issued by companies and tend to offer higher interest rate payments to bondholders, but they also involve more risk.
- MUNICIPAL BONDS: These are issued by states, cities, and local government agencies to pay for public projects such as repairing roads, schools, parks, etc. These are considered safe, and the risk of default is low.
- TREASURY BONDS: These bonds are issued by the U.S. government. They are considered one of the safest investments because the government has never defaulted on a debt. In order to lose your investment, there would have to be a total market collapse. The payments on interest rates tend to be lower on these types of bonds. These bonds, in particular, tend to rise in value when the stock market is volatile or declining.

Below is a list of large, well-diversified bond investments worth researching further:[38]

SAMPLE BOND FUNDS

	TYPE OF FUND	MINIMUM INVESTMENT REQUIRED	FEE PER YEAR (% OF AMOUNT INVESTED)	LINKS FOR ADDITIONAL INFORMATION
VANGUARD TOTAL BOND MARKET INDEX FUND (VBTLX)	Mutual Fund	$3,000	0.05%	investor.vanguard.com/mutual-funds/profile/VBTLX
FIDELITY U.S. BOND INDEX FUND (FXNAX)	Mutual Fund	No Minimum	0.025%	fundresearch.fidelity.com/mutual-funds/summary/316146356
VANGUARD INTERMEDIATE-TERM BOND (BIV)	ETF	No Minimum	0.05%	investor.vanguard.com/etf/profile/BIV
FIDELITY TOTAL BOND (FBND)	ETF	No Minimum	0.36%	screener.fidelity.com/ftgw/etf/goto/snapshot/snapshot.jhtml?symbols=FBND
ISHARES CORE U.S. AGGREGATE BOND (AGG)	ETF	No Minimum	0.04%	www.ishares.com/us/products/239458/ishares-core-total-us-bond-market-etf
FIDELITY TOTAL BOND (FTBFX)	Mutual Fund	No Minimum	0.45%	fundresearch.fidelity.com/mutual-funds/summary/31617K881
VANGUARD TOTAL BOND MARKET ETF (BND)	ETF	No Minimum	0.035%	investor.vanguard.com/etf/profile/bnd
VANGUARD HIGH-YIELD TAX-EXEMPT (VWAHX)	ETF	$3,000	0.17%	investor.vanguard.com/mutual-funds/profile/VWAHX

Mutual Funds, Index Funds, and Exchange Traded Funds (ETFs)

Let's start with what a fund is. A fund is comprised of hundreds or even thousands of stocks and/or bonds in a single holding. Some funds will focus on publicly traded companies with the largest values, while other funds will focus on specific sectors such as technology, retail, or healthcare, to name a few. Certain funds will focus on investments geographically, such as international stocks or stocks in developing countries. Let's say, for example, you wanted to invest in companies that target the obesity epidemic specifically. Well, there is a fund for that, *ticker symbol* (SLIM). If you wanted to invest in all healthcare-related companies in the S&P500, there is a fund for that, ticker symbol (S5HLTH). The options of funds are almost endless.

Funds are the key to both simplifying and diversifying your investments.

There are many different types of funds, but they all fall into two main categories: actively managed funds and passive funds. Actively managed funds are run by investment managers who constantly make decisions on adding investments to and removing investments from their funds. This involved management tends to make the cost of owning these funds more expensive for the investor, as opposed to a passively managed fund which normally tries to track a large, existing index. Since these funds try and mimic indexes like the S&P500, the costs to own these funds tend to be cheaper since it does not involve an active management strategy to try and 'beat the market.'

> *Ticker symbol:* the abbreviation used to uniquely identify a publicly traded company on a stock exchange. It is normally a combination of one to five letters used to buy or sell shares of a company.

MUTUAL FUNDS

Mutual funds are an example of actively managed funds. The investments in these funds are constantly changing in an effort to beat average market index returns. As stated earlier, these funds tend to have a higher cost for investors. These costs are referred to as a fund's *expense ratio*. Mutual funds may also require a high minimum cost to invest. Some mutual funds will require a minimum initial investment of $1,000 or more, depending on the fund. Regarding taxes, these funds are structured to lead to higher *capital gains* taxes because of the frequency of trades. When an investment within a mutual fund is sold for a gain, capital gains taxes are passed down to all fund investors.

Expense ratio: the administrative fee associated with managing a fund.

Capital gains: the profits from the sale of property or an investment like stocks, bonds or real estate.

INDEX FUNDS

An index fund is an example of a passively managed fund. Index funds aim to mirror the performance of an index, such as the S&P 500, Nasdaq, or Dow Jones Industrial Average. Index funds are considered passively managed funds since the manager of these funds will just buy most or all of the stocks within an index. When these market indexes increase or decrease, the index fund mimicking them will do the same.

They are similar to mutual funds in that they are not traded throughout the day like stocks. They are bought and sold by investors at a price set at the end of each day. Many index funds also require an initial minimum investment that can be a barrier to entry for some. Like mutual funds, capital gains taxes are passed on to investors when investments within the fund are sold for a gain. These occur much less often in an index fund since fewer trades tend to occur in a passive fund. One of the most critical differences between passive index funds and actively managed mutual funds is the annual cost to own the fund. Since index funds are passively managed, they cost significantly less to own. We have reserved an entire chapter to discussing passive index funds, which is the backbone of our own *portfolio*.

Portfolio: a collection of investments owned by an individual, and managed as a collective whole with specific investment goals in mind.

EXCHANGE-TRADED FUNDS (ETFS)

Another type of fund that has gained a lot of popularity in recent years are exchange-traded funds, often referred to as ETFs. They're popular for a few reasons. For one, ETFs offer the convenience of being able to trade like stocks throughout the day. They offer the convenience of being easy to purchase through your mobile investment account or through a *robo-advisor* app. You can find both index funds and actively managed funds in the form of an ETF, although most ETFs are passively managed. The passive approach results in lower costs (expense ratio) to the investor. ETFs are also structured differently than mutual funds for tax purposes. Unlike mutual funds, you do not pay taxes on capital gains until you sell the ETF.

ETFs To Stay Away From

In your research, you may come across leveraged or inverse ETFs. Leveraged ETFs were created to double or triple the returns of an index. Sounds amazing, right? Yes, but there's a catch. These are dangerous investments designed for day traders who are willing to take an enormous risk. They are not meant for buy-and-hold strategies. Because these ETFs reset daily, they are built to naturally erode returns over time. Leveraged ETFs are the epitome of a high-risk gamble. Hopefully, you avoid this gamble altogether.

> *Robo-advisors:* investment management companies
> that rely on algorithm-driven computer modeling to manage
> your portfolio rather than human financial advisors.

STOCKS, BONDS, AND FUNDS

✓ Shares of stock are small slices of ownership in a company.

✓ The S&P 500 index represents 500 of some of the largest, publicly traded U.S. companies.

✓ The internet has made investing accessible to the general public through access to information and reductions in transaction costs via online brokers.

✓ Bonds are a type of investment in which you lend money to the bond issuer in exchange for interest payments. Bonds are generally considered less risky than stocks and act as a counterbalance to the stock market.

✓ Exchange-traded funds (ETFs) trade like stocks but are funds that contain multiple investments. ETFs allow you to purchase a large number of stocks within a single investment vehicle.

✓ Bear and bull markets are part of the life cycle of investing. It is important not to make emotional trades during times of volatility. Remain steadfast in a long-term approach.

✓ Passive index funds are historically more likely to outperform actively managed funds over time.

Scan for a full list of the links and tools listed.

Chapter 21
RETIREMENT ACCOUNTS

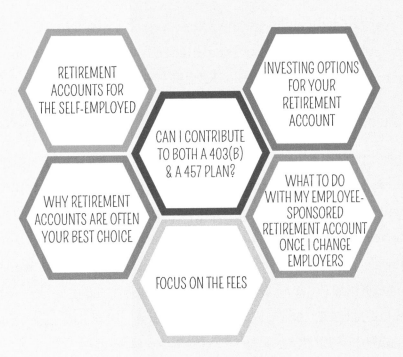

When starting your investment journey, retirement accounts are the place to begin. For many people, the benefits provided under these plans are as good as it gets in the investment world. I'll explain why below, but first, let's talk about what exactly a 401(k), a 403(b), and a 457(b) are. All three are employer-sponsored retirement plans that offer workers a tax break when they invest towards retirement. The main difference between 401(k) and 403(b) boils down to what kind of business your employer is. Private companies normally offer 401(k)s, while 403(b)s are only provided by non-profit organizations. Hospitals and education institutions are examples of companies that offer 403(b)s.

There is a third, less-common retirement plan sometimes provided by state and local governments as well as non-profits known as a 457(b). All three of these plans can only be offered by an employer, so you can't sign up for them as an individual.

Retirement Accounts for the Self-Employed

If you are self-employed, there are several retirement account options available. Here, we'll discuss the three most common retirement accounts for the self-employed: Simple IRAs, SEP IRAs, and Individual IRAs

SIMPLE IRAS AND SEP (SIMPLIFIED EMPLOYEE PENSION) IRAS[39]

These plans are very similar to a traditional IRA. You are granted a deduction on your taxable income when you place money into a retirement account. Like a traditional IRA, your money grows tax-free within the account. When you make withdrawals during retirement, those withdrawals are taxed as ordinary income. You can make the same type of investments (buying and selling stocks and bonds) as you would in a traditional IRA, and the withdrawal penalties are the same as well. We discuss traditional IRAs in detail in the next chapter.

The main difference between Simple and SEP IRAs are your contribution limits. For 2021, Simple IRA contributions cannot exceed $13,500. SEP IRA account contributions cannot exceed the lesser of 25% of the employee's income or $58,000. It's worth noting that *elective salary deferrals* and *catch-up contributions* are not permitted in SEP plans.

> *Elective salary deferrals:* amounts contributed to a retirement plan by the employer at the employee's request. Elective deferrals are typically excluded from an employee's gross income unless they are for a Roth contribution.
>
> *Catch-up contributions:* a type of retirement savings contribution that allows for additional contributions on top of what is normally allowed. These types of contributions are usually permitted for people nearing retirement age.

INDIVIDUAL (SOLO) 401(K)[40]

An individual (solo) 401(k) is similar to a standard employer-sponsored 401(k) plan. The main advantage here is that you can make contributions as both the employee and the employer. So, as an employee, your contribution can be up to the lesser of $19,500 or 100% of your salary. Then you get to put on the employer hat and contribute an additional 25% of the employee's income.

Another advantage to these is that many individual 401(k) plans offer the option of Roth or traditional contributions, meaning you can choose to contribute pre-tax or after-tax funds to these retirement accounts, depending on when you prefer to take the tax advantage. This is discussed in detail in our next chapter. If you have employees aside from yourself and your spouse, the individual 401(k) is not an option.

Keep in mind that if you also have retirement accounts with an employer, your contribution limits are per person and not per plan. This very brief introduction to self-employed retirement accounts is by no means exhaustive. Still, it should help you understand that many options are available to you if you are self-employed. If you have employees, seek advice from a tax professional since you will need to consider reporting requirements and which account would be best suited for your company.

Why Retirement Plans Are Often
Your Best Choice

Retirement accounts are a great opportunity to take advantage of the out-of-sight, out-of-mind principle. Once you designate how much to save from your paycheck, you can set up an automatic transfer, for your retirement contribution, straight to your retirement account; without the money ever hitting your checking account. That way, you are not tempted to spend that money and won't have the hassle of regularly transferring it out of your checking account.

Another potential benefit to retirement accounts is matching contributions. Many employers will offer to match a part of what you contribute to your retirement plan. If your employer offers you a matching contribution, run—don't walk—to your HR office and get set up with an account. Seriously. Here's why.

Let's assume your employer offers you a match on the first 5% of your salary contributed to a 401k. We will also assume your salary is $150,000 a year. If you contribute 5% of your paycheck over a year, that would be $7,500. With your contribution match, your employer provides an additional $7,500 in your 401k.

BEFORE WE EVEN TALK ABOUT EARNINGS (GROWTH) FROM YOUR INVESTMENTS OVER TIME, YOU HAVE MADE A 100% RETURN ON YOUR INVESTMENT WITH THIS MATCH.

With all the investment opportunities out there, this is as good as it gets. One trip to the HR department and a bit of paperwork, and you've doubled your money. Another way to look at it is you are getting a 5% raise from your employer just for contributing to your retirement. This is an important part of why these employer-sponsored retirement plans are always your first step in investing.

If your employer does offer matching contributions, there is usually a vesting period. This is how long it takes for the employer's matching contribution to be available in your account. The amount you contributed will be available immediately in your retirement account, but the employer match will likely take longer.

Using the example we just discussed, if the employer matches your $7,500 contribution, that full amount will be in your retirement account based on your employer's vesting schedule. Your employer might have a vesting schedule over four years. That means that you might receive 25% of the $7,500 each year. After four years, the total amount of $7,500 would be fully vested and available to you.

$7,500 VESTED OVER 4 YEARS

At the end of year 1, $1,875 of the $7,500 offered through your employer match would be available in your retirement account.	At the end of year 2, an additional $1,875 would be available in your retirement account, totaling $3,750.	At the end of year 3, an additional $1,875 would be available, bringing the total up to $5,625.	At the end of year 4, the full $7,500 would be vested and available to you in your retirement account.
YEAR 1	YEAR 2	YEAR 3	YEAR 4
$1,875 (25% Vested)	$3,750 (50% Vested)	$5,625 (75% Vested)	$7,500 (100% Vested)

Employers create a vesting period as an incentive for employees to stick around. If you leave an employer, any money that is not vested will no longer be available to you. This can make it difficult to leave an employer if you have been taking advantage of the employer's match for several years. The benefits compound every year. Below illustrates how the benefit compounds over time.

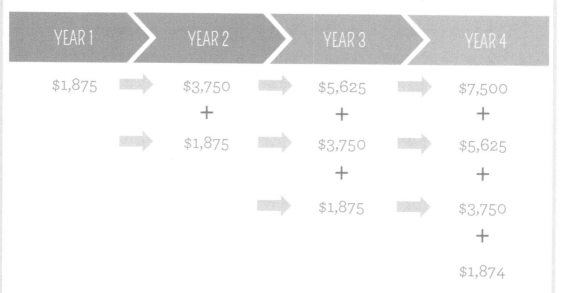

If you take advantage of the employer match every year, this is what the vesting schedule would look like over 4 years.

YEAR 1	YEAR 2	YEAR 3	YEAR 4
$1,875	$3,750	$5,625	$7,500
	+	+	+
	$1,875	$3,750	$5,625
		+	+
		$1,875	$3,750
			+
			$1,874

At the end of your fourth year, you would have $18,749 fully vested from your employer's match. If you include the $7,500 per year you contributed, you have a total of $48,749.

Another critical benefit to retirement plans is the tax breaks. With both a 401(k) and a 403(b), your tax break can either take place at the time you contribute money (with a traditional account), or the tax break occurs when you withdraw funds in retirement (with a Roth account). Whether your tax break is on the front end or the back end, it represents a substantial opportunity to keep more of your earnings in your pocket.

Here is an example to illustrate the tax advantages of saving in a traditional retirement account compared to saving in a regular taxable investment account like Etrade or Fidelity:

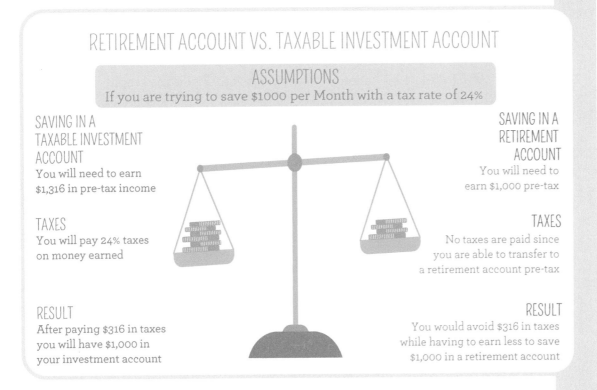

RETIREMENT ACCOUNT VS. TAXABLE INVESTMENT ACCOUNT

ASSUMPTIONS
If you are trying to save $1000 per Month with a tax rate of 24%

SAVING IN A TAXABLE INVESTMENT ACCOUNT
You will need to earn $1,316 in pre-tax income

SAVING IN A RETIREMENT ACCOUNT
You will need to earn $1,000 pre-tax

TAXES
You will pay 24% taxes on money earned

TAXES
No taxes are paid since you are able to transfer to a retirement account pre-tax

RESULT
After paying $316 in taxes you will have $1,000 in your investment account

RESULT
You would avoid $316 in taxes while having to earn less to save $1,000 in a retirement account

A tax-related benefit specifically for a 457(b) is unlike the other retirement accounts discussed; there are no penalties for withdrawals when switching employers if you are under the required 55 years old.

You can also contribute significantly more with an employer-sponsored retirement account than you can with an investment retirement account (IRA). For 2021, on 401(k)s, 403(b)s, and 457(b)s, you can contribute $19,500 a year (or $26,000 if you are 50 or older). Your employer can contribute up to $57,000 in contributions. (If you're over 50, it is $63,500 with the catch-up contribution offered.) That's compared to $6,000 a year for an IRA ($7,000 if you're over 50).

A lesser-known benefit to retirement accounts is the credit protection most plans offer. These plans are protected by the federal government under the Employment Retirement Income Security Act (ERISA). Private creditors (credit card companies or lenders that may come after you during bankruptcy) are not allowed to touch any funds in your retirement account; that money is protected.

Can I Contribute to Both a 403(b) and a 457 Plan?

Yes. If your employer offers both, you can contribute and max out both retirement plans. Many employers require that you max out your 403(b) first. In 2021, that maximum is $19,500. The 457(b) plans also have a maximum contribution of $19,500. If you are over 50, you can contribute an additional $6,500 to each plan per year.[41]

Investing Options for Your Retirement Account

For an employer-sponsored retirement account, your investment options will depend on your employee plan. Some companies have three or four *funds*, while others offer dozens to choose from.

When you are enrolled in a 401k plan, your employer will choose a default investment if you do not make a selection (usually a *target-date fund*). However, we advise taking the time to select the fund that best meets your needs. Choosing investments can feel overwhelming, but here is a systematic approach that can help.

Choosing your retirement account investments really boils down to your *risk tolerance* and your time horizon. In general, the less time you have until retirement, the less risk you will want to take on. Many companies such as Vanguard (personal.vanguard.com/us/FundsInvQuestionnaire) and Charles Schwab (www.schwab.com/public/file/P-778947/Investor ProfileQuestionnaire.pdf) offer risk tolerance questionnaires that can provide guidance on which type of funds to choose for your retirement account.

Fund: comprised of hundreds or even thousands of stocks and/or bonds in a single holding.

Target-date fund: a fund aimed at people planning for retirement. These funds have select investments based on an approximate date that an investor plans to start withdrawing money.

Risk tolerance: the amount of loss and uncertainty an investor is comfortable taking with their investments.

Different financial advisors will recommend slightly different percentage allocations. The American Association for Individual Investors provides some sample portfolios for aggressive, moderate, and conservative investors.[42]

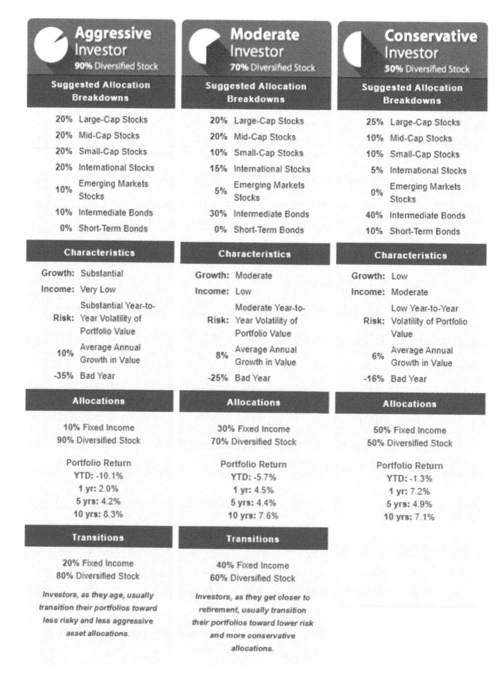

"Asset Allocation Models to Maximize Your Returns." American Association of Individual Investors. www.aaii.com/asset-allocation. Accessed 15 April 2021

Focus on the Fees

The *expense ratio* associated with the fund is more critical for your investment strategy than choosing the fund itself. I know we covered this in the previous chapter, but it is worth repeating. Several well-diversified index funds are likely to produce similar results, but you'll see a substantial difference in results from the seemingly minor differences in fund fees. These small fees can add up quickly. Here is our example once again to highlight the importance of fees over time.

SMALL FEES OVER TIME

ASSUMPTIONS

Initial Investment: $10,000	Time Horizon: 30 Years
Yearly Contribution: $25,000	Interest Rate: 6% per Year

RETIREMENT FUND WITH EXPENSE RATIO OF 0.10%

FEES PAID

You would pay $40,056 in fund fees over 30 years

VS

RETIREMENT FUND WITH EXPENSE RATIO OF 0.75%

FEES PAID

You would pay $280,951 in fund fees over 30 years

Expense ratio: the administrative fee associated with managing a fund.

What to Do with My Employer-Sponsored Retirement Account Once I Change Employers

When you leave a job, you get to keep all your retirement contributions as well as the amount vested by your employer. You must decide whether to transfer your funds to another account or leave the money where it is. Transferring your retirement account to another account is known as a rollover. You can roll over your 401k to another 401k with a new employer or to an individual retirement account (IRA). Let's talk about what to consider when making this choice.

OPTION 1: KEEPING YOUR 401K IN ITS CURRENT ACCOUNT

If you have more than $5,000 in your account and you like your plan's portfolio, you may be able to keep it as is, even if you are no longer with that employer. Although normally there are no transfer fees when rolling over your account, compare the account fees with the new IRA or 401k. Since many 401ks offer similar funds, going with a plan with lower fees can save you thousands of dollars in the long run, as we showed you in the example earlier. IRAs tend to have lower maintenance fees, but they do not have the same level of legal protection from creditors and bankruptcy that 401ks offer.

Some employers offer company stock in your 401k. If you have a considerable amount of company stock and you are weighing your options on whether to transfer your 401k, we recommend discussing your options with a financial or tax advisor familiar with the concept of net unrealized appreciation (NUA).

NUA is the difference between what you paid for the company stock and what the stock price is currently at. This gain is treated differently for tax purposes in a 401k than it is a regular trading account.

This also matters when you withdraw money from the stock. Normally, distribution rules would tax your distribution as ordinary income. However, the NUA rule allows your distribution to be taxed at the capital gains rate instead. This is important because your capital gains tax rate usually is much lower than your ordinary income tax rate.

Again, there are very specific IRS requirements to take advantage of this, and we recommend discussing this scenario with a tax or financial professional.

OPTION 2: TRANSFERRING YOUR 401K TO A NEW EMPLOYER'S 401K PLAN

Since most of us will work for many employers throughout our careers, it doesn't make much sense to keep track of multiple retirement accounts. Consolidating retirement accounts will help you simplify and manage your account.

If you opt to transfer your old 401k to a new one, avoid having a check written out to you when rolling over an account since you may incur penalties if you do not deposit the correct amount within 60 days. Instead, transfer the money from one *custodian* to the new custodian for your 401k.

OPTION 3: TRANSFERRING YOUR 401K TO AN INDIVIDUAL RETIREMENT ACCOUNT (IRA)

IRAs typically offer considerably more investment options, such as individual stocks, ETFs, mutual funds, and index funds. Also, many IRAs will have lower fees than 401ks do.

Custodian: a person responsible for an asset, in this case ownership of a retirement account

OPTION 4: CASHING OUT YOUR RETIREMENT ACCOUNT

We have to (begrudgingly) mention that you also have the option of cashing out your retirement. This is a bad idea for numerous reasons. For one, if you're withdrawing the funds before you are 59½, you will pay taxes on that withdrawal as well as a 10% penalty.

It might be tempting to see that lump sum and imagine all the things you could do with it; the funds saved up in a retirement account will likely determine what level of comfort you enjoy as you reach retirement. Starting all over will wipe out the *compound interest* on the savings you have generated.

> *Compound interest:* the interest earned on both the original principal amount plus the interest already added to the principal amount. The compounding component can be thought of as interest earned on interest over time.

Chapter 21 Recap

RETIREMENT ACCOUNTS

✓ Taking advantage of employer-sponsored retirement plans is key when investing for your future.

✓ If your employer offers matching contributions to your retirement, contribute enough to max out the match. Few times in life are you given such a fantastic investment opportunity.

✓ When selecting investments, start by assessing your risk tolerance. Then, find funds that match your comfort level.

✓ When selecting funds, assess the fees your plan charges. Avoiding excessive fees is imperative to maximizing your investment returns.

✓ Carefully consider fees and stock options when rolling over your retirement account.

Scan for a full list of the links and tools listed.

Chapter 22
ROTH & TRADITIONAL IRAs

An individual retirement account (IRA) is another important tool for your retirement strategy. Like a 401(k), an IRA offers tax advantages that you cannot secure with a regular taxable investment account. The main difference between a 401(k) and an IRA is that a 401(k) is an employer-sponsored retirement plan, while you as an individual can open an IRA at any time. There are several types of retirement accounts, but we'll focus on the two most popular flavors: the traditional and the Roth.

IRAs, 401(k) plans, and 403(b) plans offer both traditional and Roth options. However, a 457(b) only provides a traditional account. In this chapter, we will cover why IRAs should be an essential part of your retirement strategy.

225

Roth IRA Tax Breaks

The main difference between the two plans is the type of tax break. Both types of accounts enjoy tax breaks, but they differ in their timing.

With a Roth IRA, you are investing with money that you have already paid taxes on. Think about your paycheck, which generally has taxes taken out by the time it hits your bank account. You make Roth IRA contributions with that after-tax money.

You might be asking, "Where is the tax break?" There are two important tax breaks with this account, the first being that the money in your Roth IRA account grows tax-free. Over time your investments will grow in value. Whether you are invested in individual stocks or large funds, normally, you have to pay a capital gains tax on any *earnings* on investments, which can vary from 15% to 37%. Not so with an IRA. You can buy and sell investments, within your Roth account, without ever paying any capital gains tax. The ability to reinvest that money that would otherwise go towards taxes can easily double what you end up with in retirement, given a period of 30 years or more.

The other tax benefit is that you won't have to pay any taxes when you are ready to withdraw your funds in retirement. This is why Roth IRAs are commonly referred to as tax-free accounts.

Earnings: money that is made from an investment. This includes interest, dividends and capital gains on a financial asset.

Traditional IRA Tax Breaks

With a traditional IRA, you capture your first tax break when you contribute to the account. This allows you to deduct the money you invest on your tax return in the year you contribute. This reduces your taxable income and, therefore, your tax bill. For example, if you make $60,000/year and contribute the max amount of $6,000 in a traditional IRA, your taxable income would be reduced to $54,000.

With a traditional IRA, your money will also grow tax-free (meaning you won't pay capital gains taxes), but you will have to pay taxes on your earnings when you make withdrawals in retirement.

To put it simply, your tax advantages with a Roth IRA occur in retirement, while your tax advantages with a traditional IRA occur when you make deposits into the account. Later in the chapter, we'll discuss what questions you should be asking when considering what type of account to open.

Are You Eligible to Contribute to an IRA?

CONTRIBUTIONS TO A ROTH IRA

The table below shows the 2021 contributions and income limits for Roth IRAs. You can only contribute to a Roth IRA if your *adjusted gross income* is less than $140,00 as an individual or $208,000 as a married couple filing taxes jointly.

ELIGIBILITY FOR A ROTH IRA[43]

IF YOUR FILING STATUS IS:	AND YOUR MODIFIED ADJUSTED GROSS INCOME (AGI) IS ...	...THEN YOU CAN CONTRIBUTE
Married filing jointly or qualifying widow(er)	Less than $198,000	$6,000 ($7,000 if you're over 50)
	Between $198,000 to $208,000	amount phases out as income increases
	More than $208,000	zero
Single, head of household, or married filing separately, and you did not live with your spouse at any time during the year	Less than $124,000	$6,000 ($7,000 if you're over 50)
	Between $125,000 to $140,000	amount phases out as income increases
	More than $140,000	zero

Adjusted gross income: gross income minus adjustments to income. Gross income includes wages, dividends, capital gains, business income, retirement distributions as well as other income. Adjustments to income include items like educator expenses, student loan interest, alimony payments or contributions to a retirement account.

CONTRIBUTIONS TO A TRADITIONAL IRA[44]

With a traditional IRA, you can open up an account as long as you have taxable income. Although anyone can contribute, there are limitations on your tax deductions based on whether you or your spouse are offered a retirement plan through your employer.

If you are not offered a retirement plan through your job, then you can deduct the following contribution amount on your taxes.

2021 TRADITIONAL IRA TAX DEDUCTIONS
IF YOU ARE NOT COVERED BY A RETIREMENT PLAN AT WORK

IF YOUR FILING STATUS IS...	AND YOUR MODIFIED AGI IS...	THEN YOU CAN TAKE...
Single, head of household, or qualifying widow(er)	any amount	a full deduction up to the amount of your contribution limit of $6,000 ($7,000 if you're 50 or older)
Married filing jointly or separately with a spouse who is not covered by a plan at work	any amount	a full deduction up to the amount of your contribution limit of $6,000 ($7,000 if you're 50 or older)
Married filing jointly with a spouse who is covered by a plan at work	$198,000 or less	a full deduction up to the amount of your contribution limit of $6,000 ($7,000 if you're 50 or older)
	more than $198,000 but less than $208,000	a partial deduction
	$208,000 or more	no deduction
Married filing separately with a spouse who is covered by a plan at work	less than $10,000	a partial deduction
	$10,000 or more	no deduction

If you file separately and did not live with your spouse at any time during the year, your IRA deduction is determined under the single filing status.

If you or your spouse are provided a retirement plan through your employer, then the IRS offers the following table to show how much you can deduct from your taxes.

2021 TRADITIONAL IRA TAX DEDUCTIONS
IF YOU ARE COVERED BY A RETIREMENT PLAN AT WORK

IF YOUR FILING STATUS IS...	AND YOUR MODIFIED AGI IS...	THEN YOU CAN TAKE...
Single or head of household	$66,000 or less	a full deduction up to the amount of your contribution limit of $6,000 ($7,000 if you're 50 or older)
	more than $66,000 but less than $76,000	a partial deduction
	$76,000 or more	no deduction
Married filing jointly or qualifying widow(er)	$105,000 or less	a full deduction up to the amount of your contribution limit of $6,000 ($7,000 if you're 50 or older)
	more than $105,000 but less than $125,000	a partial deduction
	$125,000 or more	no deduction
Married filing separately	less than $10,000	a partial deduction
	$10,000 or more	no deduction

If you file separately and did not live with your spouse at any time during the year, your IRA deduction is determined under the single filing status.

Should I Open a Roth or Traditional Retirement Account?

Answering the following questions will help you to decide which IRA may be a good fit for you.

ARE YOU ELIGIBLE FOR BOTH TRADITIONAL AND ROTH IRAs?

Your income and whether your employer offers a retirement plan will determine your eligibility.

DO YOU THINK YOUR TAX RATE WILL BE HIGHER OR LOWER IN THE FUTURE?

In other words, do you think you'll be making more money in retirement than you are now? This is relevant because more income in retirement will put you in a higher tax bracket.

If you feel confident that your income will continue to increase into retirement, then you may want to consider a Roth IRA. That way, you have already paid income taxes on what you are contributing, and you can avoid higher income taxes on withdrawals in the future when you're at a higher tax rate.

If you would rather pay the taxes in the future and believe you are at a higher tax bracket now than you will be in retirement, consider a traditional IRA. This way, you delay paying taxes until retirement when your tax bracket is at a lower rate.

You can always contribute to both a traditional and Roth account simultaneously if you are uncertain what your financial picture will look like in retirement.

IS FLEXIBILITY FOR WITHDRAWALS IMPORTANT TO YOU?

Roth IRAs are generally considered more flexible than traditional IRAs. If you need to withdraw funds early for an emergency, you will be paying considerably fewer taxes compared to withdrawals with a traditional IRA. For one, you won't be paying any taxes on the amount you contributed since that money has already been taxed. You will still have to pay capital gains taxes on your profits if you are withdrawing early. Also, a Roth IRA does not require you to start making withdrawals at 72 like a traditional IRA will.

There is also some flexibility around what is considered a *qualified withdrawal*. If you are withdrawing funds before you're 59 ½, you can typically expect a 10% penalty on just the earnings portion of what you made. You will also have to pay taxes on those earnings. If you withdraw funds (including earnings) after you are 59 ½, those withdrawals are tax-free and penalty-free, provided that the account is at least 5 years old.

Examples of qualified withdrawals, which will allow you to avoid the early withdrawal penalty, are a first-time home purchase, certain college expenses, and expenses related to the birth or adoption of a child.

> *Qualified withdrawal:* withdrawals from a retirement account without penalty after having met account requierments.

Clear as mud? The following infographics should help clarify the rules around withdrawals, penalties, and taxes for both a Roth and a traditional IRA.

WITHDRAWAL PENALTIES AND TAXES
ROTH IRA

IMPORTANT NOTE: With a Roth IRA you can withdraw your original contributions at any time without penalty or taxes. This is because you already paid taxes on the money you used to fund the account. Penalty and taxes are on the **EARNINGS** portion in your account.

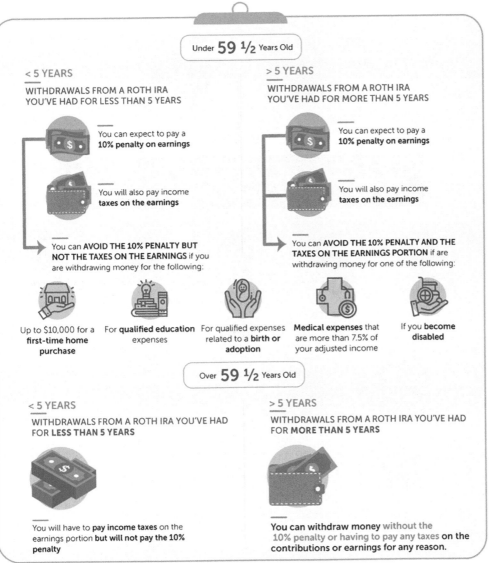

Under **59 ½** Years Old

< 5 YEARS
WITHDRAWALS FROM A ROTH IRA YOU'VE HAD FOR LESS THAN 5 YEARS

You can expect to pay a **10% penalty on earnings**

You will also pay income **taxes on the earnings**

You can **AVOID THE 10% PENALTY BUT NOT THE TAXES ON THE EARNINGS** if you are withdrawing money for the following:

> 5 YEARS
WITHDRAWALS FROM A ROTH IRA YOU'VE HAD FOR MORE THAN 5 YEARS

You can expect to pay a **10% penalty on earnings**

You will also pay income **taxes on the earnings**

You can **AVOID THE 10% PENALTY AND THE TAXES ON THE EARNINGS PORTION** if are withdrawing money for one of the following:

Up to $10,000 for a **first-time home purchase**

For **qualified education** expenses

For qualified expenses related to a **birth or adoption**

Medical expenses that are more than 7.5% of your adjusted income

If you **become disabled**

Over **59 ½** Years Old

< 5 YEARS
WITHDRAWALS FROM A ROTH IRA YOU'VE HAD FOR **LESS THAN 5 YEARS**

You will have to **pay income taxes** on the earnings portion **but will not pay the 10% penalty**

> 5 YEARS
WITHDRAWALS FROM A ROTH IRA YOU'VE HAD FOR **MORE THAN 5 YEARS**

You can withdraw money without the 10% penalty or having to pay any taxes **on the contributions or earnings for any reason.**

Source: www.irs.gov/publications/p590b | Current as of August 2020

©2020 MoneyOverMilkshakes.com

WITHDRAWAL PENALTIES AND TAXES

TRADITIONAL IRA

Under **59 ½** Years Old

You can expect to **pay a 10% penalty** on contributions and earnings.

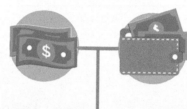

You will also have **pay income taxes** on both contributions and earnings as well.

You can **avoid the 10% penalty but not the taxes on the earnings** if you are withdrawing money for the following:

Up to $10,000 for a **first-time home purchase**

For **qualified education** expenses

For qualified expenses related to a **birth or adoption**

Medical expenses that are more than 7.5% of your adjusted income

If you **become disabled**

Over **59 ½** Years Old

If you are between **the age of 59 ½ to 70** there is **no penalties** on any withdrawals but since you originally put in pre-tax dollars you will have to **pay income taxes** on both the contributions and earnings.

Once you are 70 ½, you must start taking out annual withdrawals. There is a 50% penalty on the amounts you are required to withdraw per year.

Source: www.irs.gov/publications/p590b | Current as of August 2020

What is a Backdoor Roth IRA?

Once you finish residency, your income will exceed the income limit to contribute to a Roth IRA. You can still invest in what is referred to as a backdoor Roth IRA.

This may sound a little sketchy but is entirely legal and frequently recommended for high-income individuals. (To put you at ease, you can find the Internal Revenue Service (IRS) FAQ page on the subject at www.irs.gov/retirement-plans/retirement-plans-faqs-regarding-iras-rollovers-and-roth-conversions.) With a backdoor IRA, you can contribute to a traditional IRA first, then transfer those investments into a Roth IRA without the usual income limitations. You can perform this conversion every year.

Why do you have to jump through all these hoops just to open a Roth IRA, you might ask? Good question.

When you convert funds from a traditional IRA to a Roth, you will need to pay taxes since the Roth is an after-tax account. Remember that you get a tax break when you put money into the traditional IRA? Since the Roth grows tax-free, you have to pay taxes on the money before it goes in, whether it comes from a traditional IRA or your own pocket.

Timing on your backdoor conversion is also important. If you allow time to pass between when you contribute to a traditional IRA and subsequently convert it to a Roth IRA, you may owe taxes on any gains made. That is why you should consider converting as soon as the funds settle on your contribution. There will be little to no taxes if you contribute first to the traditional IRA, and then once the funds settle, immediately turn around and roll over those funds into a Roth IRA. The taxes would be on any gains you've made in the account, and there will not be significant gains to tax if you are transferring those funds within a short period of time.

If it is your first time converting a traditional IRA to a Roth, it is a good idea to discuss how a conversion will affect your specific tax situation with a professional tax advisor. You don't want to convert too much so that the conversion moves that contribution to the next tax bracket or convert too little where you are not taking full advantage of the conversion. Make sure to dot your i's and cross your t's.

The Pro-Rata Rule As It Applies to Backdoor IRAs

The Pro-Rata Rule is the calculation the IRS uses to determine the taxes you owe when performing a Roth conversion (a.k.a., backdoor conversion). For tax purposes, the IRS will look at all of your IRA accounts and will consider them as one lump sum for calculation purposes. The IRS will then look at how much of your IRA accounts have after-tax funds in them versus how much are pre-tax funds to determine your tax bill when transferring funds to a backdoor Roth IRA.

For example, let's say you have $100,000 spread across multiple IRA accounts, and 80% has pre-tax funds (401(k) or traditional IRA), while 20% contains after-tax funds (Roth). That means, regardless of the amount you are converting, 80% of the funds converted are taxable. So your total funds in all your IRAs will determine the taxable amount transferred over. You should also be aware that having more than one traditional IRA may also affect your taxes.

Withdrawing Funds for Education Expenses

Both Roth and traditional IRAs allow you to withdraw funds for qualified education expenses without paying the 10% early withdrawal penalty. Note that having an IRA will not affect the FAFSA until you withdraw the funds.

Withdrawals will be counted as income and will result in a reduction of eligible aid for the student. Money above $6,570 in student income will reduce financial aid eligibility by 50% of the additional income. This is why you should wait to withdraw until the student no longer has to apply for financial aid.

While you cannot use IRA funds to pay off student loans after graduation, you can make withdrawals to pay off loan payments while the student is in school. This includes the account holder's own education expenses, as well as those of their spouse, child, or grandchild. You are better off saving for college using a 529 plan rather than an IRA in most cases, but the option is there if needed.

Should I Contribute to a 401(k) or an IRA?

This need not be an either-or situation. If you have an employer-sponsored 401(k) available to you with a matching contribution, our personal strategy is always to contribute up to the maximum amount of the match to take advantage of the free money. These guaranteed, risk-free returns are as good as investing gets. If your employer is offering a 100% match on what you contribute, you'll make a 100% return on your contributions once the money is vested.

If your employer does not offer any matching contributions or additional stock options through a 401(k), consider contributing to an IRA account first. An IRA has considerably more investment options than most 401(k)s. Since one of the key criteria in choosing investments should be to find funds with low fees, you'll have a lot more options to choose from with an IRA. Once we max out our individual IRAs, we go back to our 401(k) and work on maxing out the remaining contribution amounts to those accounts.

How to Choose a Low-Cost IRA

IRAs are offered by banks, investment firms, and (more recently) online investment platforms.

When choosing an IRA, you will want to keep an eye on the following:

1 MANAGEMENT FEES. These fees are generally in the form of a percentage of the amount invested.

2 COST PER TRADE. Some companies will charge a fee every time you buy or sell an investment.

3 MINIMUM AMOUNT required to open the account or invest in funds.

We know this is a lot to digest, but don't let that overwhlem you until putting off the decision until later. Feel free to review the chapter again, pick a plan and start investing so that you can capitalize on your investments. Time is your friend here.

Here are a few organizations worth exploring when shopping for an IRA, as well as a breakdown of the features they offer:[45]

SHOPPING FOR LOW-COST IRAs

	ALLY INVEST	BETTERMENT	FIDELITY	VANGUARD	CHARLES SCHWAB
OFFER SELF-MANAGED IRA?	Yes	No	Yes	Yes	Yes
OFFER ROBO-ADVISOR IRA?	Yes	Yes	Yes	Yes	Yes
ANNUAL FEE	No fee	0.25% - 0.40%	No fee for self-directed; robo-advisor fees below	$20/year but waived w/ e-delivery; robo-advisor fee: 0.20%	No fee for self directed; robo-advisor fee min $5k
FEE FOR TRADING STOCKS AND ETFs	No trading fee	No trading fee	No trading fee	No trading fee	No trading fee
TRADING BONDS	$1 per bond (minimum of $10)	No fee	$1 per bond (minimum of $10)	$1 per bond	$1 per bond (minimum of $10)
TRADING OPTIONS	No trading fee but $0.50 per contract fee	N/A	No trading fee but $0.65 per contract fee	No trading fee but $1 per contract fee	No trading fee but $0.65 per contract fee
MUTUAL FUNDS	$0 fee for load funds $9.95 per trade for no-load funds	No fee	No fee	No fee	$9.95 per trade
ACCOUNT CLOSURE FEE	$25	No fee	No fee	No fee	$25
TRANSFER OUT FEE	$50	No fee	No fee	No fee	$50 full; $25 partial
INVESTMENT MINIMUMS	$100 for robo-advisor; none for self-managed account	None for standard; $100,000 for premium	$10	None for self-managed; $3,000 for robo-advisor	$3,000 for robo-advisor
ADDITIONAL NOTES	Robo-advisor: must choose from selection of portfolios	No self-managed option; premium offers access to CFAs	Fidelity has four options of robo-advisory fees based on account balance	Personal advisor premium fee: 0.3%	Broker-assisted trades are $25 per trade

ROTH AND TRADITIONAL IRAs

✓ Both Roth and traditional IRAs offer tax-free growth when buying and selling investments within the account.

✓ Roth IRAs provide an additional tax break upon withdrawals in retirement, while Traditional IRAs offer a tax break in the year you make contributions.

✓ For 2021, income eligibility phases out for a Roth IRA at $140,000 per year for single filers ($208,000 for those married filing jointly). Not eligible? Consider a backdoor Roth IRA.

✓ A backdoor IRA is an option for those that are not eligible for a Roth IRA. This involves contributing to a traditional IRA, then transferring those funds to a Roth IRA.

✓ Be aware of early withdrawal penalties for both traditional and Roth IRA accounts.

Scan for a full list of the links and tools listed.

Chapter 23
INDEX FUNDS

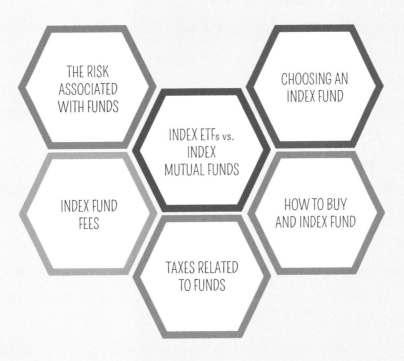

"By periodically investing in an index fund, the know-nothing investors can actually outperform most investment professionals."
—WARREN BUFFET, CHAIRMAN AND CEO OF BERKSHIRE HATHAWAY
ONE OF THE MOST SUCCESSFUL INVESTORS IN A GENERATION WITH A NET WORTH OF $108 BILLION[46]

Throughout this chapter, I have sprinkled in the words of much wiser professional investors to support my claims on index funds. I'm hoping their words and mine resonate with you when it comes to creating an investment strategy. You might remember that at the beginning of the book, I teased an investment strategy that is simple to understand, can save you tens of thousands of dollars over time, and has statistically outperformed 90% of professional investment advisors over the long term. Well, here it is: index funds are the secret sauce. This chapter will discuss why index funds should be the backbone of any solid investment strategy.

As a reminder, a fund is comprised of hundreds or thousands of stocks and bonds in a single holding. This can help considerably when simplifying and diversifying your investments.

Index funds can take the form of a mutual fund or an exchange-traded fund (ETF), and they aim to mirror an index's performance, such as the S&P 500, Nasdaq, or Dow Jones Industrial Average. Index funds are considered passively managed funds since the manager of these funds just buys most or all of the stocks within an index. When these market indexes increase or decrease, the index fund mimicking them will do the same.

Investing primarily in index funds removes the need to check in on your investments constantly. Actively managed funds, as expected, involve portfolio managers buying and selling investments regularly to try and beat the market. An active investment strategy comes with considerably higher fees.

As we mentioned previously, actively managed mutual funds are unlikely to outperform index funds over an extended period of time. The SPIVA Scorecard for 2020 (www.spglobal.com/spdji/en/documents/spiva/spiva-us-year-end-2020.pdf) compared how actively managed funds performed against the S&P 500 index. Over a 10-year period, 82% of actively managed large-cap funds underperformed the S&P 500 index.

If you only take away one statistic from this book regarding investments, let it be this: OVER A 20-YEAR PERIOD, OVER 94% OF ACTIVELY MANAGED LARGE-CAP FUNDS UNDERPERFORMED THE S&P 500.

Index Fund Fees

Since index funds are passively managed, they have lower fees than an actively managed fund. These fees may seem trivial at first, but they add up over time. They are an important reason why passive funds outperform actively managed funds over time.

The price you pay to invest in a fund is known as an expense ratio, expressed as a percentage of the total amount invested. The fee is typically based on what you have invested over a year and can be charged at the beginning of the year (frontloaded) or at the end of the year (back-end loaded).

According to the Investment Company Institute, the average expense ratio for index funds in 2019 was 0.07% compared with 0.74% for actively managed funds.[47] ACTIVELY MANAGED FUND FEES ARE 10 TIMES HIGHER THAN THOSE OF INDEX FUNDS!

Let's see what the difference in percentages means for your portfolio. Assuming you are well into your career, let's assume you have $1,000,000 invested. You would pay $7,400 per year with an actively managed fund versus $700 per year with an index fund. Over 10 years, if you take the difference in fees between the two funds, you will pay an additional $67,000 with an actively managed fund. But that's not all you're losing out on since that does not include the difference in returns between the funds. That $67,000 would have been at work in the market, earning you more money had you not spent it on fees.

Don't let the seemingly small percentages fool you. Fees matter a great deal to your overall rate of return.

Taxes Related to Funds

Index funds generally offer less of a tax burden than actively traded funds since, by definition, actively traded funds are continuously adding and removing investments. When an actively traded fund (outside of a retirement account like 401(k)s or IRAs) sells a holding for a profit, it will pass on that profit to its shareholders. If you are a shareholder, you will need to pay capital gains tax on that profit. Index funds don't do nearly as much buying and selling, so they don't generate as large of a capital gains tax bill.

The Risk Associated with Funds

Index funds tend to offer lower risk than actively traded funds since they are invested in companies representing an entire index, such as the S&P 500. Because of this, index funds tend to have more holdings and be less susceptible to losses from a single company.

Additionally, fund managers try to time and beat the market. There are inherent risks for potential errors in a manager making a large number of trades over an extended amount of time.

Index ETFs vs. Index Mutual Funds

ETFs and mutual funds are very similar, but there are a few key differences. Exchange-traded funds (ETFs) are generally easier to trade. You can buy or sell an ETF throughout the trading day, while mutual funds are usually bought or sold at one price set for each day.

If you are not constantly trading and you have a long-term investment strategy, this is rarely problematic. Some mutual funds have a minimum amount that needs to be invested. (Below are some examples.) An ETF does not usually have a minimum—only the cost of a single share.

Choosing an Index Fund[48]

Below are a few of the most popular, well-diversified index funds. The first five track the performance of the S&P 500, while the remaining three track the performance of the entire U.S. stock market.

SAMPLE INDEX FUNDS

	TYPE OF FUND	MINIMUM INVESTMENT REQUIRED	COST PER YEAR (% OF AMOUNT INVESTED)	LINKS FOR ADDITIONAL INFO
VANGUARD 500 INDEX ADMIRAL (VFIAX)	Mutual Fund	$3,000	0.04%	investor.vanguard.com/ mutual-funds/profile/ VFIAZ
FIDELITY 500 INDEX FUND (FXAIX)	Mutual Fund	No Minimum	0.015%	fundresearch.fidelity.com/ mutual-funds/summary/ 315911750
SPDR S&P 500 ETF TRUST (SPY)	ETF	No Minimum	0.0945%	www.ssga.com/us/en/ individual/etfs/funds/ spdr-sp-500-etf-trust-spy
VANGUARD S&P 500 ETF (VOO)	ETF	No Minimum	0.03%	investor.vanguard.com/ etf/profile/VOO
ISHARES CORE S&P 500 ETF (VOO)	ETF	No Minimum	0.04%	www.ishares.com/ us/products/239726/ ishares-core-sp-500-etf
VANGUARD TOTAL STOCK MARKET INDEX FUND ADMIRAL (VTSAX)	Mutual Fund	$3,000	0.04%	investor.vanguard.com/ mutual-funds/profile/ VTSAX
FIDELITY ZERO LARGE CAP INDEX (FNILX)	Mutual Fund	No Minimum	0%	fundresearch.fidelity.com/ mutual-funds/summary/ 315911628
VANGUARD TOTAL STOCK MARKET ETF (VTI)	ETF	No Minimum	0.03%	investor.vanguard.com/ etf/profile/VTI

These are low-cost options compared to many actively managed mutual funds that are 10 to 20 times the annual *expense ratio*.

Expense ratio: the administrative fees associated with managing a fund.

"Our standard prescription for the know-nothing investor with a long-term time horizon is a *no-load* index fund. I think that works better than relying on your stockbroker. The people who are telling you to do something else are all being paid by commissions or fees."
—CHARLIE MUNGER; VICE-CHAIRMAN OF BERKSHIRE HATHAWAY
ESTIMATED NET WORTH OF $2.2 BILLION[49]

"Invest in low-turnover, passively managed index funds... and stay away from profit-driven investment management organizations... The mutual fund industry is a colossal failure... resulting from its systematic exploitation of individual investors... as funds extract enormous sums from investors in exchange for providing a shocking disservice... Excessive management fees take their toll, and manager profits dominate fiduciary responsibility."
DAVID F. SWENSON, CHIEF INVESTMENT OFFICER AT YALE UNIVERSITY
RESPONSIBLE FOR INVESTING YALE'S ASSETS THAT TOTAL OVER $30 BILLION[50]

No-load: A fund sold directly by the investment company without any sales charges or commssions.

How to Buy an Index Fund

There are several options to purchase an index fund. You may purchase index funds through your IRA or 401(k) or buy funds directly from the sponsor's website, such as Vanguard or Fidelity. Another option is through a broker, such as E-Trade or Charles Schwab, with a taxable investment account. Index *ETFs* can be purchased anywhere you can buy stocks, including online brokers. There is no minimum besides the cost of a single share. For example, the ETFs mentioned above are $100 to $300 per share.

I hope that between the information provided in the chapter, the data in the SPIVA Report, and the advice from some of the most successful investors of our time, index funds are carefully considered as part of your *long-term investment* strategy.

Exchange Traded Fund (ETF): A fund that allows you to purchase a large number of securities under a single investment. ETFs are traded throughout the day.

Long-term investment: stocks, bonds, or funds that are held for more than a year.

INDEX FUNDS

✓ Index funds offer investors a great way to mimic overall market returns over time.

✓ Index funds are passive funds that offer lower fees than many actively traded funds.

✓ Index funds generally cost less in taxes than actively traded funds that continuously buy and sell investments in a taxable account.

✓ Index funds tend to offer lower risk than actively traded funds due to fewer trades and more diversification in their holdings.

✓ Index funds can be purchased through a 401(k), IRA, or taxable investment account.

Scan for a full list of the links and tools listed.

Chapter 24

HEALTH SAVINGS ACCOUNTS (HSA) & FLEXIBLE SPENDING ACCOUNTS (FSA)

It can be difficult to look at a savings account that helps you save for healthcare-related bills or childcare-related expenses and consider it a key element to your investment strategy, but that is exactly how these accounts should be viewed. This chapter discusses how health savings accounts and flexible spending accounts are some of the most undervalued opportunities available to many of us.

What is a Health Savings Account (HSA) or a Flexible Spending Account (FSA)?

Health savings accounts (HSAs) and flexible spending accounts (FSAs) are both pre-tax savings accounts that are tied to your employer. Health savings accounts (HSAs) allow you to transfer part of your pre-tax income to a savings account to help pay for health-related expenses.

Flexible spending accounts (FSAs) will similarly allow you to save pre-tax money for certain expenses. There are two major types of FSAs. One type of FSA will allow you to contribute pre-tax income to pay for childcare-related expenses. The other kind of FSA will allow for the same pre-tax benefit but for healthcare-related expenses. These are separate accounts and will vary depending on your employer's plan. Your HR department can give you details on what accounts your employer offers.

WHY HSAs AND FSAs SHOULD BE AN IMPORTANT PART OF YOUR INVESTMENT STRATEGY

Many of us would rather cross our fingers and hope that hospital bills are not in our future over preemptively saving for these occasions. Unfortunately, that is almost guaranteed not to be the case. According to an analysis of the Bureau of Labor Statistics Consumer Expenditures Survey by data company Clever, the average American household spends $5,000 on healthcare annually. This includes health insurance, prescription drugs, medical services, and medical supplies.[51]

Even if you are young, healthy, and running marathons, you will need the savings in retirement. A 65-year-old couple in good health will need $387,644 to pay for healthcare costs for the remainder of their lives, according to HealthView Services, a provider of healthcare cost projection software. "That amount includes premiums for Medicare Part B (medical insurance) and D (prescription drug coverage), dental insurance and out-of-pocket costs related to doctor's exams, hearing services, and more."[52]

The tax benefit can likewise be hard to appreciate at first, but consider how much more you would have to save if the pre-tax benefit did not exist. If you wanted to save the equivalent of $1,000 pre-tax, you would need to earn around $1,316, assuming an effective tax rate of 24% because you would still have to pay taxes on the money earned.

HEALTH SAVINGS ACCOUNT vs TAXABLE INVESTMENT ACCOUNT

ASSUMPTIONS
If you are trying to save $1,000 with a tax rate of 24%

SAVING IN A HSA ACCOUNT
You will need to earn $1,000 pre-tax

TAXES
No taxes are paid since you are able to transfer to an HSA pre-tax

RESULT
You would have saved yourself $316 in taxes while having to earn less to save $1,000 in an HSA account

SAVING IN A TAXABLE INVESTMENT ACCOUNT
You will need to earn $1,316 pre-tax

TAXES
You will need to pay 24% income tax on money earned

RESULT
After paying $316 in taxes, you can deposit $1,000 in a taxable investment account

If you are not saving for healthcare-related expenses in an HSA account, you'll be paying for those expenses with money that has been unnecessarily reduced by taxes by up to 30%; or worse, use a credit card with a high-interest rate that takes months to pay off. When those bills come due, that is money that you'll have to divert from savings and other investments.

HSAs are also the only account that I am aware of that offer three separate tax breaks on the account. First, your money is deposited into the account pre-tax, reducing your taxable income. Second, you can then invest the money in the stock market, and the interest on that money will grow tax-free. Finally, you can withdraw the funds for qualified health-related expenses tax-free. The triple tax advantage HSA accounts offer is extremely rare in the investment world.

A full list from the IRS website of medical expenses that can be used with an HSA can be found at www.irs.gov/pub/irs-pdf/p502.pdf.

What is Required to Open an HSA or FSA?

Your employer must offer a flexible spending account—you cannot open a flexible spending account on your own. Alternatively, you can open an HSA on your own; however, you must be enrolled in a high-deductible health plan to qualify. HSAs are designed to offset the high costs of such plans. The minimum *deductible* on HSA-eligible health plans for 2021 is $1,400 for an individual and $2,800 for a family. Check with your employer's HR department on whether they offer pre-tax savings accounts and whether your health plan qualifies for an HSA account. If your health plan does qualify, you can open an HSA with a bank or brokerage and provide the account information to your HR department so that they can transfer pre-tax dollars from your paycheck into the account.

Can You Open Up Both Accounts?

Not normally. If both are available, you will need to choose one or the other.

Deductible: the amount of money you pay out-of-pocket when a claim is made.

Health Savings Account vs. Flexible Spending Account

The biggest advantage of a flexible spending account is the ability to save money for health-related expenses with pre-tax dollars in combination with a low-deductible health plan. If you have ongoing health issues or you expect upcoming hospital bills to be considerable, the combination of a flexible spending account and a low-deductible plan can cost you less out of pocket.

If you and your family are relatively healthy, you might consider a high-deductible health plan with an HSA account. You will pay less in premiums monthly (the trade-off with a high deductible), but you do have to build up savings in your HSA account to cover the out-of-pocket deductible and expenses. The more money you save in your HSA account, the better this decision looks.

HSA accounts roll over every year and do not expire—even if you change employers. A flexible spending account, on the other hand, does not roll over. It is usually a use-it-or-lose-it arrangement, so you forfeit any money left over at the end of the fiscal year that you haven't used toward health-related expenses. There are some exceptions to this in which an account will allow you to roll over a certain amount to the following year, but that is not often the case.

Another difference is that HSAs can be invested in the stock market while FSAs do not have the option. As mentioned, the HSA account enjoys three separate tax breaks on the account. A flexible spending account also offers pre-tax contributions and tax-free withdrawals. However, there is no interest earned on these accounts since they do not offer options for growth in the stock market on your contributions.

Here is a side-by-side comparison to help distinguish the two accounts:

HEALTH SAVINGS ACCOUNT vs FLEXIBLE SPENDING ACCOUNT

	HEALTH SAVINGS ACCOUNT (HSA)	FLEXIBLE SPENDING ACCOUNT (FSA)
ELIGIBILITY REQUIREMENTS	Must have a qualified high-deductible health plan	Must be offered by employer
2021 CONTRIBUTION LIMIT	Individual: $3,600 Family: $7,200 (For ages 55 or older, an additional $1,000 catch-up contribution is allowed)	$2,750
ROLLOVER	Money not used in the account will roll over to the following year	Money not used in the account will be lost at the end of the year (many plans offer a grace period)
MAKING CHANGES TO CONTRIBUTION AMOUNTS	You can change your contribution amounts at any time	You can only change your contribution amounts during open enrollment, or with a qualifying status event
TAX ADVANTAGES	Triple tax advantage: pre-tax contributions, no tax on interest or earnings, and no tax on withdrawals for qualified expenses	Pre-tax contributions and no tax on withdrawals for qualified expenses (FSAs do not offer earnings on contributions)
ACCESSIBLE FUNDS	You can only access the funds you have contributed so far	You have access to the full amount you choose to contribute for the year
EMPLOYMENT STATUS	You can take your HSA account with you as you change employers as long as you have a high-deductible health plan	Your account is tied to a specific employer and you will lose the account when changing employers

SOURCE: www.irs.gov/pub/irs-drop/rp-20-32.pdf and www.irs.gov/pub/irs-drop/rp-20-45.pdf

Pandemic-Related Exceptions

The spending package passed by Congress during the COVID-19 pandemic allows employers to carry over unused funds for healthcare- and childcare-related FSA accounts. This is for plans in 2020-2021 as well as 2021-2022. The bill also allows for midyear election changes without having a change in status event. ULTIMATELY THIS IS UP TO EMPLOYERS THOUGH. It is optional, so you'll want to check with your employer to see if they offer any extensions to benefits.

Whether you're saving for childcare or healthcare-related expenses, take the time to understand what accounts your employer offers. These pre-tax accounts are a financial opportunity that should be considered carefully. Planning ahead and not paying taxes on these expenses should be an integral part of your overall financial strategy.

HEALTH SAVINGS ACCOUNTS (HSA) AND FLEXIBLE SPENDING ACCOUNTS (FSA)

✓ An HSA is a pre-tax savings/investment account to help pay for health-related expenses.

✓ An FSA is a pre-tax savings account to help pay for either health-related expenses or childcare-related expenses.

✓ You cannot normally have both and HSA and a FSA account simultaneously.

✓ An HSA account enjoys three separate tax breaks on the account. Money is deposited pre-tax, money will grow tax-free on investments, and you can withdraw the funds for qualified health-related expenses tax-free.

✓ Pandemic related exceptions may allow you to carry over unused benefits on an FSA account.

Scan for a full list of the links and tools listed.

Chapter 25
ASSET ALLOCATION

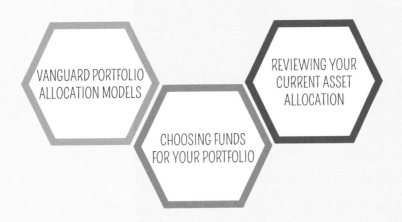

Asset allocation determines how much of your savings and retirement funds should go towards different investments such as stocks, bonds, and mutual funds. This is where diversification comes in. The concept of diversification is to have investments in different asset classes act differently from each other to balance out risk. As some investments go up, others come down.

Historically, bonds have posed less risk but yielded lower returns compared to stocks. Since 1926, a *portfolio* of 100% bonds has returned 6.1% per year on average. Stocks have historically provided higher returns at around 10.3% per year on average.[53] However, stocks also come with higher volatility and higher risk. The goal of asset allocation is to create a good mix of stocks and bonds through various funds that provide suitable returns at a level of risk you are comfortable with.

Portfolio: a collection of investments owned by an individual, and managed as a collective whole with specific investment goals in mind.

Vanguard Portfolio Allocation Models

To begin determining your asset allocation, ask yourself where you are on your investment journey in relation to your retirement. We like Vanguard's straightforward approach to allocation models. They have three broad categories for different stages of life: income, balanced, and growth models. The income model is geared towards those closer to retirement that want to preserve what they have while generating an income from their investments. The growth model is geared toward those with many years to go before reaching retirement age. The balanced portfolio sits in the middle, with investments that are still generating income and a mid-range time horizon for investments.

Income

An income portfolio consists primarily of dividend-paying stocks and coupon-yielding bonds. If you're comfortable with minimal risk and have a short- to midrange investment time horizon, this approach may suit your needs. Keep in mind, depending on the account, dividends and returns can be taxable.

100% bonds

- 0% Stocks
- 100% Bonds

Historical Risk/Return (1926–2020)

Average annual return	6.1%
Best year (1982)	45.5%
Worst year (1969)	−8.1%
Years with a loss	19 of 95

20% stocks / 80% bonds

- 20% Stocks
- 80% Bonds

Historical Risk/Return (1926–2020)

Average annual return	7.2%
Best year (1982)	40.7%
Worst year (1931)	−10.1%
Years with a loss	16 of 95

30% stocks / 70% bonds

- 30% Stocks
- 70% Bonds

Historical Risk/Return (1926–2020)

Average annual return	7.7%
Best year (1982)	38.3%
Worst year (1931)	−14.2%
Years with a loss	18 of 95

"Vanguard Portfolio Allocation Models." Vanguard.com. investor.vanguard.com/investing/how-to-invest/model-portfolio-allocation. Accessed of 20 May 2021.

Balanced

A balanced portfolio invests in both stocks and bonds to reduce potential volatility. An investor seeking a balanced portfolio is comfortable tolerating short-term price fluctuations, is willing to tolerate moderate growth, and has a mid- to long-range investment time horizon.

40% stocks / 60% bonds

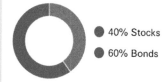

- 40% Stocks
- 60% Bonds

Historical Risk/Return (1926-2020)

Average annual return	8.2%
Best year (1982)	35.9%
Worst year (1931)	–18.4%
Years with a loss	19 of 95

50% stocks / 50% bonds

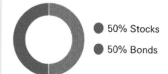

- 50% Stocks
- 50% Bonds

Historical Risk/Return (1926-2020)

Average annual return	8.7%
Best year (1982)	33.5%
Worst year (1931)	–22.5%
Years with a loss	20 of 95

60% stocks / 40% bonds

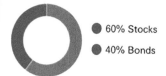

- 60% Stocks
- 40% Bonds

Historical Risk/Return (1926-2020)

Average annual return	9.1%
Best year (1933)	36.7%
Worst year (1931)	–26.6%
Years with a loss	22 of 95

"Vanguard Portfolio Allocation Models." Vanguard.com. investor.vanguard.com/ investing/how-to-invest/model-portfolio-allocation. Accessed of 20 May 2021.

Growth

A growth portfolio consists of mostly stocks expected to appreciate, taking into account long-term potential and potentially large short-term price fluctuations. An investor seeking this portfolio has a high risk tolerance and a long-term investment time horizon. Generating current income isn't a primary goal.

70% stocks / 30% bonds

- 70% Stocks
- 30% Bonds

Historical Risk/Return (1926-2020)

Average annual return	9.4%
Best year (1933)	41.1%
Worst year (1931)	−30.7%
Years with a loss	23 of 95

80% stocks / 20% bonds

- 80% Stocks
- 20% Bonds

Historical Risk/Return (1926-2020)

Average annual return	9.8%
Best year (1933)	45.4%
Worst year (1931)	−34.9%
Years with a loss	24 of 95

100% stocks

- 100% Stocks
- 0% Bonds

Historical Risk/Return (1926-2020)

Average annual return	10.3%
Best year (1933)	54.2%
Worst year (1931)	−43.1%
Years with a loss	25 of 95

"Vanguard Portfolio Allocation Models." Vanguard.com. investor.vanguard.com/investing/how-to-invest/model-portfolio-allocation. Accessed of 20 May 2021.

Vanguard's risk questionnaire[54] will help you determine your *risk tolerance* and time horizon. We like Vanguard's approach to asset allocation, but there are other options out there, and different investment firms may have their own allocation strategy.

> *Risk tolerance:* the amount of loss and uncertainty an investor is comfortable taking with their investments.

Choosing Funds for Your Portfolio

With an asset allocation plan to guide you, the next step is to choose the funds that make up your portfolio. Believe it or not, you can accomplish a well-diversified portfolio with a single fund, if that is your preference. A target-date fund is one example of this. This single fund is comprised of thousands of stocks and bonds, providing a well-diversified portfolio. These funds will have your expected year of retirement in the name of the fund. For example, if you plan on retiring in 30 years, you would pick a fund with 2050 in its name or the year closest to that since these funds usually are listed in 5-year increments. Most 401k and other retirement accounts offer target-date funds.

Aside from good *diversification* in stocks and bonds, the other major advantage to target-date funds is they provide automatic rebalancing. This means the fund will periodically shift your holdings to more conservative investments as you approach retirement age to preserve your capital. This rebalancing will ensure you have the appropriate balance of stocks and bonds for your risk tolerance and time horizon. (We go into more detail on rebalancing in the next chapter.)

Risk tolerance: the amount of loss and uncertainty an investor is comfortable taking with their investments.

Diversification: the concept of not putting all your eggs in one basket. In other words to have investments in different asset classes that perform well at different times. This helps to reduce risk and volatility.

Although target-date funds can be a great, no-hassle solution to investing, be careful with the *expense ratios* associated with these funds. Many 401(k)s will choose a target-date fund for you by default if you do not choose one yourself when the account is created. We were automatically placed in a target-date fund with an expense ratio of 0.755%. You may be able to find target-date funds with expense ratios as low as 0.10% to 0.15%. The difference in fees may seem insignificant, but the example below illustrates how they are not.

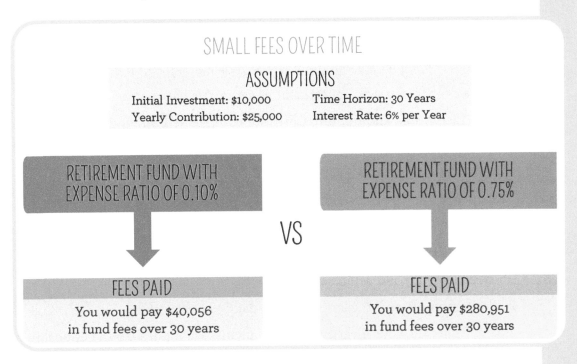

SMALL FEES OVER TIME

ASSUMPTIONS

Initial Investment: $10,000   Time Horizon: 30 Years
Yearly Contribution: $25,000   Interest Rate: 6% per Year

RETIREMENT FUND WITH EXPENSE RATIO OF 0.10%

VS

RETIREMENT FUND WITH EXPENSE RATIO OF 0.75%

FEES PAID
You would pay $40,056 in fund fees over 30 years

FEES PAID
You would pay $280,951 in fund fees over 30 years

In the example above, the difference between a fund with a fee of 0.10% and one with a fee of 0.75% will be close to $241,000 in fees over 30 years. Managers in the industry want you to believe these small percentages are inconsequential.

If you're looking for more control over your investments, you also have the option of selecting multiple funds to meet your chosen asset allocations.

Expense ratio: the administrative fees associated with managing a fund.

Some professionals may choose as little as a single index fund for stocks and a single index fund for bonds. Although two holdings in a portfolio may seem underdeveloped, this may still be a well-diversified portfolio invested in hundreds or even thousands of individual stocks and bonds.

If you want more control and are willing to spend more time analyzing your investments, selecting funds, and rebalancing your portfolio, you can dive deeper into your investment choices. You can continue to go down the rabbit hole and get unnecessarily complicated, which is what many investment advisors recommend: more funds, more stocks, more bonds, more buying, more selling, more transaction fees, more advisor fees—all of which is frankly much ado about nothing.

The SPIVA Report has demonstrated it is unnecessary if your goal is to simply outperform the majority of investment professionals. All the active buying and selling of individual stocks has not proven to provide better returns over the long run than passive index funds.

That said, your investments become more complicated and critical in retirement. If you are fast approaching retirement, you will definitely want to review your strategy with a financial advisor as your goals shift from growth to income.

Reviewing Your Current Asset Allocation

You'll need to figure out how much you currently have in stocks and bonds. If all you have is a 401(k) with Vanguard, Fidelity, or a brokerage with an online portal, that will be pretty easy since they will display your asset mix online.

If your investments are spread throughout multiple plans and companies, you have a few options to get a full and current picture. You can pull up an excel spreadsheet (templates.office.com/en-US/Investment-tracker-TM00414392) and enter in your investments one by one to get a full picture of your asset allocation. However, our preferred method is to use a free online tool to do all the hard work for you.

Personal Capital is one online tool that will provide you with your existing asset mix once you link your accounts to their platform. As of the time of publication of this book, this tool was free. Personal Capital offers additional investment services at a fee and can help you with asset allocation and rebalancing, but you can also just collect the full picture and manually make the necessary trades to save yourself the fee. I personally use the free version to keep track of our asset mix for multiple retirement accounts in one place.

Personal Capital also offers budgeting tools, but it is primarily an investing and retirement application. Mint and YNAB far exceed Personal Capital when it comes to budgeting. However, if you have a good handle on your budget and you are only willing to link all your accounts to one platform, we recommend Personal Capital for the investment and retirement tools they offer for free.

If you want the best of both worlds, consider using both Personal Capital for tracking your retirement goals and an app like Mint or YNAB for regular budgeting and goal setting.

Chapter 25 Recap

ASSET ALLOCATION

- ✓ Your asset allocation choices should be determined by your risk tolerance, age, and retirement goals.

- ✓ Consider starting with Vanguard's asset allocation models. This can be done by completing Vanguard's risk questionnaire.

- ✓ A diverse portfolio does not have to consist of a large number of individual holdings. Diversification can exist within a small number of funds.

- ✓ The more stocks, bonds, and mutual funds you place in your portfolio, the more time and research will be required in order stay up to date on the investments. Investment advisors tend to favor this approach because it justifies their fees.

- ✓ Review your current asset allocation mix by logging into your online retirement portal. If you own multiple accounts in different places, consider summarizing them in an excel sheet or using an app like Personal Capital to bring together a full picture of all of your accounts.

Scan for a full list of the links and tools listed.

Chapter 26
REBALANCING YOUR PORTFOLIO

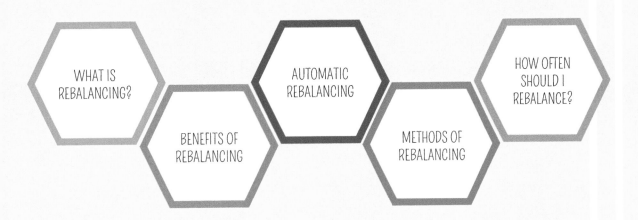

What is Rebalancing?

Over time, your *asset allocation* will change—even if you don't add to your account or make any changes in your holdings. Some investments will do better than others, which will change your original asset allocation.

For example, let's assume you invested $10,000 and chose an asset allocation mix of 70% stocks and 30% bonds. Over the last year, the money you invested in stocks has done very well, but there was no change in the value of your bonds. The value of your stocks went from $7,000 to $9,000, which has increased your percentage of stocks from 70% to 75% of your total portfolio.

> *Asset allocation:* determines how much of your savings and retirement funds should go towards different investments such as stocks, bonds, and mutual funds.

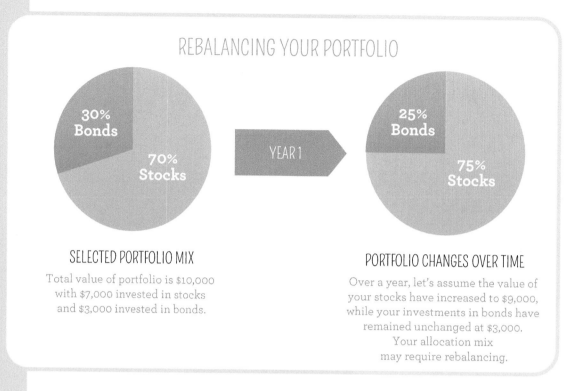

REBALANCING YOUR PORTFOLIO

SELECTED PORTFOLIO MIX

Total value of portfolio is $10,000 with $7,000 invested in stocks and $3,000 invested in bonds.

PORTFOLIO CHANGES OVER TIME

Over a year, let's assume the value of your stocks have increased to $9,000, while your investments in bonds have remained unchanged at $3,000. Your allocation mix may require rebalancing.

Your portfolio is now "overweight" on stocks in relation to your original allocation target. Rebalancing is bringing back your portfolio to the original allocation mix, which is 70% stocks and 30% bonds in this example.

There are three ways to rebalance your portfolio:

1 SELL investments in the asset category that has increased

2 BUY investments that are under-weight to increase the allocation to that category

3 ADJUST your future contributions to the portfolio to increase or decrease different asset classes to get back in line with the original asset mix

Benefits of Rebalancing

Rebalancing has two major benefits. First, it will help control the portfolio's risk over time. Let's say the 70% of stocks in your portfolio have continued to do well over several years. Let's assume that (without rebalancing) your portfolio is now 90% stocks and 10% bonds. If there is a *market correction*—and there always is—you may potentially be overexposed in stocks. That correction in stocks might be particularly ugly, leaving you wishing you had rebalanced your account to include more money in safer investments such as bonds to mitigate the correction.

The other significant benefit of rebalancing is that it forces you to buy low and sell high. Rebalancing forces you to sell investments that have done well, locking in those gains, and hold investments that are at discounted levels, giving them time to recover and increase in value.

It sounds simple enough, but without a plan in place, we tend to invest emotionally, resulting in jumping into a stock at an elevated price after it becomes popular or newsworthy. Conversely, we also tend to sell stocks when the market is on a downturn, and we panic, locking in losses when prices are low.

Automatic Rebalancing

Some investments will automatically rebalance, such as target-date funds. Many 401(k)s offer an auto-rebalancing feature. You will need to review your specific plan to see if this feature is available for your account.

> *Market correction:* the term used when the market has increased to a point in which it is overvalued. The correction is bringing that value back down to a more modest valuation.

TAX IMPLICATIONS OF REBALANCING

Remember that with retirement accounts, you can buy and sell as much as you want without tax implications, as long as you do not actualize your returns for cash.

With a regular, taxable investment account, you have to consider the tax implications of selling. Liquidating investments within these accounts can result in *short-term* or *long-term* capital gains taxes. We cover this in more detail in our chapter dedicated to TAXES.

Online *robo-advisors* like Acorns, Betterment, or Wealthfront also offer automatic rebalancing, but be aware of how frequent rebalancing occurs and what fees and tax implications are associated with rebalancing on these accounts.

Methods of Rebalancing

Your method of rebalancing can be based on either time or a set threshold. Time-based rebalancing (better known as periodic rebalancing) is done by setting fixed dates at regular intervals, such as quarterly, bi-annual, or annually, to rebalance your *portfolio*.

The second method is to rebalance after there has been a particular percentage change to your portfolio. For example, if one asset class has

---

Short-term trading: the buying and selling of an investment over a period of time that can range from seconds to several days. For tax purposes, short-term trading is an investment held for less than one year.

Long-term investment: stocks, bonds, or funds that are held for more than a year.

Robo-advisors: investment management companies that rely on algorithm-driven computer modeling to manage your portfolio rather than human financial advisors.

Portfolio: a collection of investments owned by an individual, and managed as a collective whole with specific investment goals in mind.

increased by 10%, this might trigger a notification and rebalancing. If your preferred method is to rebalance based on when a certain percentage is reached (such as an increase of 5% or 10%), then the number of times you would rebalance would depend on market movements, not regular, timed intervals.

How Often Should I Rebalance?

There is no hard-set rule on how often you should rebalance. Many advisors recommend rebalancing at least once or twice a year. If you create a well-diversified portfolio, you may not even need to rebalance that often.

Vanguard published an interesting white paper[55] where they looked at comparing different rebalancing strategies: monthly, quarterly, yearly, and not ever touching your portfolio. Here are the oversimplified takeaways from the paper:

1. There wasn't a single strategy that consistently outperformed other methods. The key was to select a strategy you're comfortable with and stick to it.

2. Frequent rebalancing can lead to lower returns, increased fees, and a heavier tax burden.

3. Choosing never to rebalance your portfolio takes on increased risk, which can lead to higher returns (if you're lucky) or lower returns during a correction (due to being overexposed).

Keep in mind that your chosen asset mix will change with age and time. So not only will you need to consider rebalancing as regular maintenance on your portfolio, but you'll want to ask yourself periodically if you are ready to make changes to your default asset allocation. This should not occur frequently and is often triggered by life-changing events like marriage, divorce, loss of a job, retirement, or having children. These events might change your risk appetite and, therefore, your asset allocation.

REBALANCING YOUR PORTFOLIO

- ✓ Rebalancing is the process of bringing your investments back in line with your original asset allocation mix.

- ✓ Rebalancing can reduce your risk to overexposure and can help lock in gains from investments that have performed well.

- ✓ Many target-date funds and robo-advisor apps offer automatic rebalancing.

- ✓ A rebalancing strategy can either be based on a set time period or a percentage threshold.

- ✓ Vanguard's study showed that no single rebalancing strategy outperformed others, but choosing a strategy and sticking with it was the key.

Scan for a full list of the links and tools listed.

Chapter 27
SAVING FOR YOUR CHILDREN

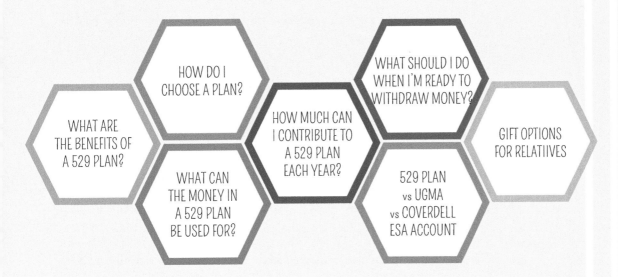

WHAT ARE THE BENEFITS OF A 529 PLAN?

HOW DO I CHOOSE A PLAN?

WHAT CAN THE MONEY IN A 529 PLAN BE USED FOR?

HOW MUCH CAN I CONTRIBUTE TO A 529 PLAN EACH YEAR?

WHAT SHOULD I DO WHEN I'M READY TO WITHDRAW MONEY?

529 PLAN vs UGMA vs COVERDELL ESA ACCOUNT

GIFT OPTIONS FOR RELATIIVES

We are all inundated with news stories of the student debt crisis. Student loan debt in the U.S. is now almost two trillion dollars. The pandemic has exacerbated the struggle that millions of borrowers face, which is to keep current on their student debt payments. If you are considering saving for your children's education, some accounts can offer substantial tax savings. Over time, even small contributions can multiply and grow into impressive sums. In this chapter, we will focus on education-related savings plans for your children and other minors.

What are the Benefits of a 529 Plan?

In a nutshell, a 529 plan is designed to save for college through an investment account that provides significant tax breaks. If you're interested in saving money for a child's education, we will break down the details of what you need to know.

Once you are familiar with what a 529 plan offers, setting up an account normally only takes 15 to 20 minutes.

The main advantage of a 529 plan over a regular investment account is the tax benefits. As we mention throughout the book, it's hard to appreciate what a big deal it is not to have to pay taxes on money earned. It's easy to dismiss since you never see the money you pay in taxes leave your hands.

WE WOULD ALL HAVE A GREATER APPRECIATION FOR THESE TAX SAVINGS IF WE WERE GIVEN OUR INCOME PRE-TAX, THEN HAD TO PHYSICALLY GIVE AWAY 20% TO 30% OF THAT MONEY.

There are tax benefits when you contribute money into a 529 plan and benefits when you withdraw funds. There are also distinct benefits for your federal taxes versus your state taxes.

When you first contribute money into a 529 plan, it's usually as simple as transferring money from your checking account to a 529 account. The money you are transferring to your new 529 plan is after-tax income; therefore, you will not have to pay taxes on that money again. This money is referred to as your contribution. In most states, your 529 contributions reduce your taxable income in the year you make the contribution. This can help to reduce the amount of taxes owed at the state level.

A 529 account is more than a savings account—it can contain investments, such as stocks, bonds, and ETFs. Ideally, as that invested money grows, you'll make more than what you contributed. This money is known as your *earnings*. Typically, you pay taxes on those earnings—but with a qualifying education expense, you are exempt from paying both federal and state taxes on those earnings.

To highlight this benefit, let's compare what the same investment would look like inside a 529 plan versus a regular, taxable investment account.

529 PLAN vs TAXABLE INVESTMENT ACCOUNT

ASSUMPTIONS

Yearly Contribution: $5,000
Time Period: 18 years

Investment Growth Rate: 7%
Federal Tax Rate: 22%

TAXABLE INVESTMENT ACCOUNT	VS	529 PLAN
EARNINGS AFTER 18 YEARS After 18 years of contributions at $3,000/year, your earnings would be $169,995 before tax		**EARNINGS AFTER 18 YEARS** After 18 years of contributions at at $3,000/year you would have $169,995
TAXES OWED ON GAINS Assuming a 22% federal tax rate, you would owe $23,142		**TAXES OWED ON GAINS** No federal taxes owed on qualified withdrawals in a 529 Plan
AFTER TAX VALUE Total amount available for withdrawal is $146,853		**AFTER TAX VALUE** The full $169,995 is available for withdrawal. That is an additional $23,142 over a taxable account.

All things being equal, by choosing a 529 plan, you would have close to an additional $23,142 over a taxable investment account, thanks to the tax savings.

The example illustrates the benefits of not paying federal taxes, but there are also benefits at the state level in the form of an income tax deduction or credit.

Depending on the state you live in, you can save an additional $200 to $1,000 in taxes at the state level. In most states, you will need to enroll in an in-state plan to receive the tax deduction.

529 PLAN DEDUCTIONS BY STATE[56]

STATES THAT OFFER TAX BREAKS FOR IN-STATE 529 PLANS:	STATES THAT OFFER TAX BREAKS FOR IN-STATE & OUT-OF-STATE 529 PLANS:	STATES THAT DO NOT OFFER TAX BREAKS FOR 529 PLANS:
Alabama, Arkansas, Colorado, Connecticut, District of Columbia, Georgia, Idaho, Illinois, Indiana, Iowa, Louisiana, Maryland, Massachusetts, Michigan, Mississippi, Nebraska, New Mexico, New York, North Dakota, Oklahoma, Oregon, Rhode Island, South Carolina, Utah, Vermont, Virginia, West Virginia, Wisconsin	Arizona, Kansas, Minnesota, Missouri, Montana, Pennsylvania	Alaska, California, Delaware, Florida, Hawaii, Kentucky, Maine, Nevada, New Hampshire, New Jersey, North Carolina, South Dakota, Tennessee, Texas, Washington, Wyoming

SOURCE: www.blackrock.com/us/individual/literature/brochure/529-plans-and-state-tax-benefits-client-piece-en-us.pdf

- There is no limit on the number of 529 plans you can open.
- There are no income limits on those who contribute to a 529 plan (unlike IRAs).
- You can change the beneficiary to any member of the original beneficiary's family. This includes siblings, cousins, parents, aunts, uncles, nieces, nephews, stepchildren, and yourself. This also includes the spouses of any of the family members listed.
- Funds can be used for trade and vocational schools as well.
- If the student (beneficiary) gets a scholarship, you can withdraw that same amount from the 529 without paying the penalty and tax-free.
- As of December 2019, you can also use money from a 529 plan to pay off student debt.[57]
- You can also withdraw up to $10,000 each year to pay private tuition for kindergarten through 12th grade.

What Can the Money in a 529 Plan Be Used for?

You can use these funds towards tuition, meals, textbooks, room and board, computers, equipment (such as printers), and internet service. You may also use the money for special needs and adaptive equipment to navigate around campus, depending on the plan. There are limitations on how much can go toward room and board, which will be based on the school's estimates. You'll need to verify exactly what is covered with your plan. If you use 529 funds for non-eligible expenses, you can expect a 10% penalty on money withdrawn, as well as having to pay income taxes on the earnings made in the account.

How Do I Choose a Plan?

Each state offers 529 plans, but you don't have to choose your state's plan. You can also select a plan in one state and use it for education-related expenses in another state. If you reside in one of the states that offer tax savings for contributing to a 529 plan, start there. If you are in a state that does not offer tax benefits on a 529 plan or your state offers multiple plans, then comparing the cost and fees is prudent.

Generally, investment options within 529 plans are limited. The most common investment option is an age-based investment, where the fund will adjust based on the student's age (similar to a target-date retirement fund). These funds invest more aggressively if the student has several years before needing to use the funds and shift to funds with lower risk as college approaches.

Most plans also have static investment options that do not modify the fund's investments over time. Some examples of a static investment are index funds based on the U.S. stock market or the global equity market. These funds often come with lower fees and tend to be larger, more established funds with more diversified holdings.

Don't let the choices overwhelm you. Honestly, most 529 plans are diversified, with hundreds of equities in each investment. Picking the perfect plan is much less important than opening an account and getting started on saving for college. You can always transfer to a different plan and adjust your investments as needed. You should compare the fees from one fund to another. Vanguard offers a side-by-side comparison of 529 plans on their website[58] where you can compare fees and investment options.

How Much Can I Contribute to a 529 Plan Each Year?

You can contribute up to $15,000 as an individual or $30,000 as a married couple per year for each 529 account you have without triggering a gift tax. (The gift tax is unnecessarily complicated since you can get around paying it by filling out the federal tax form 709. An individual is exempt from paying federal gift taxes until they gift $11.58 million within their lifetime, as long as they fill out the form to claim against that reduction officially.)

You can also super-fund the account for future years. With this option, you contribute up to $75,000 as an individual or $150,000 as a married couple in one year by choosing to treat the contribution as if it were over a five-year period. If you do this, you cannot contribute additional funds during the subsequent five-year period. This is advantageous because the quicker you get that money invested, the quicker it can start to grow.

OTHER ITEMS WORTH NOTING ABOUT A 529 PLAN

Students must be enrolled at least half time or more to use funds from the plan. In addition, the account owner—not the beneficiary—has control over the 529 plan.

If your funds are limited and you are debating whether to contribute to a 529 plan or your retirement, prioritize your retirement first. If this sounds selfish to you, remember the safety announcements you hear when you board a plane: put your oxygen mask on first so that you are in a position to help your child. Your retirement should be the priority, so you are less of a burden on your children in your later years. Hopefully, with the advice we're providing and the high income of a physician, you consider contributing to your retirement and a college fund simultaneously.

What Should I Do When
I'm Ready to Withdraw Money?

KEEP YOUR RECEIPTS. You will need them for reimbursement for your 529 plan provider and tax purposes since you are responsible for reporting these expenses to the IRS.

TIME YOUR WITHDRAWALS. If you plan to apply for financial aid while in school, the timing of your withdrawals is important. Withdrawals from a 529 plan will reduce your financial aid package for the following year, so if you can, consider making your 529 withdrawal during your last year when you are no longer applying for financial aid.

CONSIDER WHO OWNS THE 529 PLAN. Withdrawing funds from a 529 plan will affect financial aid in different ways, depending on who owns the plan. Approximately the first $20,000 in a 529 plan falls under the FAFSA's Asset Protection Allowance and will not affect financial aid. If a parent or legal guardian owns the plan, this tends to have the least negative effect on financial aid the following year, reducing the aid by a maximum of 5.64% of the value of the plan.

If the plan is owned by the student, withdrawals can reduce aid by up to 20%. For everyone else (aunts, uncles, grandparents, etc.) who owns the plan, withdrawals are counted as a student's non-taxable income and will reduce the amount of aid by 50% of the withdrawal amount from the 529 plan.

CONSIDER THE AMERICAN OPPORTUNITY TAX CREDIT. An undergraduate student (or parent that claims the student as a dependent) can claim a $2,500 tax credit if they spend $4,000 on qualified college-related expenses in a year, excluding 529 plan withdrawals.

If you want to take advantage of this tax credit and are in a position to do so, consider paying at least $4,000 of college expenses out of pocket before using money from your 529 plan. This hoop may not be worth jumping through if you're a physician, however. In 2020, if you make more than $90,000 as an individual or $180,000 as a couple, the tax credit is not available to you.

READ THE FINE PRINT. Keep in mind that the details of each 529 plan can change over time. Every 529 plan has a customer service line to answer any questions specific to the particular plan you are interested in. Give them a call to answer any questions we did not cover here.

529 Plan vs. UGMA/UGTA vs. Coverdell ESA Account

Other savings accounts, such as the Coverdell ESA or the Uniform Gift to Minors Act (UGMA)/Uniform Transfers to Minor Act (UTMA) accounts, are presented as alternatives to a 529 savings plan. To be frank, none of these accounts should be considered as a replacement for a 529 plan since the advantages of 529 plans far outweigh them. Here is a brief comparison of all three accounts.

529 PLAN vs UGMA vs COVERDELL ESA

	529 PLAN	UGMA/UGTA	COVERDELL ESA
INCOME TAX BENEFITS	No federal or state taxes on earnings; additional deductions on state taxes for contributions in most states.	Taxed to minor. First $1,050 is tax free; next $1,050 is taxed at child's rate. Above $2,100 taxed at either parents' income rate or capital gains tax rate.	No federal or state taxes on earnings. Contributions are not tax deductible.
HOW MUCH CAN YOU CONTRIBUTE EACH YEAR?	No annual limit; lifetime limit varies by state, ranging from $300,000 to $400,000	No limit	Annual contribution limit of $2,000 per child
WHAT CAN MONEY BE USED FOR?	Tuition, meals, textbooks, room/board, computers, and related equipment (such as printers, internet service, and special needs equipment)	No restrictions except that it must benefit the child/account holder	Tuition, meals, textbooks, room/board, computers, and related equipment (such as printers, internet service, and special needs equipment)
PENALTIES FOR NON-QUALIFIED EXPENSES	You must pay income tax and a 10% penalty on withdrawn earnings	Not using money for the child appropriately is fraud and opens you up to criminal prosecution and civil lawsuits	You must pay income tax and a 10% penalty on withdrawn earnings
INCOME RESTRICTIONS	No income restrictions	No income restrictions	Cannot contribute if income is above $110,000 for individual or $220,000 as a couple filing jointly
INVESTMENT OPTIONS	Choice of investments developed by plan manager; you can choose how much to allocate from their options	Any investments available in a brokerage account (stocks, bonds, mutual funds, etc.)	Any investments available in a brokerage account (stocks, bonds, mutual funds, etc.)
FINANCIAL AID IMPACT	Low impact on financial aid if parents own the plan; 5.64% counted towards financial aid calculation	High impact on financial aid; can reduce financial aid by 20% as child is the owner	Low impact on financial aid; 5.64% counted towards financial aid calculation
ADDITIONAL NOTES	You can transfer beneficiary to family members; can be used for education expenses in K-12. Can also use to pay off student debt.	Parent acts as custodian until child takes full ownership of the account around 18 (depending on the state); ownership cannot be transferred	You can transfer beneficiary to family members; can be used for education expenses in K-12. Can use to pay off student debt.

Gift Options for Relatives

We thought it might be helpful to provide a few tips for the relatives (grand-parents, aunts, uncles, or family friends) that are interested in contributing to college expenses. There are different tax consequences and effects on financial aid eligibility, depending on who has ownership of the funds.

1. If you hold a 529 plan for the student in your name, the student does not have to list that 529 as an asset on their FAFSA.

> NOTE, HOWEVER, THAT WHEN YOU WITHDRAW MONEY FROM THE 529, the student must report that as unearned income on their FAFSA the following year. This will reduce the amount of aid by 50% on the amount withdrawn from the 529 plan. For example, if you (as a relative) have a 529 savings plan and withdraw $10,000 to pay for the student's tuition, the following year, the student's aid will be reduced by $5,000.

2. Instead of holding the 529 plan yourself, you could also contribute to the student's parent's 529 plan. If you were to donate a gift to a parent-owned 529 plan, this only reduces the student's financial aid eligibility by 5.64%. This will significantly decrease the negative impact on the student's financial aid eligibility.

3. Another option recommended by many financial advisors is to use the funds from the 529 plan in the student's last year of school. This will help avoid the negative impacts of their financial assistance eligibility since the student will no longer require financial aid the following year.

SAVING FOR YOUR CHILDREN

✓ A 529 plan is a great way to save and invest for your children's college expenses. It takes 20 minutes to set up an account and create a recurring, automatic transfer from your bank.

✓ The benefits of a 529 plan include no taxes on earnings in the account and no taxes upon withdrawal. Most states offer tax breaks at the state level as well.

✓ Most plans allow you to change the beneficiary to siblings, cousins, parents, aunts, uncles, nieces, nephews, stepchildren, or yourself.

✓ You can use up to $10,000 from most 529 plans to pay off student debt (including your own or your spouse's) by updating the beneficiary.

✓ A 529 plan can affect a student's eligibility for financial aid, depending on who owns the plan and when withdrawals are made.

Scan for a full list of the links and tools listed.

Chapter 28
INTRODUCTION TO TAXES

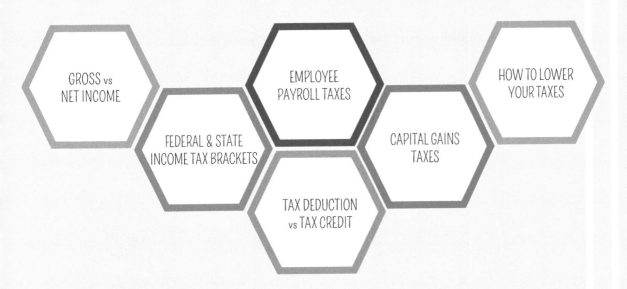

This chapter will help to bring together all the different concepts on taxes we mention throughout the book. If you have a specific tax question on your particular situation, we always recommend discussing it with a tax professional. Having said that, this chapter will help give you added confidence and awareness on the subject to ask the right questions.

Gross vs. Net Income

Throughout the book, we perform calculations that involve your income. It is important to distinguish between gross income and net income, considering the substantial difference between the two.

Your gross income is the amount before any taxes or deductions are taken out. Your net income, on the other hand, is your take-home pay. This is your income after federal, state, Social Security, and Medicare taxes are withdrawn. Additional payroll deductions for health insurance, 401(k) plans, and flexible spending accounts can also lower your net income. Whenever you are discussing your income, make sure you are distinguishing between gross or net income. The difference between the two can be 30% or more, or put in another way, 3 to 4 months of annual income.

Federal & State Income Tax Brackets

In this section, we'll discuss state and federal income taxes. The federal income tax brackets for 2021 are as follows:

TAX RATE	FOR UNMARRIED INDIVIDUALS	FOR MARRIED INDIVIDUALS FILING JOINT RETURNS	FOR HEAD OF HOUSEHOLDS
10%	Up to $9,950	Up to $19,900	Up to $14,200
12%	$9,951 to $40,525	$19,901 to $81,050	$14,201 to $54,200
22%	$40,526 to $86,375	$81,051 to $172,750	$54,201 to $86,350
24%	$86,376 to $164,925	$172,751 to $329,850	$86,351 to $164,900
32%	$164,926 to $209,425	$329,851 to $418,850	$164,901 to $209,400
35%	$209,426 to $523,600	$418,851 to $628,300	$209,401 to $523,600
37%	Over $523,600	Over $628,300	Over $523,600

Source: www.irs.gov/pub/irs-drop/rp-20-45.pdf

Using the table above, you might assume that if you are unmarried and you make $250,000 a year, you'll be taxed at 35% on your entire income. This is not the case. Federal income taxes use marginal tax rates.

In other words, it is a progressive tax rate system that taxes your income at different rates.

For example, using the example of a single person making $250,000 annually, the federal income tax rate would look something like this:

10%	Your first $9,950 of income would be taxed at 10%, which equals $995 in taxes
12%	The next $30,574 of income would be taxed at 12%, which equals $3,669 in taxes
22%	The next $45,849 of income would be taxed at 22%, which equals $10,086 in taxes
24%	The next $78,549 of income would be taxed at 24%, which equals $18,852 in taxes
32%	The next $44,499 of income would be taxed at 32%, which equals $14,240 in taxes
35%	The last $40,579 of income would be taxed at 35%, which equals $14,203 in taxes

You can expect to pay $62,045 in taxes on $250,000 of income before any tax deductions or credits

So, although your marginal tax rate is 35%, your effective tax rate is actually 25% because not every dollar you made was taxed at the same rate.

On the state level, each state has its own tax rates.[59] State income taxes can range from 3.07% in Pennsylvania to 13.30 % in California. As of the publishing of this book, there are seven states that do not charge a state income tax: Alaska, Florida, Nevada, South Dakota, Texas, Washington, and Wyoming. New Hampshire and Tennessee do not assess a tax on earned income, but they do tax income from dividends and interest on investments. The remaining 41 states have either a flat income tax or a marginal (progressive) tax system like the federal tax rate system.

Employee Payroll Taxes

	% OF INCOME	TAX % ON ANNUAL INCOME OF $250,000 IN NEW YORK
FEDERAL INCOME TAXES	10% to 37%	24.8%
STATE INCOME TAXES	0% to 13.3%	6.33%
SOCIAL SECURITY	6.2%	6.2%
MEDICARE TAXES	1.45% to 2.35%	2.35%
TOTAL	17.65% to 58.85%	39.68%

In the tables above, we've put together a list of the various taxes you can expect to be taken out of your paycheck as an employee. There are a couple of important caveats to the percentages listed above. In the far-right column, we discuss what taxes would look like if you made $250,000 annually as a single person in New York. We have the effective tax rate listed at 24.8% because we take all the marginal tax rates from the example above and divide the total amount of tax owed by the total income ($62,045 / $250,000). Although the marginal tax rate would be considered 35%, not every dollar is taxed at that rate, and the effective tax rate is around 25%. New York state taxes are also on a progressive tax rate system, so we have listed the 2020 effective rate of 6.33%.

We show the percentages that the employee pays on Social Security and Medicare, but bear in mind your employer is paying the same percentages on their end. Your employer also pays federal and state unemployment tax as well as workers compensation, which (as an employee) you do not have deducted from your paycheck.

These percentages are before any federal or state tax deductions or credits. Think of these percentages as a starting point, and it's your job to find opportunities to reduce your taxes by every legal means available to you.

Tax Deduction vs. Tax Credit

Both tax deductions and tax credits reduce your tax burden, but there are important distinctions between them. A tax deduction lowers your taxable income, which in turn reduces your tax liability. A tax credit, on the other hand, is a dollar-for-dollar reduction on the tax bill owed. A tax credit usually is more valuable in reducing your tax liability.

You can claim tax deductions in one of two ways: by taking the standard tax deduction or itemizing each deduction. Standard deductions were created to streamline certain expenses that you can deduct from taxable income. Rather than identifying every tax-deductible expense, the standard deduction alternative was created. This deduction can be taken with no questions asked. Current standard deduction amounts are as follows:

FILING STATUS	2020 STANDARD DEDUCTION	2021 STANDARD DEDUCTION
SINGLE OR MARRIED FILING SEPARATELY	$12,400	$12,550
MARRIED FILING JOINTLY	$24,800	$25,100
HEAD OF HOUSEHOLD	$18,650	$18,800

Choose the method that offers the larger tax deduction. If you choose to itemize your tax deductions, you will be required to fill out additional tax forms and provide receipts to substantiate those deductions.

Capital Gains Taxes

So far, we've only spoken about taxes on earned income from a salary or wages. Other forms of income will also be taxed; capital gains taxes are taxes on your investments. When you sell a capital asset for more than you purchased it for, you've made a profit known as a capital gain. Examples of capital assets are shares of stock, a business, or in some cases, your home or land. Capital gains tax rates will depend on the type of asset and how long you owned it. There are both short-term and long-term capital gains tax rates.

Short-term capital gains are defined as purchasing and selling a capital asset within one year or less. The tax rate is pretty straightforward in that it is the same as your ordinary federal income tax bracket, which will likely mean you'll pay more than 25% on those capital gains.

Long-term capital gains are defined as owning the asset for more than a year before selling it. Your long-term capital gains tax rate will either be 0%, 15%, or 20%, depending on your filing status and taxable income.

Here is some additional detail on long-term capital gains tax rates.

2021 LONG-TERM CAPITAL GAINS TAX RATES

SINGLE FILERS		MARRIED, FILING JOINTLY		HEAD OF HOUSEHOLD		MARRIED, FILING SEPARATELY	
CAPITAL GAINS TAX RATE	ANNUAL INCOME	CAPITAL GAINS TAX RATE	ANNUAL INCOME	CAPITAL GAINS TAX RATE	ANNUAL INCOME	CAPITAL GAINS TAX RATE	ANNUAL INCOME
0%	$0 to $40,400	0%	$0 to $80,800	0%	$0 to $54,100	0%	$0 to $40,400
15%	$40,401 to $445,850	15%	$80,801 to $501,600	15%	$54,101 to $473,750	15%	$40,001 to $250,800
20%	$445,851 or more	20%	$501,601 or more	20%	$473,751 or more	20%	$250,801 or more

Short-term capital gains rates can be more than double long-term rates. This should be motivation to hold on to capital assets (such as stocks) for more than a year. If you bought a stock and sold it within a year, you will likely pay over 25% in taxes on that profit. On the other hand, if you sell that same stock after owning it for more than a year, you would most likely be paying only 15% on the profit from that sale.

In addition, you will most likely meet the income criteria to pay the net investment income tax of 3.8% on capital gains. The 2021 annual income level criteria for this additional tax are:

SINGLE: $200,000
MARRIED, FILING JOINTLY: $250,000
MARRIED, FILING SEPARATELY: $125,000

How to Lower Your Taxes

1. TAKE A LONG-TERM APPROACH TO INVESTMENTS

The difference in your capital gains rate can be substantial, depending on whether you hold your assets short or long term. Holding on to capital assets for more than a year can reduce your capital gains taxes by half.

2. REDUCE YOUR TAX LIABILITY WHEN SELLING YOUR HOME[60]

If you can, avoid paying capital gains taxes when you sell your home. This is not hard to do if you meet the following criteria:

- The house is your primary residence
- You have owned the property for more than 2 years, and it has also been your primary residence for 2 of the last 5 years before you sell it
- You did not buy the house through a like-kind 1031 exchange
- You have not already sold a house in the last 5 years and claimed the capital gains exclusion
- You have not renounced your citizenship in the U.S. for federal tax purposes

There are exceptions if you were in the military, Peace Corps, or an intelligence branch, or if you sold the home because of job relocation, a health issue, or an "unforeseeable event." You may still qualify for the capital gains exclusion under these circumstances.

If you meet the criteria above, you can exclude up to $250,000 of profit if you are single or $500,000 if you are married on the capital gain from selling your home.

To further reduce your capital gains taxes on your home, keep receipts on any home improvements completed on your house. If you do end up paying capital gains tax, you can subtract the cost of home improvements from your purchase price to reduce your capital gains tax.

The capital gains calculation looks like this:

$$\text{SALES PRICE OF HOME} -$$
$$(\text{PURCHASE PRICE OF HOME} + \text{HOME IMPROVEMENTS})$$
$$= \text{CAPITAL GAIN/LOSS}$$

3. UNDERSTAND THE TERM STEP-UP IN BASIS

Step-up basis is the term used to calculate your capital gains taxes for assets that are inherited. The capital gains calculation is the difference between the original purchase price of the home and the home's sales price. Let's see this in action.

Say you inherited a home from your parents. Once they pass away, the capital gains tax could be substantial if they bought the house 20 years ago for $50,000 and you inherit the house at a current value of $250,000. (This can apply to other capital assets, such as stock in a company that your parent or grandparent bought many years ago.) The step-up in basis adjusts the original purchase price to the current market price upon the transfer of inheritance. This reduces capital gains taxes significantly.

This benefit is a good reason to consider transferring assets upon death in order to take advantage of the step-up in basis rule, rather than transfer to an heir while you are still alive.

Here is an illustration of the previous example:

UNDERSTANDING THE STEP-UP IN BASIS RULE

ASSUMPTIONS

Your parent purchased a home 20 years ago for $50,000. Today that home is worth $250,000. Once you own the property, you sell the home for $250,000

IF HOME IS TRANSFERRED TO AN HEIR WHILE ALIVE	VS	CAPITAL GAINS TAX IF HOME IS INHERITED AFTER DEATH
TRANSFERRING (GIFTING) A HOME		**INHERITANCE OF A HOME**
Your parent transfers their home into your name while they are still alive		Your parent passes away and you inherit their home
SELLING HOME AFTER TRANSFER		**STEP-UP IN BASIS UPON INHERITANCE**
Once you sell the home, you may owe capital gains tax on the profit $250,000 (Sales Price) - $50,000 (Purchase Price) = $200,000 (Profit)		If you sell the house, you no longer consider the original purchase price in the capital gains calculation due to the step-up in basis rule
CAPITAL GAINS TAX		**CAPITAL GAINS TAX**
Depending on your income, you could owe $30,000 to $40,000 in taxes		New cost basis is the market value of the home when your parent died, so no taxes owed $250,000 (Sales Price) -$250,000 (New Cost Basis) = $0 (Profit)

4. TAX LOSS HARVESTING

This term means using your capital losses to offset capital gains, which results in less taxable income from your capital assets. For example, if you invested in a stock that has not done well, meaning its current price is below your purchase price, then you have the option to "harvest" or sell that stock at a loss.

That loss can be used to offset capital gains made from other stocks you have sold for a profit. Using this method, you can also reduce your tax liability by up to $3,000 per year on your ordinary income. If your losses exceed $3,000 in one year, you can carry over additional losses to the following year.

Tax-loss harvesting can only be done in taxable investment accounts, not retirement accounts such as 401(k)s or IRAs, since they already grow tax-deferred.

The one caveat to keep in mind is the Wash-Sale Rule, which states that you cannot use the stock or security to offset a capital loss with a capital gain of the same stock.

5. TAX-ADVANTAGED ACCOUNTS

We have several chapters dedicated to better understanding RETIREMENT ACCOUNTS, 529 COLLEGE SAVINGS PLANS, and HEALTH SAVINGS ACCOUNTS, but we will briefly touch upon the tax advantages of those accounts again here. When you think about a tax-advantaged account, remember that you either get the tax break on the front end or the back end, meaning that contributions are taxed before they go into the account or after they are withdrawn. With a Roth or 529 college savings plan, you contribute money that has already been taxed through your paycheck, which allows your earnings to grow tax-free, and your qualified withdrawals are tax-free.

With a traditional retirement account, the tax advantages are upfront. You get to reduce your taxable income by the amount you contribute to a traditional 401(k) or IRA. You accomplish both saving for your future and lowering your current tax bill at the same time. You will have to pay taxes on your withdrawals during retirement, but that can be advantageous since your tax bracket may be lower in retirement. Traditional retirement accounts reduce your current taxable income during your working years when your tax rate is at its highest and allows you to make withdrawals at a much lower tax rate in retirement.

A health savings account (HSA) has been referred to as the holy grail of tax-advantaged accounts. No other account has the triple tax advantage that an HSA provides. First, it is funded with pre-tax dollars. Next, your earnings grow tax-free within the account. Finally, you do not pay any taxes when you withdraw money for a qualified healthcare-related expense. If you have a high-deductible health insurance plan, investigate this option to optimize your taxes.

6. FORMING A BUSINESS

Starting a business can offer you not only asset and liability protections, but it can also turn some of the expenses you already pay into business expenses that can reduce your taxable income.

For example, by setting up a home office for your business, you can deduct a percentage of your mortgage interest, property taxes, utilities, internet, and homeowner's insurance based on the square footage of the office. You can also deduct maintenance and repairs for the office space. As of 2021, the IRS allows a simplified option for home office deductions of $5 per square foot up to 300 square feet.[61]

To take advantage of the deductions, the office space should be the principal place of business with regular and exclusive use. Travel-related expenses such as hotel, meals, and gas can also be deducted for your business as long the primary purpose of the trip is business-related.

7. HAVE SOME CHILDREN

Just kidding. We're trying to be funny here. (If you think having kids is an effective financial strategy, you are not remotely aware of how much children cost to raise.)

If you do have children though or are planning to have a child, for the 2021 tax year, the American Rescue Plan offers a tax credit of $3,000 per child ($3,600 per child under 6 years old) for each qualifying dependent under the age of 17. The tax credit begins to phase out at adjusted *gross incomes* of $75,000 on single returns, $112,500 on head-of-household returns, and $150,000 on joint returns.

8. GIVE MONEY TO CHARITY[62]

Giving money to a charity of your choice will allow you to deduct your donations from your taxable income. For the 2021 tax year, you can deduct up to $300 per taxpayer on cash donations before you have to itemize your deductions. You can typically deduct up to 60% of your adjusted gross income via gifts to charity.

Gross income: the amount of money earned before taxes or other deductions are taken out.

INTRO TO TAXES

✓ When using income in a calculation make sure you identify whether you need to calculate gross or net income.

✓ Federal taxes are calculated on a progressive tax rate system that taxes your income at different rates rather than a flat rate.

✓ The difference between holding a capital asset for more than a year (long-term) or less than a year (short-term) can cost you double in taxes.

✓ Tax credits tend to be more valuable than tax deductions.

✓ You can either take the standard tax deduction or itemize your deductions, selecting the method that has the largest deduction for you.

✓ There are many ways to reduce your taxes. We present 8 action items to review.

✓ Consider consulting a tax advisor to maximize the tax credits and deductions available to you.

Scan for a full list of the links and tools listed.

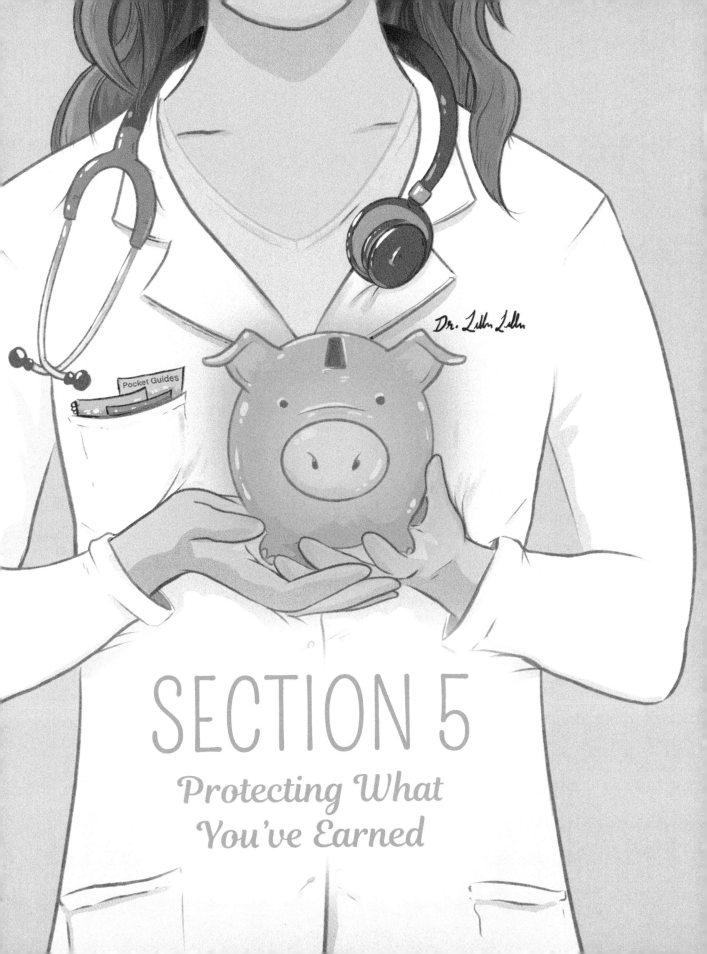

SECTION 5

Protecting What
You've Earned

As you start to accumulate wealth and consider investments, businesses, and alternate sources of income, you open yourself up to liability and potential lawsuits. We practice in the most litigious country in the world. On top of that, no other professionals are sued more often than physicians. Creating a strategy to protect what you've earned is as vital as generating the wealth to begin with.

Lawyers, financial advisors, and insurance agents love to tell horror stories of physicians losing everything to lawsuits. As horrifying as some of these stories might be, you need to be careful not to be oversold on these forms of protection. You can definitely go too far with too much insurance. There's no need to create overly complicated business structures to protect your assets, especially early in your career. For many of us, a solid auto, home, and umbrella policy will provide sufficient coverage for catastrophic events.

In this section, we will cover the following:

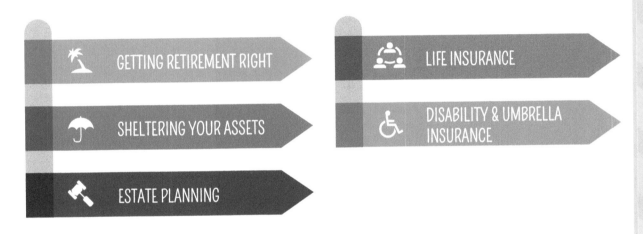

GETTING RETIREMENT RIGHT

SHELTERING YOUR ASSETS

ESTATE PLANNING

LIFE INSURANCE

DISABILITY & UMBRELLA INSURANCE

Chapter 29
GETTING RETIREMENT RIGHT

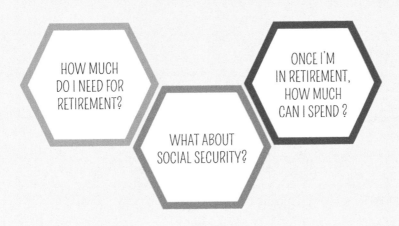

HOW MUCH DO I NEED FOR RETIREMENT?

WHAT ABOUT SOCIAL SECURITY?

ONCE I'M IN RETIREMENT, HOW MUCH CAN I SPEND ?

How Much Do I Need for Retirement?

There are many ways to calculate how much money you need for retirement. One quick way to do this is to figure how much money you *spend* (not earn) in a year and multiply that by 25. You really shouldn't use this calculation for much more than to appreciate the sticker shock of how big of a number it is. This back-of-the-napkin calculation will make most people sweat a little. It's daunting but achievable with regular monthly deposits into retirement and savings accounts.

For a more in-depth look at how big your nest egg needs to be, you need to consider the following:

1 PRE-TAX ANNUAL INCOME

2 CURRENT AGE

3 RETIREMENT AGE

4 THE AMOUNT YOU ARE REGULARLY SAVING FOR RETIREMENT (MONTHLY OR YEARLY)

5 RATE OF RETURN ON INVESTMENTS (MOST CALCULATORS DEFAULT THIS TO 5% OR 6% A YEAR)

6 HOW MUCH YOU WANT TO SPEND EACH YEAR IN RETIREMENT

For that last question, remember that you will be spending much less in retirement than you do now. If your income consists primarily of investments rather than a salary, you will be paying less in income taxes. When you are retired, you are also no longer saving for retirement. You have likely paid off your mortgage by now (or are close to it), and your expenses for your children should decrease substantially once they have graduated from college. With the children out of the house, you may downsize your home, saving on property taxes and utilities. At this point in your life, you will not be paying for life or disability insurance either.

You can use a retirement planner template[63] as a starting place. The calculations tab will give you a closer look at the numbers.

You can also use an online calculator[64] to clean up the calculations and present you with visually appealing summaries and charts. We like a couple of calculators online that take different approaches. We like the SmartAsset calculator. It provides a good level of detail, and you can include your savings in your 401(k), IRA, and pensions. You can also choose to include or exclude Social Security benefits. The summary provided has great information, starting with how much money you should be saving each month to reach your retirement goals.

We also like NerdWallet's calculator. The output summary is less detailed, but it covers the basics and is easy to use and adjust.

These calculators are only as good as the information you provide. The real goal here is to stress the importance of saving for retirement and get a reasonable estimate of how much you should begin putting away each month.

What About Social Security?

Whether or not you have confidence that Social Security will still be available when you retire, it is helpful to assume that it will not be. It is not impossible to conceive a scenario in which there are no Social Security retirement benefits (or one in which they are considerably reduced). Just look at the annual report by the Social Security Board of Trustees. The retirement fund is projected to run out in 2034.[65] That is 13 years from now (2021).

Even if it is still available, the maximum benefit in 2020 is $3,000 to $3,700 a month, depending on whether you start receiving benefits at the full retirement age of 67 or wait until you are 70. This will not nearly cover the lifestyle you have become accustomed to as a physician. Planning retirement without Social Security allows those benefits to be the icing on the cake for your retirement package.

Once I'm in Retirement, How Much Can I Spend?

To determine how much you can spend in retirement, we'll use another calculation, known as the 4% rule. This rule is based on the Trinity Study that was intended to calculate a safe withdrawal rate for retirement accounts. Once you have reached retirement, you can spend 4% of your savings each year. This assumes a retirement period of 30 years, so if you retire at 67, you should have funds until you're 97. (While most of us won't have this concern, if you do make it into your 100s, hopefully your children aren't deadbeats.)

This rule of thumb also takes *inflation* into account. Let's see how this plays out. If you start your retirement with $2 million, you would withdraw $80,000 your first year. If the cost of living rises 2% that year, you will increase your withdrawal the following year by $80,000 plus 2% cost of living increase. So, in year two, you would withdraw $81,600.

The calculation does have its limitations. It is based on historical trends with a *portfolio* of 50% stocks and 50% bonds. It also assumes a very inflexible withdrawal amount that is similar every year, not taking into account unexpected financial situations. It also does not take Social Security benefits or other income-generating investments into account. Having said that, the 4% rule is a good starting point.

Inflation: the decreased purchasing value of money over time. Think of the difference in costs to go to the movie theater 75 years ago compared to now.

Portfolio: a collection of investments owned by an individual, and managed as a collective whole with specific investment goals in mind.

Chapter 29 Recap

GETTING RETIREMENT RIGHT

- ✓ A back-of-the-napkin calculation to determine how much you need to retire is to multiply how much you spend (not earn) in a year by 25.

- ✓ For a more in-depth review of what you need for retirement, use an online calculator.

- ✓ Consider calculating your retirement without Social Security benefits and allow them to be icing on the cake in retirement.

- ✓ The 4% rule contends that you can spend 4% of what you have saved in retirement per year, plus annual inflation, which should give you around 30 years of funding.

Scan for a full list of the
links and tools listed.

Chapter 30
SHELTERING YOUR ASSETS

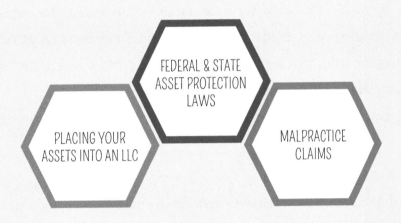

This chapter will focus on the legal protections offered by forming a company as well as asset protection laws at the federal and state level you should be aware of. We'll also touch on professional malpractice claims and how to protect yourself from related lawsuits.

Placing Your Assets into an LLC

Business entities like a limited liability company (LLC) were created under the law to allow entrepreneurs to build businesses without risking all of their personal assets. Today, there wouldn't be many small businesses if entrepreneurs were constantly worried about losing their house, retirement accounts, children's college fund, and personal assets just for taking a chance on a professional endeavor.

In the eyes of the law, an LLC is treated as a completely separate entity from its members, much like another individual. To form an LLC, you will need a legitimate business purpose. The most common is owning a property for the sole purpose of renting to others. By placing the property in an LLC, you protect your personal assets from lawsuits related to the rental property. You also protect your rental property if you were to be sued personally.

If you are personally sued, the assets within an LLC are owned by the entity and are protected. On the other hand, if a renter sues you on one of your properties that is part of an LLC, your liability will be limited to the assets within the company.

LLCs are pretty easy to set up.

1 CHOOSE A NAME and make sure it's available to register. You can search this on the Secretary of State's website or do an internet search for your state and "register company name."

2 CHOOSE A REGISTERED AGENT. This is someone who agrees to receive official documents on behalf of the LLC. You can act as the agent or pay a registered agent a fee of around $100 a year if you prefer not to have your personal address on file.

3 CREATE AN OPERATING AGREEMENT for your LLC. This document lays out owner-ship interest, voting rights, and other ways your business will be run. There are plenty of templates online to use.

4 FILE PAPERWORK with the Secretary of State and obtain a certificate of exis-tence for the LLC.

5 OBTAIN A FEDERAL EMPLOYER IDENTIFICATION NUMBER (FEIN) for tax purposes.

Another option is to have a company like LegalZoom walk you through the process. They offer several different packages, including one that covers registering your business with your state, forming an operating agreement, filing your FEIN number, and exploring what permits and licenses you need. This package costs $300 to $400. Local lawyers also offer LLC packages that range between $500 to $1,000, depending on where you live and what they offer.

When you set up a business under an LLC or a corporate entity, there needs to be a clear separation of business and personal transactions. There is a term called "piercing the corporate veil," which refers to a court's decision to remove the protections of an LLC and hold the owners of the LLC personally responsible. This happens when there is no clear separation between the owners and the company. To get started, open up a business bank account and keep your personal and business transactions separate from each other.

You are asking for trouble if you use your business bank card to purchase vacation packages or other items unrelated to your business. It should also be clear when you are transacting business on behalf of the LLC. Contracts, invoices, and other business-related paperwork should clearly show that you represent the LLC. Forming a limited liability entity will not protect you from negligence, fraud, or illegal activities.

Federal & State Asset Protection Laws

Federal and state asset protection laws will shield certain assets, such as retirement accounts, from creditors during bankruptcy. Retirement accounts like your 401(k) and IRA accounts offer protection from lawsuits and creditors through the ERISA Act.[66] There are exceptions to the protection provided. One exception to that rule is divorce; money accumulated in a retirement account while married can be accessed during a divorce settlement. Malpractice and personal liability laws are created at the state level and differ from state to state.

There are also home equity protection laws known as homestead laws designed to protect your primary residence only. States such as Florida, Oklahoma, Arkansas, Kansas, and Texas cover up to 100% home equity protection from many creditors, while other states offer varying degrees of protection. You should be aware of the homestead laws in your state, as well as laws that govern personal liability and retirement account protection from lawsuits in your state.

Malpractice Claims

Medical malpractice occurs when a healthcare professional is negligent in their duties, fails to take appropriate action, or causes harm to a patient through substandard treatment. In other words, claims center around improper treatment, failure to diagnose, or failure to warn patients of known risks.

About one in three practicing physicians have been sued. That number increases considerably for physicians performing surgeries. Here is a look at lawsuits by specialty from an AMA benchmark survey.[67]

Specialty	Percentage of Physicians			Number of Claims per 100 Physicians
	Ever Sued	Sued 2+ Times	Sued in Last 12 Months	
	(1)	(2)	(3)	(4)
Anesthesiology	36.3%	17.9%	1.3%	64
Emergency medicine	51.7%	25.7%	3.0%	108
Family practice	33.4%	13.8%	1.1%	55
General surgery	63.2%	50.1%	8.0%	205
Internal medicine	31.7%	14.8%	3.1%	57
Internal medicine sub-specialties	25.5%	11.0%	1.0%	44
Obstetrics/Gynecology	63.6%	44.1%	6.7%	162
Pediatrics	17.8%	6.0%	1.0%	28
Psychiatry	16.1%	5.9%	1.9%	25
Radiology	37.6%	21.4%	0.4%	82
Surgical sub-specialties	47.4%	25.0%	3.3%	110
Other specialties	19.5%	5.8%	2.5%	29
Observations	3211	3145	3147	3145

Source: Author's tabulation of data from the AMA's 2016 Benchmark Survey
www.ama-assn.org/sites/ama-assn.org/files/corp/media-browser/public/government/
advocacy/policy-research-perspective-medical-liability-claim-frequency.pdf

The time period in which a patient can file a malpractice claim varies from state to state. It averages around 2 years from the date of occurrence in most states, but it can range from 1 to 10 years.[68] For OBGYNs like Amanda, it can be 20 years.

WHO SHOULD CONSIDER MALPRACTICE INSURANCE?

All residency programs are required to provide medical liability coverage. It is important to note that there are limits to the coverage, and the amount of coverage will vary by program. Although it is unlikely that a claim will exceed the coverage that your program offers, it's a possibility. In that case, the resident may be personally liable.

After residency, normally your employer will offer group malpractice insurance coverage and may not ever have to worry about purchasing your own malpractice insurance. However, if you are self-employed, you may have to buy your own malpractice insurance. This is often one of the largest costs associated with running your own practice.

MALPRACTICE INSURANCE OPTIONS

Malpractice insurance is purchased to protect physicians from lawsuits from a patient or patient's family that decides to sue you. Malpractice claims are personal, and the formation of a limited liability company will not shield you from malpractice claims. That is why malpractice insurance is necessary for liability protection. There are essentially two types of malpractice insurance:

1. OCCURRENCE POLICY: This covers claims that happened during the period you had coverage, even if the claim occurs years later when that policy no longer covers you. The "tail" coverage on these policies refers to this extended time period of liability coverage permitted to you, regardless of whether you still participate in that policy.

2. CLAIMS-MADE POLICY: This only covers claims that are made while you are covered on that policy. If a claim is made and you no longer have that policy, you will not have coverage unless you purchase "nose" coverage. Nose coverage will cover malpractice claims on procedures performed while covered under a previous policy but were not reported until after starting a new policy.

Nose and tail coverage are essentially the same and cover the same period. The difference is when you purchase the coverage. Nose coverage is purchased at the beginning of new coverage, while tail coverage is purchase at the end of an existing policy. Make sure you know what kind of policy you currently have in place or will have in place with a new position.

You want to ensure there are no gaps in coverage that will expose you to a lawsuit without insurance coverage.

WHAT DOES MALPRACTICE INSURANCE NORMALLY INCLUDE?

Malpractice insurance typically covers legal fees such as attorney fees and court costs. Some policies will also cover a patient's medical bills related to the lawsuit. It is critical to know what is excluded from your malpractice insurance. Many policies do not cover injuries a patient might have while in your office not related to medical care. Criminal acts, sexual misconduct, and misrepresentation on the application for malpractice insurance are generally excluded from coverage.

HOW MUCH DOES MALPRACTICE INSURANCE COST?

A recent report[69] from the American Medical Association (AMA) indicates there has been a surge in premiums in the last couple of years. There is a lot of interesting data in the report, but here is a summary of the findings for 2020. As you can see insurance premiums vary wildly depending on geographic area.

OB/GYN	ANNUAL PREMIUMS FOR $1M/$3M POLICIES FOR 2020
California (Los, Angeles, Orange)	$49,804
Connecticut	$134,054
Florida (Miami-Dade)	$205,380
Illinois (Cook, Madison, St. Clair	$179,497
New Jersey	$90,749
New York (Nassau, Suffolk)	$174,552
Pennsylvania (Philadelphia)	$119,466

Source: Policy Research Perspectives (www.ama-assn.org/system/files/2021-03/prp-mlm-premiums-2020.pdf) by Jose R. Guardado, PhD (American Medical Association)

GENERAL SURGERY	ANNUAL PREMIUMS FOR $1M/$3M POLICIES FOR 2020
California (Los, Angeles, Orange)	$41,775
Connecticut	$90,577
Florida (Miami-Dade)	$205,380
Illinois (Cook, Madison, St. Clair	$120,258
New Jersey	$60,810
New York (Nassau, Suffolk)	$154,056
Pennsylvania (Philadelphia)	$85,930

Source: Policy Research Perspectives (www.ama-assn.org/system/files/2021-03/prp-mlm-premiums-2020.pdf) by Jose R. Guardado, PhD (American Medical Association)

INTERNAL MEDICINE	ANNUAL PREMIUMS FOR $1M/$3M POLICIES FOR 2020
California (Los, Angeles, Orange)	$8,274
Connecticut	$18,878
Florida (Miami-Dade)	$51,345
Illinois (Cook, Madison, St. Clair	$41,272
New Jersey	$15,900
New York (Nassau, Suffolk)	$33,852
Pennsylvania (Philadelphia)	$24,873

Source: Policy Research Perspectives (www.ama-assn.org/system/files/2021-03/prp-mlm-premiums-2020.pdf) by Jose R. Guardado, PhD (American Medical Association)

WHERE SHOULD I LOOK FOR MALPRACTICE INSURANCE?

Whether it is life, disability, or malpractice insurance, using an independent broker who is not financially incentivized to push you towards a particular policy or company is a practical choice. You'll want to speak with a broker that specializes in medical malpractice insurance. You can start your search online for "independent medical malpractice insurance brokers." You'll want to find a highly rated reputable company that can be verified with AM Best,[70] the world's largest credit rating agency.

Physicians must take the time to be thorough when making this decision. Although it can be time-consuming, understanding your coverage can help you avoid financially devastating lawsuits in the long run.

SHELTERING YOUR ASSETS

✓ Placing your assets into an LLC can shield those assets from personal liability. A common example of this is forming an LLC for rental properties.

✓ Forming an LLC takes very little time and costs between $100 to $500, depending on how much assistance you need.

✓ In most cases, your retirement accounts (such as your 401(k) or IRA) are protected from lawsuits and creditors.

✓ Homestead laws vary from state to state, but many offer home equity protection from creditors for your primary residence.

✓ About one in three practicing physicians have been sued.

✓ Make sure you have malpractice coverage during transitional periods in your career.

Scan for a full list of the
links and tools listed.

Chapter 31
ESTATE PLANNING

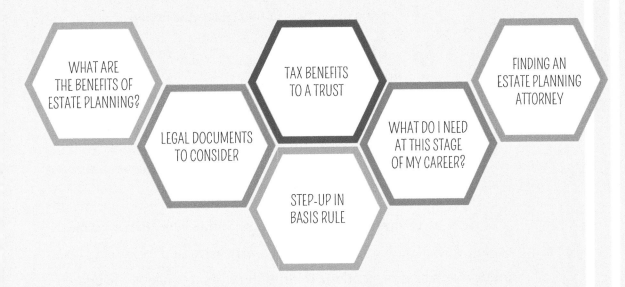

WHAT ARE THE BENEFITS OF ESTATE PLANNING?

LEGAL DOCUMENTS TO CONSIDER

TAX BENEFITS TO A TRUST

STEP-UP IN BASIS RULE

WHAT DO I NEED AT THIS STAGE OF MY CAREER?

FINDING AN ESTATE PLANNING ATTORNEY

DEATH, MONEY AND INHERITANCE. No, this isn't an episode of a true-crime podcast. We're talking about estate planning. Estate planning is all about having a legal and financial plan in place when you are either incapacitated or deceased. You'll want to minimize both the costs and time involved in transferring your assets to your family. It is not uncommon to have assets tied up in probate court for years. An estate plan is a thoughtful approach to your finances during what can be a difficult and chaotic time for the family.

There are three functions to estate planning:

1 TO PROVIDE INSTRUCTION
for end-of-life care or mental incapacitation

2 TRANSFERRING OF ASSETS
upon death

3 TO ESTABLISH GUARDIANSHIP
for children

This has to be one of the top "I'll deal with this later" items for most people. Estate planning can be confusing, expensive, and depressing. The truth is that many people don't want to think about what will happen if they die. Although the process can be emotionally taxing at first, it can also provide you with a sense of relief once you know that you have taken the necessary precautions to ensure your family is well cared for.

What are the Benefits of Estate Planning?

1. AVOIDING PROBATE COURT

Estate planning allows you to determine what happens to your assets upon your death. Without proper legal documents in place, these decisions are made by the state. The process of a court determining how assets from an estate are distributed is known as probate. Going through probate can be time-consuming, complicated, and expensive as the surviving family will need to hire a lawyer to represent you in probate.

For modest estates, a flat fee can cost your family anywhere from $2,500 to $10,000 or more in legal fees, depending on how much the estate is worth and how complicated the situation is. If the estate is worth several million dollars and the lawyer charges 5% of the estate's value, you could end up paying over $100,000. Creating the correct legal documents will help you avoid probate.

2. DETERMINING LEGAL GUARDIANSHIP FOR YOUR CHILDREN

You will want to ensure that minor children are cared for by declaring a guardian. The last thing you want is to leave it up to the courts to decide who will obtain custody should something happen to you and your spouse.

3. SAVING YOUR FAMILY FROM DIFFICULT DECISIONS

There are difficult decisions to be made if you are incapacitated. Having made those decisions in advance can eliminate a substantial amount of stress for your family. Also, determining decisions around your wealth can eliminate disagreements and tension for family members.

4. PEACE OF MIND

An added benefit of estate planning is the peace of mind it provides while you're alive. By having a plan in place, you'll know that you've taken steps to organize what will surely be a confusing and upsetting event if something should happen.

Legal Documents to Review

TRUSTS

A trust is a legal entity that exists to protect the possessions in your estate. Although a will communicates your wishes, a trust becomes the legal owner of the assets in your estate. In our opinion, the biggest advantage to forming a trust is avoiding probate. This becomes even more valuable if you have property or investments in multiple states because you would be required to go through probate in each state.

With a trust, you can designate a trustee to manage the assets on your behalf. You can also provide stipulations in your trust, such as the amount of money given to a beneficiary each year. Or perhaps you would prefer that your children not receive their inheritance until they reach a certain age—your trust can set that up too.

Trusts are private, whereas wills are public records and can therefore be accessed through probate court.

There are many types of trusts, but we have chosen to focus on the more popular categories:

IRREVOCABLE: This type of trust cannot be amended or canceled without the permission of the beneficiary. Once those assets are placed in a trust, they no longer legally belong to you. It is an entity unto itself and even pays taxes separately. This affords you the benefit of legal protection from creditors and lawsuits since the property is no longer yours. For some, the idea of not owning the asset is unsettling, but as the trustee, you are still able to maintain control of the assets. This is true whether the trust contains a house you live in or a *brokerage*/investment account you are making decisions on.

REVOCABLE: This type of trust can be canceled or amended at any time for any reason. This type of trust does not afford the same protections from creditors that an irrevocable trust does, but it offers privacy and flexibility to make changes when needed. Most importantly, the assets placed in the trust should help you to avoid probate court.

LIVING TRUST: This trust is made to use during your lifetime. You can use the assets while alive and pass on the assets to a beneficiary upon death. This type of trust can be revocable or irrevocable.

TESTAMENTARY TRUST: It takes effect once you pass away, as assets will be transferred to the beneficiary under your trust's direction. An executor of your choosing will manage the trust. This type of trust is irrevocable.

> *Brokerage:* an institution that acts as a middleman to connect buyers and sellers of investments such as stocks, bonds, or funds.

It is important to note that once a trust has been set up, maintenance is still required. You will need to update the trust when new assets are acquired. Some people create a "pour over" will, which captures the assets not included in your trust and transfers them to the trust upon your death. An irrevocable trust will require more maintenance than a revocable trust as it requires separate filings for taxes. Once you've set up a trust, it's important to transfer the title of your assets over to your trust for it to become functional.

LAST WILL AND TESTAMENT

A will is a legal document that describes how you would like your assets distributed upon your death. A will can also assign guardianship for your children that are minors and allow you to select the beneficiaries of your assets. A will is much cheaper and easier to set up than a trust, but keep in mind that a will is public record, and your family may still have to go through probate, which can be costly after hiring a lawyer. In addition, a will only covers decisions upon your death and will not cover decisions that need to be made if you are alive, incapacitated, or mentally disabled.

ADVANCED CARE DIRECTIVE

This document will help your family make medical decisions for you if you are unable to do so. These directives tend to focus on if you want life-sustaining interventions, such as a ventilator to support your breathing or a feeding tube. You can also determine who will make these decisions for you.

An advanced directive can take the form of:

LIVING WILL: This document covers financial and medical decisions while you are alive but unable to make decisions.

POWER OF ATTORNEY: This designates an individual that will make financial and medical decisions on your behalf. Power of attorney will no longer be in effect upon your death.

WHERE TO STORE THESE DOCUMENTS

Make sure you have all your documents in a secure location that is easily accessible. Think about a protected place in your home, such as in a safe that your family members can access. Do not store the documents in a safety deposit box as it is sealed upon your death and will require a court order to open. Discuss the location of all important documents with your spouse or a close relative.

IF THE DOCUMENTS CAN'T BE FOUND, YOUR FAMILY WILL BE FORCED TO GO THROUGH PROBATE.

Tax Benefits to a Trust

Many people believe that a trust comes with tax benefits, but this is only the case for irrevocable trusts. As you transfer assets to an irrevocable trust, they are no longer part of your estate. This reduces the value of your estate to help keep you below the federal estate exemption amount—the amount you can pass onto your heirs before you have to pay federal estate tax. The truth is most of us will never need the tax benefit since the federal exemption is $11.58 million per person or $22.4 million for married couples in 2020. Know that estate taxes at your state level will vary from state to state.[71] Many states do not have a separate estate tax, but some states do. You can find estate tax information related to your state here.[72]

TRANSFER OF RETIREMENT ACCOUNTS

Most retirement accounts will pass outside probate as long as you have selected beneficiaries. This includes 401(k)s, 403(b)s, IRAs, and life insurance policies. The beneficiaries listed in your accounts or policies will supersede anything you have listed in your will.

Step-Up in Basis Rule

We briefly discussed the step-up in basis in our TAX section. Before we dive in any deeper, let's revisit the concept of capital gains tax. When you sell an asset for a profit, you pay capital gains tax on the profit you made. The step-up in basis adjusts the price of the asset, so capital gains taxes on inherited assets don't gouge you.

This loophole allows you to leave a mutual fund or property as an inheritance and reduce (or even eliminate) the capital gains tax. This is typically carried out by placing those assets in a trust and having your heirs legally inherit them.

Here is an example we used earlier in the book to illustrate how much money this can save your heirs.

UNDERSTANDING THE STEP-UP IN BASIS RULE

ASSUMPTIONS

Your parent purchased a home 20 years ago for $50,000. Today that home is worth $250,000. Once you own the property, you sell the home for $250,000

IF HOME IS TRANSFERRED TO AN HEIR WHILE ALIVE	VS	CAPITAL GAINS TAX IF HOME IS INHERITED AFTER DEATH

TRANSFERRING (GIFTING) A HOME

Your parent transfers their home into your name while they are still alive

INHERITANCE OF A HOME

Your parent passes away and you inherit their home

SELLING HOME AFTER TRANSFER

Once you sell the home, you may owe capital gains tax on the profit

$250,000 (Sales Price) - $50,000 (Purchase Price) = $200,000 (Profit)

STEP-UP IN BASIS UPON INHERITANCE

If you sell the house, you no longer consider the original purchase price in the capital gains calculation due to the step-up in basis rule

CAPITAL GAINS TAX

Depending on your income, you could owe $30,000 to $40,000 in taxes

CAPITAL GAINS TAX

New cost basis is the market value of the home when your parent died, so no taxes owed

$250,000 (Sales Price) -$250,000 (New Cost Basis) = $0 (Profit)

In that example, you could save up to $40,000 in taxes by planning for the future and taking advantage of the tax law.

What Do I Need at This Stage of My Career?

Like insurance policies or investment strategies, it's important to get what you need, but no more. Your estate planning will get more complex over time as you accumulate wealth, explore investments, or start a business. If you have children, you should at the very least establish a guardian for them in the event that both parents pass away. This can be done in a will. (A living trust cannot appoint a personal guardian for minor children.)

If your situation is straightforward (i.e., you are just beginning your career and have little more than debt to your name), then you do not need all the bells and whistles that some attorneys will try and sell you. In most cases, if you're married at the time of your death, your assets will automatically transfer to your spouse. An online service like Legal Zoom[73] might be a good fit early in your career and will be much more affordable than an in-person attorney. Their estate plan packages range from about $200 to $400.

Once you have begun to accumulate assets, you should consider a trust. Although a trust is ordinarily expensive to set up, your family would have to pay for a lawyer in probate if you don't have one. In many cases, the cost between the two is a wash. The big difference is that you can determine what happens with your assets before you pass away in a trust. It also saves your family the hassle of going through probate court.

An in-person attorney might be best suited for individuals who are further along in their careers. If you have accumulated assets such as retirement accounts, property, or a business, an attorney can create a customized plan. They are aware of state laws, tax implications, and legal issues you might come across. Before hiring an attorney, research the cost of the packages offered, as they can vary greatly. If you meet with a lawyer and feel like things are getting unnecessarily complicated, go get a second opinion. Initial consultations usually are free of charge.

Finding an Estate Planning Attorney

Look for an attorney that specializes in estate planning. If you have found a good financial advisor, ask for a referral. (Just don't feel obligated to use their services if you don't click with that attorney.) Also, consider referrals from lawyers or accountants you have worked with in the past. Barring those, you can always use the tried-and-tested method of reaching out to a facebook group or neighbors on the Nextdoor app. We always look closely at the reviews, which can tell you a lot about how the attorney runs their business.

Don't forget to ask up front how much they charge for estate planning. I personally would not entertain an hourly rate. Estate plans are done in packages, and attorneys should offer a set fee explaining what services are included in that fee.

HOW OFTEN SHOULD YOU MEET WITH YOUR ESTATE ATTORNEY?

Ideally, every time you take on a new asset or investment, it should be added to your estate. Once everything is put into place, you only have to check in every few years to make revisions and examine any changes to laws that will affect your estate.

Having said that, if your situation becomes complicated, we recommend seeking the advice of an estate attorney. Hopefully, after reading this, you are better positioned to ask the right questions, challenge their suggestions, and ensure the attorney is a good fit for your family.

ESTATE PLANNING

✓ Estate planning is having a plan in place for your family when you are no longer around.

✓ You can avoid probate by placing your assets inside a trust.

✓ Trusts can offer legal protection from creditors and lawsuits.

✓ A last will and testament will not allow you to avoid probate court, but it will give the judge direction for decisions on your assets.

✓ Most retirement accounts will pass outside probate as long as you have selected beneficiaries. This includes 401(k)s, 403(b)s, IRAs, and life insurance policies. The beneficiaries listed will supersede anything you have listed in your will.

✓ Be aware of the tax benefits with the step-up in basis rule and inheritance of assets.

✓ Be cautious about being oversold on protection measures early in your career when you have few assets to protect.

Scan for a full list of the links and tools listed.

Chapter 32

LIFE INSURANCE

The Basics of Life Insurance

Life insurance is a contract between yourself and the insurance company, which states that in exchange for monthly premiums (payments), your beneficiary will receive a lump sum of money if you pass away. While no one likes to think about their death, preparing for the future means making sure that your family is cared for.

As a physician, your salary is most likely the primary source of income. If something happens to you, having a policy will provide you with peace of mind, knowing that your family will be financially supported during a difficult time.

There are two basic types of life insurance policies: term policies and whole-life (or permanent) policies. Like most financial products, these can get unnecessarily complicated, so we'll try and unpack the details for you in the sections ahead.

TERM LIFE INSURANCE

These policies are purchased for a specific period of time, usually between 5 and 30 years. These tend to be the cheapest option and are easy to understand. Your main decisions are based on how long you want the policy to last and what you would like the payout amount to be if you died. There is no cash value with these policies, which means that it is not an asset that increases in value over time. If you are still alive when the policy expires, you do not recover any money paid into the policy.

WHOLE-LIFE (PERMANENT) INSURANCE

These policies do not expire and will last your entire life as long as you continue to pay the premium. These tend to be more expensive policies since the insurance company is almost guaranteed to pay out. Many of these policies have a cash value feature, which means that a portion of the premium you pay will go into an investment account and grow in value over time. If you are looking for ways to save and invest, using a life insurance policy should not be your primary method.

Whole-life policies can be further broken out into subcategories: variable and universal policies. Both of these offer a cash-value component, but they differ in how the cash value increases. A variable policy offers flexible investment options in stocks, bonds, and mutual funds. By contrast, a universal policy offers growth based on an interest rate put in place by the insurance company.

If you want the flexibility of both term and whole-life policies, you can get a hybrid, called a convertible life insurance policy. This will allow you to start with a term life insurance policy and later convert it into a whole life policy.

Using a life insurance policy as an investment strategy is rarely a good idea. The additional fees and higher premiums for these policies can be 5 to 10 times higher than a comparable term life policy. We present much more cost-effective options for investing in our INVESTING FOR YOUR FUTURE section and using life insurance to insure your income in the event of your untimely death.

Understanding How the Cost of Premiums is Determined

Your health, age, hobbies, and gender (sorry, men—you're statistically riskier than women) are factors determining how much you will have to pay for life insurance. To apply for life insurance, you'll fill out a questionnaire and a health screening, which will help determine your premium. The health screening is usually done by a third-party testing company that will come out to your house, draw blood, and take vitals. Once completed, you will receive an industry 'grade' based on your health and lifestyle. The best rates will be given to those with higher grades, and the poorest ratings with the highest premiums will be those given a substandard grade.

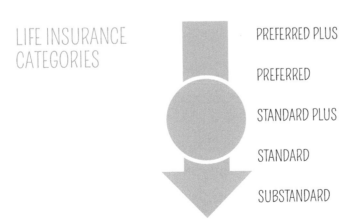

LIFE INSURANCE CATEGORIES

PREFERRED PLUS

PREFERRED

STANDARD PLUS

STANDARD

SUBSTANDARD

How to Shop for Life Insurance

If your experience is similar to ours, agents for insurance companies may come to give a presentation or buy you dinner and drinks while you are in residency, trying to sell you a policy. We would never say no to a free dinner, and we found the conversations informative. These may be good policies that you are presented with, but they only provide one of many options out there. And to be honest, if the agent is taking you out for fancy dinners, that money is probably coming from higher premiums.

Broker websites like **PolicyGenius** and **HealthIQ**[74] can help you compare different life insurance policies from various companies. Before you select a company, you will want to make sure that they will be around in several decades. You can get a sense of their stability through their credit ratings at **S&P Global** or **AM Best**, which are rating agencies specifically for the healthcare industry.

Choosing A Plan

Life insurance agents typically get paid based on the premium amount of your policy. Since whole-life policies have higher premiums, agents often push whole-life policies or frame them as the best option. In general, when you compare insurance policies, you should be raising an eyebrow if your agent recommends the plan that also happens to be the most expensive option. Here are some questions to consider when choosing a plan:

HOW MUCH LIFE INSURANCE SHOULD YOU GET?

The first question to ask yourself is, "Does anyone depend on me financially?" If the answer is no, the money you would put towards monthly premiums could go towards investments. If others depend on you financially, many advisors recommend a policy around 10 to 15 times your annual income. So, if your yearly income is $200,000, that would equate to a policy between $2 million and $3 million. For a more detailed dive, you can use an online life insurance coverage calculator. PolicyGenius.com has a calculator we like that is about halfway down the page.[75]

CAN I SWITCH MY PLAN?

Yes, you can always switch to a new policy that may save you money on your premiums. You'll want to compare the plans to make sure you are not being offered a lower rate because the new policy offers less coverage. You also will want to consider that you'll need to take another medical exam.

SHOULD I LOCK IN A LOW RATE WHILE I'M YOUNG AND HEALTHY?

If you have people who depend on you financially, you should consider a policy regardless of your age. Remember, your premiums will depend on the 'health grade' you are given after your medical exam. The older you get, the more likely you are to develop health problems and the more expensive your life insurance policy will be.

IF MY EMPLOYER OFFERS LIFE INSURANCE, SHOULD I LOOK THERE FIRST?

You will want to explore your employer's group life insurance policy if one is available. Some employers will pay for part or all of the monthly premiums. Do not just assume your employer's coverage is the cheapest option. Compare the employer's plan with other plans on third-party brokerage sites like PolicyGenius. Be aware that you may lose your policy through work if you are no longer employed there.

Avoid These Mistakes

You need to understand that insurance companies make a profit when they do not have to pay out on existing policies, so it's in your best interest to be mindful of the details of your policy so you can avoid costly mistakes. Missing a premium payment is one way to forfeit your policy. It is very important to find out the company's rules on late payments. They should offer a grace period of at least 30 days. Find out about their reinstatement policy as well. What is their reinstatement policy if you miss the grace period window? Will they require a new medical exam?

The other mistake to avoid is falsifying information on your questionnaire or medical exam. You may be tempted to sugarcoat your current health conditions to get the cheapest policy available. Upon your death, insurance companies will comb through all the information you provided. Their research may include pulling medical records, state and federal public records, social media posts, and interviewing friends and family—all searching for a misrepresentation of the information you provided that will void the policy. (Remember, the insurance company makes money when they don't have to pay.) If you have a hobby that might be considered risky or a health condition, just be upfront about it during the screening period. That way, you'll sleep well at night, knowing you won't pay a monthly premium for years just to have your policy voided upon your death.

How to Save Money on Life Insurance Policies

Life insurance policy pricing can vary based on multiple factors. Below are six items to consider to help you save money once you have decided to purchase a policy.

HOW TO SAVE MONEY ON LIFE INSURANCE

01 TERM LIFE IS CHEAPER THAN WHOLE LIFE
This is not always true, but it generally is. If you are looking for investment opportunities, look in a brokerage account, not a whole life insurance policy.

02 YOUR AGE
The younger you are, the cheaper the rate you can lock in.

03 ONLINE BROKER
An independent online broker will help you compare prices from different companies.

04 DISCOUNTS
It never hurts to ask for any and all discounts. For example, do they provide a discount to pay premiums annually rather than monthly?

05 FIXED RATES
Look for a policy with premiums that do not increase over time.

06 QUIT SMOKING
A Policygenius study released in 2018 showed that smoking had the highest impact on life insurance premiums. Smokers pay 342% more on their monthly premiums than a person with no conditions.

Nobody likes to think about dying. The COVID-19 pandemic has reminded many of us of our own mortality and how our children's lives will be effected if something happens to us. For us personally, when we think about passing away, it puts our mind at ease to know that if something were to happen, our family would be financially provided for after a tragedy.

LIFE INSURANCE

✓ Life insurance can provide peace of mind. It is a great comfort to know that your loved ones will have financial security if the unexpected occurs.

✓ Avoid whole life policies with investment options. The fees and higher premiums are rarely worth it compared to other investment options.

✓ Your health, age, hobbies and gender are all factors in determining how much you will have to pay for life insurance.

✓ Missing a premium payment or not being upfront about health conditions can void your life insurance policy.

✓ Ask about discounts that your life insurance provider can offer.

Scan for a full list of the links and tools listed.

Chapter 33

DISABILITY & UMBRELLA INSURANCE

The Basics of Disability Insurance

Few professions involve such a high cost of education, with the expectation of a return on investment a decade or more down the line. This leaves you open to substantial financial risk. A disability can be more financially destructive than even death for your family. In most cases, your federal student debt is forgiven if you die. However, with a disability, you may lose most or all of your income while still having to pay off your student debt. Therefore, a solid disability policy should be a high priority for those starting residency.

Disability can be broken down into short-term and long-term categories. A short-term disability normally lasts 3 to 6 months. A long-term disability normally takes effect 3 months after an injury; however, this can vary by policy. Short-term disability policies are usually provided by employers and not often purchased by individuals. This chapter focuses on long-term disability policies as they pose the greatest threat with the most significant financial impact.

Employer Coverage

Many employers offer some form of disability insurance. This can be in the form of short-term or long-term disability coverage. Keep in mind that employer coverage concludes when you are no longer employed with that company. If you buy a disability policy as an individual, it will follow you throughout your career.

If you have employer coverage, ask your private insurance company how your policy will be affected. Some private policies limit your benefits based on your employer coverage.

How to Calculate How Much Insurance You Need

If you meet with an insurance agent, you will undoubtedly hear the horror story of a resident without disability insurance who was days away from graduating and became disabled in an accident. These stories are enough to scare you senseless, and although agents sometimes exaggerate, these things do happen. The fact is that you are more likely to become disabled (whether it's temporary or permanent) than you are to die before retirement. Having said that, keep a level head when researching your options and find a policy that is a good fit for you.

I've heard many times from insurance professionals that you should have a policy that covers 60-70% of your after-tax income, but it really depends on your particular circumstances. If you have a spouse that has a substantial income, then you might consider a lower percentage. If you feel that your family will solely rely on your income, you may want to consider increasing the recommended percentages to accommodate for your current lifestyle.

Understanding your expenses is the key to selecting the disability coverage that works best for you. Hopefully, you've read our section on budgeting and have a good idea of your monthly expenses. You'll want a policy that, at the very least, will cover your primary expenses. Remember to tabulate mortgage payments, bills, and any student or personal debt payments.

How to Shop for Disability Insurance

You should be comparing the insurance policies available to you in school, residency, or through your employer with the policies offered by an independent online broker. Just because your employer provides disability insurance doesn't mean that's the policy that will work best for you. The same websites that offer life insurance quotes will also provide numbers on disability insurance. Websites like PolicyGenius, LeverageRX, and HealthIQ are a few options of many available.[76]

How Much Do These Policies Cost?

When we began exploring our options, we quickly discovered that disability policies were not cheap. These are expensive policies because the potential payout is considerable over many years. As a general rule, expect to pay 1-3% of your annual salary per year in disability policy premiums.

Also, if your employer is paying for the disability insurance, then the benefits you receive on a disability policy are taxable in many cases. If you purchase a private policy yourself, those benefits are usually tax-free if you pay the premiums with after-tax dollars. Make sure you compare policies apples-to-apples with the actual take-home amounts on each policy.

When to Buy Disability Insurance

A good time to begin exploring your options is while you are in medical school or in residency. Most universities offer group long-term disability insurance. You are not required to take a physical if you purchase your policy through school. These policies also tend to be cheaper than private policies, although shopping around is prudent.

In residency, the university should offer you guaranteed insurance coverage while in training. Many private insurance policies allow you to lock in a disability benefit in medical school and residency at a discount. If you are purchasing a private policy in medical school or residency, you make sure you have the option to increase your disability benefits in the future without having to undergo a physical examination.

Understanding Your Policy Options

Most long-term disability policies will pay out up until you are around 65 years old. You'll be offered a base policy with the option of additional riders. A rider is an 'add-on' to your policy.

Here is a list of terms and common riders to most disability policies.

RECOVERY BENEFITS (PARTIAL OR RESIDUAL DISABILITY): This term is used to describe if you are disabled temporarily and will need to supplement the loss of income for a period of time until your salary reaches the levels you were at before you were disabled.

For example, let's assume you had an accident, and you could not work for a year. Your principal disability insurance policy would cover lost wages while you were unable to work. The recovery benefits would begin when you were able to return to work. During your absence, you may have lost patients, and it might take some time for you to return to your prior income level. The recovery benefit can help to make up the difference in income.

FUTURE PURCHASE OPTION: This benefit will allow you to increase your coverage later without taking another medical exam. This is particularly beneficial if you are purchasing the policy in medical school or residency. You will be able to increase the amount of your benefit as your income increases.

NON-CANCELABLE: This means that your rates cannot increase while your policy is in effect.

RETIREMENT PROTECTION DISABILITY INSURANCE: This option will make regular payments into a retirement account if you become disabled and no longer have earned income to contribute.

OWN-OCCUPATION FEATURE: This term implies that you will still receive a disability benefit if you are unable to work in your specific field, even if you are able to work in other capacities. For example, if you can no longer perform surgeries but can still work in a clinic, a true own-occupation policy will pay you for the loss of income from what you were making performing surgeries.

> WE WOULD PERSONALLY NEVER ENTERTAIN ANY POLICY THAT DOES NOT HAVE A TRUE OWN-OCCUPATION FEATURE.

STUDENT LOAN RIDER: This benefit will have your insurance company make student debt payments while you are disabled.

COST OF LIVING ADJUSTMENT: This rider will increase your disability benefit yearly to account for inflation (based on the National Consumer Price Index).

LEVEL VS. GRADED: If you feel you cannot afford the monthly fixed premiums, you can explore a graded option, which means your premiums are cheaper the first few years and gradually increase over time. Over the life of the policy, graded plans will cost you more. If you can afford the monthly premiums on a fixed plan, we recommend that option because it is more costeffective over time.

Questions to Ask About Your Policy

How your policy defines disability is very important since the definition will vary from policy to policy. You should know what types of disabilities are excluded in the definition.

It is also essential to understand the details of your recovery benefits. How long does the benefit period last? How much loss of income is required for the recovery benefit to kick in? For example, this benefit usually takes effect if you make 75% or less than you made before the disability. Keep in mind that to receive recovery benefits, you have to show your loss of earnings was caused by the disability and not by other factors.

Prior health conditions will most likely be excluded if those conditions lead to a disability. Make sure you clarify exactly what is excluded due to your medical history and your family's medical history.

While we are on the subject of exclusions, many policies will exclude disabilities due to pregnancy, foreign travel, or excursions such as scuba diving or jet skiing. Educate yourself on what the policy excludes. You will also want to find out exactly when your benefits begin. The waiting period for long-term disability usually is 90 days, but this can vary by policy.

Find out how other sources of income will affect your disability benefits and whether they will deduct that income from your benefits. You will also want to determine how your disability is affected if you have group insurance with an employer. Your policy should allow you full benefits, even if you have a group policy.

How to Save Money on Disability Policies

If you can save up for 3 to 6 months of expenses in an emergency savings account, you will not need a short-term disability policy and can avoid that cost.

Regarding long-term disability, you do not have to purchase the maximum amount you are eligible for. Understanding your needs for your budget and expenses can help you select an affordable policy with adequate coverage. Keep in mind that a disability policy is in place to provide financial security if a catastrophe occurs. Once you're financially independent, a disability policy will no longer be necessary.

Umbrella Insurance

Umbrella insurance policies act as extended coverage of your auto and homeowner's insurance policies, and it covers areas that your home or auto policies will not. Umbrella policies can help protect you against lawsuits, injury and hospitalization costs, liability coverage on rental units, and even lawsuits related to libel or slander.

Certain activities increase your likelihood of being sued. (Just being a physician is one.) If you have a pool, a trampoline, or a dog, accidents can happen. Your babysitter accidentally slips on ice in your driveway and decides to sue you, or your neighbor trips and falls in your yard. You may be coaching a little league sports team or seeking jet ski adventures on your vacations, you should consider a policy that will cover these activities.

I know you're thinking, "How much freaking insurance do I need?! Life, disability—now this?" We would hesitate to recommend umbrella insurance if it wasn't so affordable. Umbrella insurance acts as a personal liability policy above and beyond existing policies and is easily added to an existing policy.

A good place to start is with your current auto and home insurance companies. Often, you can get significant discounts for owning multiple policies with the same company. Policies can range from $150-$300 a year for $1-$3 million worth of coverage. I feel these policies are affordable considering the coverage. It's important to note that umbrella policies for personal liability do not cover malpractice claims.

OTHER FORMS OF FINANCIAL SUPPORT

It is worth noting that if you have an injury or become disabled, other forms of financial support may be available to you. Workers' compensation, which is mandated by law for employers, could be an option, but only if you are injured on the job. Social Security can also offer financial support if you become disabled, but it's important to note that qualifying can be difficult. If you qualify, the benefits for disability max out at around $2,190 per month[77] as of 2021.

Your student debt can be forgiven if you qualify for a total and permanent disability discharge. This would require a physician's certification that states your disability has lasted or can be expected to last for a continuous period of at least 60 months. Disabilities less severe would not qualify for student loan forgiveness.

As a medical professional, your personal liability coverage should be considered as carefully as professional liability coverage. This chapter and this entire section can be summed up by hoping for the best but preparing for the worst.

Chapter 33 Recap
DISABILITY AND UMBRELLA INSURANCE

- ✓ Keep a level head when insurance agents share horror stories of residents becoming disabled.

- ✓ Short-term disability normally lasts 3 to 6 months. Long-term disability takes effect 3 months after an injury, and most policies last until you are 65.

- ✓ Explore your disability policies through your medical school or residency before shopping for private insurance.

- ✓ Make sure you are familiar with the 8 disability contract terms we discuss in the chapter.

- ✓ Ask a lot of questions about your policy. How long does the benefit last? When does the recovery benefit kick in? Are there exclusions of current health conditions? How much loss of income is required before benefits kick in?

- ✓ Do not consider a policy that is not a true own-occupation policy.

- ✓ A short-term disability policy is no longer needed once you save 3 to 6 months' worth of income in an emergency account.

- ✓ An umbrella policy is relatively inexpensive and can cover you for $1 to $2 million of personal liability for a few hundred dollars a year.

Scan for a full list of the links and tools listed.

CLOSING THOUGHTS

We hope you have found value in the information we provided in the book. Our goal was always to write a book that offers the financial guidance we wish we had many years ago. We have strived to provide a comprehensive list of personal finance topics in one easily accessible spot, along with practical tips to get you started and push you towards your financial goals.

During our research for the book, we could not find any personal finance websites that were not sponsored by financial institutions or did not accept payments from finance-related companies to promote their products or services. That is why we plan on continuing to provide content with our own, unbought opinions on personal finance topics through our MoneyOverMilkshakes.com website.

If you enjoyed the book and would like to keep updated on personal finance topics, please consider subscribing. We'll keep you posted on topics such as budgeting, saving, taxes, student loans, scholarships, and much more.

Thank you again for reading this book. We plan on making it a living document, updating it regularly to give you access to the most recent and accurate information.

Now, put down the book and take the next step in your personal finance journey. If we've done our job well, you now know what that is and how to do it. (Still need some guidance? Follow the checklists in the next section.)

Nick & Amanda
Co-Founders of MoneyOverMilkshakes.com

YOUR CHECKLIST

We covered so many different topics in the book. If you read the book cover to cover, you might be asking yourself, "Where do I start?"

We created this section to give you an actionable, step-by-step approach to address all of the information we covered. We've added links that will take you directly to helpful websites on relevant topics. We've also linked back to chapters, so you can go back and refer to them for additional information.

It would be impossible to customize the list for every possible situation, so please consider this a general list. Check off these items as you complete them.

The Early Years:
Pre-Med and Medical School

FAFSA (CHAPTER 1)

- ☐ Set annual calendar reminder for October 1st to submit FAFSA
- ☐ Create an FSA ID for both students and parents
- ☐ You can fill out your FAFSA online, or download the MyStudentAid app for mobile devices for Apple products and Google Android products
- ☐ If you are a male and 25 years or younger, you must be registered with the Selective Service to eligible for financial aid. You can register or verify your status on their website
- ☐ Get Title IV Institution Codes for each of the schools you are applying to that you will need on the FAFSA
- ☐ Use the IRS Data Retrieval Tool option in the application to save time filling out your FAFSA
- ☐ Use the FAFSA forecaster tool to estimate how much financial aid you will qualify for

FEDERAL VS. PRIVATE LOANS (CHAPTER 2)

- ☐ Review the pros and cons of private and federal student loans before selecting a loan
- ☐ Ask the following questions when applying for a private loan:
  - · Can I make pre-payments without being charged a penalty?
  - · Can I pay off my loan early without penalty?
  - · Is the interest rate variable or fixed?
  - · What are the options to defer loans during times of financial hardship?

- ☐ Can I defer payments until after graduation?

SCHOLARSHIPS AND GRANTS (CHAPTER 3)

- ☐ Choose medical school scholarships to apply for, such as the list compiled by Fastweb or the list gathered by Scholarships.com

- ☐ Since scholarships and grants are awarded on a first-come, first-served basis, add a calendar reminder on the deadlines for the scholarships you plan to apply for

- ☐ Run a search online for local community foundations and businesses that offer scholarships

- ☐ Set up a meeting with your academic counselor or financial aid office to discuss local scholarship opportunities

MEDICINE AND THE MILITARY (CHAPTER 4)

- ☐ If you're interested in learning more about practicing medicine in the military, check out these links to help you get started for the U.S. Army, U.S. Air Force, or U.S. Navy

- ☐ Speak with a colleague or peer that has first-hand experience practicing medicine in the military. If you do not know anyone directly, LinkedIn is full of military physicians happy to answer your questions

WORKING THROUGH SCHOOL (CHAPTER 5)

- ☐ Select the work-study option on the FAFSA application to be eligible for federally subsidized work-study income

- ☐ When comparing a work-study position with another job, make sure to calculate the tax savings of 7.3% offered by many work-study jobs

- ☐ Consider applying for a job while in school that offers tuition assistance

APPLICATION & INTERVIEW COSTS (CHAPTER 6)

- ☐ Find the closest **MCAT testing location** to you
- ☐ Verify whether you qualify for **AAMC's fee assistance program**
- ☐ Ask whether interviewing for medical school remotely is an option to potentially save thousands of dollars
- ☐ Avoid using a high-interest credit card to pay for interview-related costs if you are unable to pay the balance off within one payment cycle
- ☐ Start saving for interviews now by setting up a recurring auto-transfer from your checking to a savings account

QUESTIONS TO CONSIDER WHEN GOING INTO DEBT (CHAPTER 7)

- ☐ Know what your expected income will be and compare it to those of other specialties.
- ☐ Calculate your total student debt. To estimate future debt not yet incurred, you can use the **Tuition and Student Fees Report** to estimate both undergraduate and medical school debt
- ☐ Assess future income by using the **Medscape Physician Compensation Report**
- ☐ Calculate your debt-to-income ratio to evaluate how much of a burden your debt will be in the future

Residency

STUDENT DEBT REPAYMENT OPTIONS (CHAPTER 8)

- ☐ If you're considering private loans, make sure you understand the terms, especially around prepayment policies, early payoff penalties, and options for deferment during times of financial hardship
- ☐ Utilize the studentaid.gov loan simulator to explore your repayment plan options
- ☐ Make small payments on your loans in residency. This will not only reduce your debt over time by tens of thousands of dollars but can count towards your forgiveness program

CONSOLIDATING/REFINANCING YOUR STUDENT LOANS (CHAPTER 9)

- ☐ When you start residency, review the pros and cons of consolidating your loans. If you are going to consolidate, early in residency is the ideal time to do so
- ☐ Use the consolidation calculator created by finaid.org to explore your options
- ☐ Contact the Federal Student Loan Support Center to answer any questions regarding a federal direct consolidation loan at 1-800-557-7394

STUDENT DEBT FORGIVENESS PROGRAM (CHAPTER 10)

- ☐ If you are participating in PSLF, verify that your residency program or employer is a qualified 501c(3) tax-exempt non-profit or public institution
- ☐ Confirm that your student loans are eligible for PSLF, and if they are not eligible, consider consolidating into a direct federal loan that is eligible

- [ ] Certify that your loan payments qualify for PSLF every year by filling out **the annual certification form**
- [ ] Utilize an online PSLF calculator to explore repayment options with PSLF in mind. We like the **studentloanhero.com calculator**
- [ ] See if your state offers **additional student loan forgiveness programs**
- [ ] When applying for jobs after residency, find out if your employer offers student debt payment assistance or student loan forgiveness
- [ ] Start making qualified payments towards PSLF early in residency

WORK AFTER RESIDENCY & CONTRACT NEGOTIATION (CHAPTER 11)

- [ ] Set a calendar reminder to start your job search 6 months before you finish residency
- [ ] Reach out to your peers from medical school and residency about job vacancies
- [ ] If you have a particular position, group, or hospital in mind, reach out to their HR/recruiting office directly before reaching out to a recruiter
- [ ] Utilize a recruiter to explore other potential opportunities
- [ ] Consider countering on your initial job offer at least once
- [ ] Hire a lawyer to review your employment contract
- [ ] Look into completing a billing course after residency

YOUR FIRST PAYCHECK AFTER RESIDENCY (CHAPTER 12)

- [ ] Create an updated set of goals after residency
  - Determine what percentage of your income will go towards your retirement goals

- Automate bank transfers to build your emergency fund and meet your savings goals
- Create a debt management strategy to pay off student debt
- Create a budget to support your goals

Setting Yourself Up for Success

FINANCIAL ADVISORS (CHAPTER 13)

☐ Consider a fee-only fiduciary advisor to support your goals. The National Association of Personal Financial Advisors website is a good place to find local advisors

☐ Understand how the financial advisor will charge you for their services

☐ Use our list of questions in the chapter to get you started during financial advisor interviews

☐ When interviewing an advisor, make sure they are easy to understand and patient with your questions. If not, find another advisor

BUDGETING (CHAPTER 14)

☐ Start a free trial of Mint, YNAB, or another budgeting tool of your choice

☐ Connect your accounts to help the system categorize your spending

☐ Calculate your financial net worth

☐ Create a recurring calendar reminder to open your budgeting app and review your expenses

☐ Keep an eye on your miscellaneous expenses and set a limit on them

SAVING (CHAPTER 15)

- ☐ Determine how much you will save every month for emergencies
- ☐ Create an emergency fund with 3 months' worth of expenses
- ☐ Open a high-yield savings accounts to hold your emergency fund
- ☐ Automate your savings by contacting your HR department and having a percentage of your paycheck go directly to your savings account
- ☐ If you struggle to contribute regularly to a savings account, consider using a micro-investing app like Acorns to automate your savings and investing

BANKING (CHAPTER 16)

- ☐ Search your bank statement for bank fees. If your bank charges overdraft fees, maintenance fees, monthly service fees, and other fees, drop them like a bad habit. They don't deserve your business. Consider an online bank like **Ally**, **Discover Bank**, or **Capital One 360**

CREDIT CARDS (CHAPTER 17)

- ☐ Ask yourself whether you can pay off an expense within one billing cycle before using your credit card
- ☐ Research **The Points Guy** as a good resource for comparing rewards on credit cards

BUYING, RENTING & HOME LOANS (CHAPTER 18)

☐ Decide whether you are going to rent or buy. Here are links to two of the calculators we like, built by Zillow and the New York Times that will help you make the decision to rent or buy a property

☐ Limit your mortgage payment to 25% or less of your monthly gross income

☐ Set a calendar reminder for when PMI should be paid off and contact the mortgage company to have it removed

☐ Create a savings account for the down payment on a home

☐ Get your free credit report from annualcreditreport.com

☐ Get an estimated credit score for free from Credit Karma or Credit Sesame

☐ Get a pre-approval for a mortgage before house-hunting

☐ Negotiate with two lenders up until the rate is locked and the underwriting process has been completed

☐ If you're considering buying points on your mortgage, use an online calculator to help make the decision

☐ Trulia has an easy-to-use mortgage calculator that will include all the fees you can expect

Investing

WHAT I'VE LEARNED AFTER 20 YEARS OF INVESTING (CHAPTER 19)

☐ Diversify your investments. Make sure that your trading accounts include funds with a large number of holdings across different markets

☐ Adopt a general buy-and-hold strategy. Short-term trading will increase your taxes, increase associated fees, and increase your risk on investments

☐ Keep it simple. This can be accomplished with a few well-diversified funds

STOCKS, BONDS & FUNDS (CHAPTER 20)

☐ Familiarize yourself with the terminology and concepts discussed in the chapter

RETIREMENT ACCOUNTS (CHAPTER 21)

☐ Calculate how much you need for retirement. Use retirement calculators like the SmartAsset calculator. We also like NerdWallet's calculator.

☐ Contribute enough to your retirement account to get your employer's match

  · Calculate how much you need to contribute to take full advantage of employer match
  · Understand your vesting period

☐ Inspect the fees (expense ratios) on the funds you are considering investing in

ROTH & TRADITIONAL IRAs (CHAPTER 22)

- [ ] Review whether you are eligible to contribute to a Roth IRA
- [ ] Determine whether you qualify for a tax deduction with a traditional IRA. Although anyone can contribute, not everyone is eligible for the tax deduction
- [ ] Review our section on questions to ask to help determine whether a Roth or traditional IRA is a better fit for you
- [ ] If you're not eligible for Roth and not eligible for tax deductions with a traditional IRA, consider a backdoor IRA
- [ ] Review the pro-rata rule when performing a backdoor conversion

INDEX FUNDS (CHAPTER 23)

- [ ] Review the SPIVA Scorecard for 2020 before considering an active trading strategy
- [ ] Review low-cost index funds to add to your retirement and investment accounts

HEALTH SAVINGS ACCOUNTS (HSA) & FLEXIBLE SPENDING ACCOUNTS (FSA) (CHAPTER 24)

- [ ] Check with your HR department on whether HSA and FSA accounts are available through your employer
- [ ] If you choose to open an HSA, verify whether you are enrolled in a qualifying high-deductible health insurance plan

ASSET ALLOCATION (CHAPTER 25)

- ☐ Take Vanguard's **risk questionnaire** to help you choose an allocation model based on your risk profile
- ☐ Review your current asset allocation mix by logging into your online retirement portal. If you own multiple accounts in different places, consider summarizing them in an excel sheet or using an app like Personal Capital to bring together a full picture of all your accounts

REBALANCING YOUR PORTFOLIO (CHAPTER 26)

- ☐ Many 401(k)s offer an auto rebalancing feature. Review your plan and activate the feature
- ☐ Your methods of rebalancing can either be based on time or a set threshold. Review a strategy and then stick with it
- ☐ Create calendar reminders to check in with your portfolio to review for rebalancing purposes

SAVING FOR YOUR CHILDREN (CHAPTER 27)

- ☐ Explore the plans within your state of residence for possible tax deductions
- ☐ Compare 529 plans on Vanguard's **website**
- ☐ Set up a 529 plan with monthly auto withdrawals

INTRO TO TAXES (CHAPTER 28)

- ☐ Take a long-term approach to investments (more than 1 year)
- ☐ Avoid capital gains taxes when selling your home

- [ ] Understand the concept of step up in basis for transferring property
- [ ] Utilize tax-advantaged accounts for retirement
- [ ] Consider forming a business for liability protection, additional retirement options, and business tax deductions

Protecting What You've Earned After Residency

GETTING RETIREMENT RIGHT (CHAPTER 29)

- [ ] For a back-of-the-napkin calculation to determine:
  - how much you need to retire is to multiply
  - how much you spend (not earn) in a year by 25

- [ ] For a more in-depth review of what you need for retirement, use an online calculator

SHELTERING YOUR ASSETS (CHAPTER 30)

- [ ] If you're starting a business or have rental properties, you can register an LLC to protect your assets. Legal Zoom is one option to streamline the setup
- [ ] If you're employed, make an effort to understand your malpractice insurance. Do you have an occurrence policy or a claims-made policy?
- [ ] When searching for malpractice insurance, consider using an independent broker who is not financially incentivized to push you towards a particular policy or company

- ☐ Narrow your conversations to brokers that specialize in medical malpractice insurance. You'll want to find a highly rated reputable company that can be verified with **AM Best**, the world's largest credit rating agency

ESTATE PLANNING (CHAPTER 31)

- ☐ Discuss with your family how to access your important documents
- ☐ Review packages offered by a local estate attorney as well as an online service like **Legal Zoom** to compare what would be appropriate for you at this stage of your career
- ☐ Make sure you have assigned beneficiaries for retirement accounts, life insurance, and disability policies, allowing these policies to avoid probate

LIFE INSURANCE (CHAPTER 32)

- ☐ Get a health screening to get a quote for life insurance
- ☐ Compare different policies from websites like **PolicyGenius**, and **HealthIQ** that are third-party, independent broker sites
- ☐ Check an insurance company's credit ratings at **S&P Global** or **AM Best** to make sure they are reputable and credible
- ☐ Find out what the policy is regarding late payments
- ☐ Set up autopay to avoid late payments
- ☐ Ask about discounts offered such as prepayments on premiums

DISABILITY AND UMBRELLA INSURANCE (CHAPTER 33)

- ☐ Check your employer's coverage. Do they offer short-term and long-term coverage?

- ☐ Calculate the amount needed on your policy by looking at your budget and expenses. Shoot for 60 to 70% of your after-tax income if your family relies on your income primarily, and less if your partner brings in a substantial income

- ☐ Compare the insurance policies you have available to you through school, residency, or your employer with that of an independent online broker with options from several companies. The same companies that provide life insurance quotes will also provide disability insurance. Websites like PolicyGenius, HealthIQ, and LeverageRX are a few options to explore

- ☐ Explore insurance options while you are in medical school or residency. Most universities offer group long-term disability insurance.

- ☐ You can reach out to an independent online broker to see what they can offer in comparison. In residency, you should be offered guaranteed insurance coverage while in training.

- ☐ If you purchase a private policy in medical school or residency, make sure you have the option to increase your disability benefits in the future without having to undergo a physical examination

References

FREE APPLICATION FOR FEDERAL STUDENT LOAN AID (FAFSA)

1   Taylor, Z. W., and Ibrahim Bicak. "First-Generation College Student Financial Aid: Results From A National Financial Aid Jargon Survey." College Student Affairs Journal 38.1 (2020): 91-109.

"Create an Account (FSA ID)." Federal Student Aid, https://studentaid.gov/fsa-id/create-account/launch. Accessed 15 April 2021.

"Many non-U.S. citizens qualify for federal student aid" Federal Student Aid, https://studentaid.gov/understand-aid/eligibility/requirements/non-us-citizens. Accessed 15 April 2021.

"What is the IRS Data Retrieval Tool (IRS DRT)?" Federal Student Aid, https://studentaid.gov/help-center/answers/article/what-is-irs-drt. Accessed 15 April 2021.

Selective Service System, https://www.sss.gov/. Accessed 15 April 2021.

"Title IV Institution Codes" FinAid, https://finaid.org/fafsa/tiv/. Accessed 15 April 2021.

"For purposes of applying for federal student aid, what's the difference between a dependent student and an independent student?" Federal Student Aid, https://studentaid.gov/apply-for-aid/fafsa/filling-out/dependency. Accessed 15 April 2021.

FAFSA4caster , https://fafsa.ed.gov/spa/fafsa4c/?locale=en_US#/landing. Accessed 15 April 2021.

"Is either of your parents a dislocated worker?" Studentaid.gov, https://studentaid.gov/2021/help/parent-dislocated-worker. Accessed 15 April 2021.

FEDERAL vs. PRIVATE LOANS

2   "Understand how interest is calculated and what fees are associated with your federal student loan." Studentaid.gov, https://studentaid.gov/understand-aid/types/loans/interest-rates. Accessed 15 April 2021.

SCHOLARSHIPS & GRANTS

3   "Medical Scientist Training Program." National Institute of General Medical Sciences, https://www.nigms.nih.gov/training/instpredoc/pages/predocoverview-MSTP.aspx. Accessed 15 April 2021.

"Fellowships & Grants." American Association of University Women, https://www.aauw.org/resources/programs/fellowships-grants/. Accessed 15 April 2021.

"FORD FOUNDATION FELLOWSHIP PROGRAMS." The National Academies of Sciences Engineering Medicine, https://sites.nationalacademies.org/PGA/FordFellowships/index.htm. Accessed 15 April 2021.

"Medical Student Grants" Collegegrants.org, https://www.collegegrants.org/medical-college-grants.html#:~:text=Grants%20for%20medical%20students%20are,research%20projects%20during%20medical%20school. Accessed 15 April 2021.

"Medical School & Pre-Med Scholarships" fastweb.com, https://www.fastweb.com/college-scholarships/articles/medical-school-and-pre-med-scholarships. Accessed 15 April 2021.

"Medical Scholarships" scholarships.com, https://www.scholarships.com/financial-aid/college-scholarships/scholarships-by-major/medical-scholarships/. Accessed 15 April 2021.

"Physicians of Tomorrow Awards" American Medical Association, https://www.ama-assn.org/about/awards/physicians-tomorrow-awards. Accessed 15 April 2021.

"Edith SeVille Coale Scholarship." Zontawashingtondc.org , https://www.zontawashingtondc.org/scholarship-edith-seville-coale-medical.html. Accessed 15 April 2021.

"Herbert W. Nickens Medical Student Scholarships." Association of American Medical Colleges, https://www.aamc.org/what-we-do/aamc-awards/nickens-medical-student-scholarships. Accessed 15 April 2021.

"Tylenol Future Care Scholarships" Tylenol.com, https://www.tylenol.com/news/scholarship. Accessed 15 April 2021.

"United Health Foundation/NMF Diverse Medical Scholars Program." National Medical Fellowships, https://www.aamc.org/what-we-do/aamc-awards/nickens-medical-student-scholarships. Accessed 15 April 2021.

"International Guest Scholarships." American College of Surgeons, https://www.facs.org/member-services/scholarships/international/igs. Accessed 15 April 2021.

"NYU Grossman School of Medicine." New York University, https://med.nyu.edu/education. Accessed 15 April 2021.

"Financial Support." Washington University School of Medicine in St. Louis, https://medicine.wustl.edu/education/financial-support/. Accessed 15 April 2021.

"Cost & Aid." Weill Cornell Medicine Medical College, https://medicaleducation.weill.cornell.edu/admissions/costs-aid. Accessed 15 April 2021.

"Tuition & Financial Aid." Cleveland Clinic Lerner College of Medicine, https://my.clevelandclinic.org/lerner-college-medicine/tuition-financial-aid. Accessed 15 April 2021.

MEDICINE & THE MILITARY

4   Uniformed Services University, https://www.usuhs.edu/. Accessed 15 April 2021.

5   "United States Army – O-3 Captain." Federalpay.org, https://www.federalpay.org/military/army/captain#:~:text=Starting%20pay%20for%20a%20Captain,a%20more%20detailed%20salary%20estimate. Accessed 15 April 2021.

6   "How Much Does a Family Health Insurance Plan Cost." Ehealthinsurance.com, https://www.ehealthinsurance.com/resources/individual-and-family/how-much-does-a-family-health-insurance-plan-cost#:~:text=Average%20family%20health%20insurance%20cost%20per%20month&text=In%202020%2C%20the%20average%20cost,location%2C%20and%20level%20of%20coverage. Accessed 15 April 2021.

WORKING THROUGH SCHOOL

7   **Companies That Help with College Tuition**
         UPS. https://www.jobs-ups.com/earn-and-learn. Accessed 15 April 2021.

         Starbucks. https://www.starbucks.com/careers/working-at-starbucks/education. Accessed 15 April 2021.

         Amazon. https://www.aboutamazon.com/working-at-amazon/career-choice. Accessed 15 April 2021.

         Verizon. https://www.verizon.com/about/careers/benefits. Accessed 15 April 2021.

         Fidelity. https://jobs.fidelity.com/page/show/benefits. Accessed 15 April 2021.

         Chipotle. https://ir.chipotle.com/news-releases?item=122436#:~:text=Between%20Chipotle's%20existing%20tuition%20reimbursement,year%20to%20go%20to%20college. Accessed 15 April 2021.

         Chick-Fil-A. https://thechickenwire.chick-fil-a.com/inside-chick-fil-a/tuition-discounts. Accessed 15 April 2021.

APPLICATION & INTERVIEW COSTS

8   "Register for the MCAT Exam" Association of American Medical Colleges, https://students-residents.aamc.org/register-mcat-exam/register-mcat-exam. Accessed 15 April 2021.

9   "AACOMAS Application Fees and Fee Waivers." American Association of Colleges of Osteopathic Medicine, https://help.liaisonedu.com/AACOMAS_Applicant_Help_Center/Starting_Your_AACOMAS_Application/Getting_Started_with_Your_AACOMAS_Application/02_AACOMAS_Application_Fees_and_Fee_Waivers. Accessed 15 April 2021.

10   "Fee Assistance Program Poverty Guidelines." Association of American Medical Colleges, https://students-residents.aamc.org/fee-assistance-program/who-eligible-participate-fee-assistance-program. Accessed 15 April 2021.

11   Lyndra Vassar."Study examines what it costs to interview for medical residency programs." American Medical Association, https://www.ama-assn.org/residents-students/match/study-examines-what-it-costs-interview-medical-residency-programs. Accessed 15 April 2021.

12   "Applicant Fees." National Residency Match Program, https://www.nrmp.org/match-fees/. Accessed 15 April 2021.

QUESTIONS TO CONSIDER WHEN GOING INTO DEBT

13   "Student Loan Debt Statistics." Educationdata.org, https://educationdata.org/student-loan-debt-statistics. Accessed 15 April 2021

14   "2020 Physician Education Debt." Association of American Medical Colleges, https://www.aamc.org/system/files/2020-10/aamc-2020-physician-education-debt.pdf. Accessed 15 April 2021.

15   "Tuition and Student Fees Report." Association of American Medical Colleges, https://www.aamc.org/data-reports/reporting-tools/report/tuition-and-student-fees-reports. Accessed 15 April 2021.

16   "Loan Payment Calculator." Finaaid.org, https://finaid.org/calculators/loanpayments/. Accessed 15 April 2021

17   "Medscape Physician Compensation Report 2021" Medscape, https://www.medscape.com/slideshow/2021-compensation-overview-6013761. Accessed 15 April 2021.

STUDENT DEBT REPAYMENT OPTIONS

18   Matt Carter."Average Student Loan Debt for Medical School" Credible.com, https://www.credible.com/blog/statistics/average-medical-school-debt/#:~:text=How%20long%20it%20takes%20you%20to%20repay%20your%20medical%20school,Standard%20repayment%20plan%3A%2013%20years. Accessed 15 April 2021.

CONSOLIDATING/REFINANCING YOUR STUDENT DEBT

19   "Loan Consolidation Calculator." Finaid.org, https://finaid.org/calculators/loanconsolidation/. Accessed 15 April 2021.

STUDENT DEBT FORGIVENESS PROGRAMS

20   "Public Service Loan Forgiveness Calculator." Studentloanhero.com, https://studentloanhero.com/calculators/public-service-loan-forgiveness-calculator/. Accessed 15 April 2021.

21   "Coronavirus and Forbearance Info for Students, Borrowers, and Parents." Federal Student Aid, https://studentaid.gov/announcements-events/coronavirus. Accessed 15 April 2021.

22   "Student Loan Forgiveness Programs by State." The College Investor, https://thecollegeinvestor.com/student-loan-forgiveness-programs-by-state/. Accessed 15 April 2021.

National Health Service Corps, https://nhsc.hrsa.gov/. Accessed 15 April 2021.

"Apply to the Faculty Loan Repayment Program." Health Resources & Services Administration, https://bhw.hrsa.gov/funding/apply-loan-repayment/faculty-lrp. Accessed 15 April 2021.

National Institutes of Health, https://www.lrp.nih.gov/. Accessed 15 April 2021.

FINANCIAL ADVISORS

23   Professor Dr. Thorsten Hens."Behavioral Finance: The Psychology of Investing." BhFS Behavioural Finance Solutions GmbH, a spin-off company of the Universities of St.Gallen and Zurich co-founded by Professors Enrico De Giorgi and Thorsten Hens, https://www.credit-suisse.com/media/assets/private-banking/docs/uk/wp-07-behavioral-finance-en.pdf. Accessed 15 April 2021.

24   Dyana Yochim & Jonathan Todd."How a 1% Fee Could Cost Millennials $590,000 in Retirement Savings." NerdWallet.com, https://www.nerdwallet.com/blog/investing/millennial-retirement-fees-one-percent-half-million-savings-impact/. Accessed 15 April 2021.

25   The National Association of Personal Financial Advisors, Credit Suisse White Paper, https://www.napfa.org/. Accessed 15 April 2021.

BUDGETING

26   Mint.com https://mint.intuit.com/. Accessed 15 April 2021.

YouNeedABudget.com. https://www.youneedabudget.com/. Accessed 15 April 2021.

Pocketguard.com. https://pocketguard.com/. Accessed 15 April 2021.

Everydollar.com. https://www.ramseysolutions.com/ramseyplus/everydollar. Accessed 15 April 2021.

SAVING

27   Roy Baumeister, Ellen Bratslavsky, Mark Muraven and Dianne Tice." Ego Depletion: Is the Active Self a Limited Resource?." Case Western University, June 16, 1997, http://faculty.washington.edu/jdb/345/345%20Articles/Baumeister%20et%20al.%20%281998%29.pdf. Accessed 24 April 2021.

28   Acorns.com. https://www.acorns.com/. Accessed 15 April 2021.
       Digit. https://digit.co/. Accessed 15 April 2021.

BANKING

29   Ally Bank. https://www.ally.com/do-it-right/banking/checking-account-fees-true-cost/. Accessed 15 April 2021.

       Citi Bank Simple Checking Account. https://online.citi.com/JRS/popups/PT_CAP_BasicBanking_.pdf. Accessed 15 April 2021.

       Bank of America Checking and Saving Account Fees. https://www.bankofamerica.com/deposits/account-fees/. Accessed 15 April 2021.

       Discover Bank CDs. https://www.discover.com/content/dam/dfs/online-banking/documents/Certificates_Of_Deposit_account_Guide.pdf. Accessed 15 April 2021.

       Citi Bank No Penalty CD. https://online.citi.com/US/ag/open-a-bank-account/no-penalty-cd-terms. Accessed 15 April 2021.

       Bank of America CDs. https://www.bankofamerica.com/deposits/bank-cds/cd-accounts/. Accessed 15 April 2021.

       "The Best Credit Cards." The Points Guy. https://thepointsguy.com/credit-cards/best/. Accessed 15 April 2021.

30   Peter Smith, Shezal Babar & Rebecca Borne." OVERDRAFT FEES: Banks Must Stop Gouging Consumers During the COVID-19 Crisis." Center for Responsible Lending, https://www.responsiblelending.org/sites/default/files/nodes/files/research-publication/crl-overdraft-covid19-jun2019.pdf. Accessed 15 April 2021.

BUYING, RENTING, & HOME LOANS

31   "Rent vs. Buy Calculator" Zillow, https://www.zillow.com/rent-vs-buy-calculator/. Accessed 15 April 2021.

       Mike Bostock, Shan Carter & Archie Tse."Is It Better to Rent or Buy?" The New York Times, https://www.nytimes.com/interactive/2014/upshot/buy-rent-calculator.html. Accessed 15 April 2021.

32   "Home Purchase Center." myFICO, https://www.myfico.com/loan-center/home-mortgage-rate-comparison/default.aspx. Accessed 20 May 2021.

33   "Free Credit Report." AnnualCreditReport.com, https://www.annualcreditreport.com/index.action. Accessed 20 May 2021.
      Credit Wise. https://creditwise.capitalone.com/home. Accessed 15 April 2021.
      Credit Karma. https://www.creditkarma.com/. Accessed 15 April 2021.
      Credit Sesame. https://www.creditsesame.com/. Accessed 15 April 2021.

34   "Mortgage Calculator." Trulia, https://www.trulia.com/mortgage-payment-calculator/. Accessed 15 April 2021.

35   "Mortgage Calculator: Should I Buy Points?" NerdWallet, https://www.nerdwallet.com/article/mortgages/should-i-buy-points-mortgage-calculator. Accessed 15 April 2021.

36   Berlinda Liu & Gaurav Sinha."SPIVA U.S. Scorecard", S&P Dow Jones Indices, https://www.spglobal.com/spdji/en/documents/spiva/spiva-us-year-end-2020.pdf. Accessed 15 April 2021.

STOCKS, BONDS, & FUNDS

37   Arielle O'Shea & Kevin Voigt. "Stock Market Basics: What Beginner Investors Should Know", NerdWallet, https://www.nerdwallet.com/article/investing/stock-market-basics-everything-beginner-investors-know. Accessed 15 April 2021.

38   "Vanguard Total Bond Market Index Fund Admiral Shares." Vanguard.com. https://investor.vanguard.com/mutual-funds/profile/VBTLX. Accessed 15 April 2021.

      "Fidelity U.S. Bond Index Fund." Fidelity.com. https://fundresearch.fidelity.com/mutual-funds/summary/316146356.

      "Vanguard Intermediate-Term Bond ETF". Vanguard.com. https://investor.vanguard.com/etf/profile/BIV. Accessed 15 April 2021.

      "Fidelity Total Bond ETF." Fidelity.com. https://screener.fidelity.com/ftgw/etf/goto/snapshot/snapshot.jhtml?symbols=FBND&type=sq-NavBar. Accessed 15 April 2021.

      "iShares Core U.S. Aggregate Bond ETF. iShares.com. https://www.ishares.com/us/products/239458/ishares-core-total-us-bond-market-etf. Accessed 15 April 2021.

      "Fidelity Total Bond Fund." Fidelity.com. https://fundresearch.fidelity.com/mutual-funds/summary/31617K881. Accessed 15 April 2021.

      "Vanguard Total Bond Market ETF." Vanguard.com. https://investor.vanguard.com/etf/profile/bnd. Accessed 15 April 2021.

      "Vanguard High-Yield Tax-Exempt Fund Investor Shares". Vanguard.com. https://investor.vanguard.com/mutual-funds/profile/VWAHX. Accessed 15 April 2021.

39   **Simple IRAs and (Simplified Employee Pension) SEP IRAs**
      "Retirement Topics – Simple IRA Contribution Limits." Internal Revenue Service. https://www.irs.
      gov/retirement-plans/plan-participant-employee/retirement-topics-simple-ira-contribution-
      limits#:~:text=The%20amount%20an%20employee%20contributes,%2412%2C500%20in%20
      2015%20E2%80%93%202018. Accessed 15 April 2021.

      "SEP Contribution Limits (including grandfathered SARSEPs). Internal Revenue Service. https://
      www.irs.gov/retirement-plans/plan-participant-employee/sep-contribution-limits-including-
      grandfathered-sarseps. Accessed 15 April 2021

      "SEP Plan FAQs." Internal Revenue Service. https://www.irs.gov/retirement-plans/retirement-
      plans-faqs-regarding-seps. Accessed 15 April 2021

40   "One-Participant 401(k) Plans." Internal Revenue Service. https://www.irs.gov/retirement-plans/
      one-participant-401k-plans. Accessed 15 April 2021.

41   "Retirement Topics – 457(b) Contributions Limits." Internal Revenue Service. https://www.irs.
      gov/retirement-plans/plan-participant-employee/retirement-topics-457b-contribution-
      limits#:~:text=More%20In%20Retirement%20Plans&text=A%20457(b)%20plan's%20
      annual,in%202020%20and%20in%202021. Accessed 15 April 2021.

42   "Asset Allocation Models to Maximize Your Returns." American Association of Individual
      Investors. https://www.aaii.com/asset-allocation. Accessed 15 April 2021.

ROTH & TRADITIONAL IRAs

43   "Amount of Roth IRA Contributions That You Can Make for 2021". Internal Revenue Service.
      https://www.irs.gov/retirement-plans/amount-of-roth-ira-contributions-that-you-can-make-
      for-2021. Accessed 15 April 2021.

44   "Traditional and Roth IRAs." Internal Revenue Service. https://www.irs.gov/retirement-plans/
      traditional-and-roth-iras. Accessed 15 April 2021.

45   **Shopping for Low Cost IRAs**
      Ally.com. https://www.ally.com/iras/. Accessed 15 April 2021

      Betterment.com. https://www.betterment.com/pricing/. Accessed 15 April 2021

      Fidelity.com. https://www.fidelity.com/why-fidelity/pricing-fees. Accessed 15 April 2021

      Vanguard.com. https://investor.vanguard.com/investing/account-fees. Accessed 15 April 2021

      Charles Schwab. https://www.schwab.com/pricing. Accessed 15 April 2021

INDEX FUNDS

46   "Bloomberg Billionaire Index.", Warren Buffet. Bloomberg.com. https://www.bloomberg.com/billionaires/profiles/warren-e-buffett/. Accessed 20 May 2021.

47   "Trends in the Expenses and Fees of Funds, 2019." Investment Company Institute. https://www.ici.org/system/files/attachments/pdf/per26-01.pdf. Accessed 15 April 2021.

48   **Sample Index Funds**
"Vanguard 500 Index Fund Admiral Shares." Vanguard.com. https://investor.vanguard.com/mutual-funds/profile/VFIAX. Accessed 15 April 2021.

"Fidelity 500 Index Fund." Fidelity.com. https://fundresearch.fidelity.com/mutual-funds/summary/315911750. Accessed 15 April 2021.

"SPDR S&P 500 ETF Trust." State Street Global Advisors. https://www.ssga.com/us/en/individual/etfs/funds/spdr-sp-500-etf-trust-spy. Accessed 15 April 2021.

" Vanguard S&P 500 ETF." Vanguard.com. https://investor.vanguard.com/etf/profile/VOO. Accessed 15 April 2021.

"iShares Core S&P 500 ETF." iShares.com. https://www.ishares.com/us/products/239726/ishares-core-sp-500-etf. Accessed 15 April 2021.

"Vanguard Total Stock Market Index Fund Admiral Shares." Vanguard.com. https://investor.vanguard.com/mutual-funds/profile/VTSAX. Accessed 15 April 2021.

"Fidelity ZERO Large Cap Index Fund." Fidelity.com. https://fundresearch.fidelity.com/mutual-funds/summary/315911628. Accessed 15 April 2021.

"Vanguard Total Stock Market ETF." Vanguard.com. https://investor.vanguard.com/etf/profile/VTI. Accessed 15 April 2021.

49   "Charles Munger." Forbes.com. https://www.forbes.com/profile/charles-munger/?sh=3bfc1bb1697a. Accessed 20 May 2021.

50   "The Yale Investment Office." Yale University. https://investments.yale.edu/. Accessed 20 May 2021.

HEALTH SAVINGS ACCOUNTS (HSA) & FLEXIBLE SPENDING ACCOUNTS (FSA)

51   Dr. Francesca Ortegen. " How U.S. Health Policy Changes Have Affected Healthcare Costs Over Time." Clever.com. https://listwithclever.com/research/healthcare-costs-over-time/. Accessed 20 May 2021.

52   Darla Mercado. "Retiring this year? How Much You'll Need for Health-Care Costs." CNBC.com. https://www.cnbc.com/2019/07/18/retiring-this-year-how-much-youll-need-for-health-care-costs.html. Accessed 20 May 2021.

      26 CFR 601.602: Tax forms and instructions. Internal Revenue Service. https://www.irs.gov/pub/irs-drop/rp-20-32.pdf. Accessed 20 May 2021.

      26 CFR 601.602: Tax forms and instructions. (Also Part I, §§ 1, 23, 24, 25A, 32, 36B, 42, 45R, 55, 59, 62, 63, 125, 132(f),135, 137, 146, 147, 148, 152, 179, 199A, 213, 220, 221, 448, 461, 512, 513, 642, 831, 877, 877A, 911, 1274A, 2010, 2032A, 2503, 2523, 4161, 4261, 6033, 6039F, 6323, 6334, 6601, 6651, 6652, 6695, 6698, 6699, 6721, 6722, 7345, 7430, 7702B, 9831; 1.148-5.). Internal Revenue Service. https://www.irs.gov/pub/irs-drop/rp-20-45.pdf. Accessed 20 May 2021.

ASSET ALLOCATION

53   "Vanguard Portfolio Allocation Models." Vanguard.com. https://investor.vanguard.com/investing/how-to-invest/model-portfolio-allocation. Accessed of 20 May 2021.

54   "Investor Questionnaire." Vanguard.com. https://retirementplans.vanguard.com/VGApp/pe/PubQuizActivity?Step=start. Accessed of 20 May 2021.

REBALANCING YOUR PORTFOLIO

55   "Getting back on track: A guide to smart rebalancing." Vanguard.com. https://personal.vanguard.com/pdf/ISGGBOT.pdf. Accessed 20 May 2021.

SAVING FOR YOUR CHILDREN

56   "Take Advantage of Your State Tax Benefits." Black Rock. https://www.blackrock.com/us/individual/literature/brochure/529-plans-and-state-tax-benefits-client-piece-en-us.pdf. Accessed 15 April 2021.

      "State Section 529 Deductions."Finaid.org. https://finaid.org/savings/state529deductions/. Accessed 20 May 2021.

57   Emma Kerr. "Paying Student Loans with 529 Plan Funds." U.S. News. https://www.usnews.com/education/best-colleges/paying-for-college/articles/what-to-know-about-paying-student-loans-with-529-plan-funds. Accessed 20 May 2021.

58   "Compare 529 College Savings Plans." Vanguard.com. https://vanguard.wealthmsi.com/comp529.php. Accessed 20 May 2021.

INTRODUCTION TO TAXES

59   Amir El-Sibaie."2021 Tax Brackets."Tax Foundation. https://taxfoundation.org/2021-tax-brackets/. Accessed 15 April 2021.

Katherine Loughead."State Individual Income Tax Rates and Brackets for 2020."Tax Foundation. https://taxfoundation.org/state-individual-income-tax-rates-and-brackets-for-2020/. Accessed 15 April 2021.

"Tax Year 2019 New York Income Tax Brackets." Taxbrackets.org. https://www.tax-brackets.org/newyorktaxtable. Accessed 15 April 2021.

60   "Publication 523 (2020), Selling Your Home. Internal Revenue Service. https://www.irs.gov/publications/p523. Accessed 15 April 2021..

61   "Simplified Option for Home Office Deduction." Internal Revenue Service. https://www.irs.gov/businesses/small-businesses-self-employed/simplified-option-for-home-office-deduction. Accessed 15 April 2021.

62   "Charitable Contribution Deductions." Internal Revenue Service. https://www.irs.gov/charities-non-profits/charitable-organizations/charitable-contribution-deductions. Accessed 15 April 2021.

GETTING RETIREMENT RIGHT

63   "Retirement Planner." Microsoft Excel. https://templates.office.com/en-US/Retirement-planner-TM67043060. Accessed 20 May 2021.

64   "Retirement Calculator." Smart Asset. https://smartasset.com/retirement/retirement-calculator. Accessed 20 May 2021.

"Retirement Calculator." Nerd Wallet. https://www.nerdwallet.com/investing/retirement-calculator. Accessed 20 May 2021.

65   Mark Hinkle. Press Release. "Social Security Combined Trust Funds Projection Remains the Same Says Board of Trustees." Social Security. https://www.ssa.gov/news/press/releases/2020/#4-2020-5. Accessed 20 May 2021.

SHELTERING YOUR ASSETS

66   "ERISA." U.S. Department of Labor. https://www.dol.gov/general/topic/health-plans/erisa#:~:text=The%20Employee%20Retirement%20Income%20Security,for%20individuals%20in%20these%20plans. Accessed 20 May 2021.

67   Jose R. Guardado, PhD. "Policy Research Perspectives: Medical Liability Claim Frequency Among U.S. Physicians." American Medical Association White Paper. https://www.ama-assn.org/sites/ama-assn.org/files/corp/media-browser/public/government/advocacy/policy-research-perspective-medical-liability-claim-frequency.pdf. Accessed 20 May 2021.

68   "When Is It Too Late to Sue for Medical Malpractice." i-lawsuit.com. https://www.i-lawsuit.com/medical-malpractice-statute-of-limitations/. Accessed 20 May 2021.

69   Jose R. Guardado, PhD. Policy Research Perspectives: New Data Show the Highest Prevalence of Medical Liability Premium Increases in 15 Years." American Medical Association. https://www.ama-assn.org/system/files/2021-03/prp-mlm-premiums-2020.pdf. Accessed 20 May 2021.

70   AM Best Rating Services. http://www.ambest.com/home/default.aspx. Accessed 20 May 2021.

ESTATE PLANNING

71   "Frequently Asked Questions on Estate Taxes." Internal Revenue Service. https://www.irs.gov/businesses/small-businesses-self-employed/frequently-asked-questions-on-estate-taxes. Accessed 20 May 2021.

72   "State Death Tax Chart." The American College of Trust and Estate Counsel. https://www.actec.org/resources/state-death-tax-chart/. Accessed 20 May 2021.

73   "Estate Plan Bundle." LegalZoom.com. https://www.legalzoom.com/personal/estate-planning/estate-planning-bundle.html#people-selection. Accessed 20 May 2021.

LIFE INSURANCE

74   PolicyGenius.com. https://www.policygenius.com/. Access 20 May 2021.
      HealthIQ.com. https://www.healthiq.com/. Accessed 20 May 2021.

75   "Life Insurance Coverage Calculator." Policygenius.com. https://www.policygenius.com/life-insurance/how-much-life-insurance-do-i-need/. Accessed 20 May 2021.

DISABILITY & UMBRELLA INSURANCE

76   PolicyGenius.com. https://www.policygenius.com/. Accessed 20 May 2021.
      Leveragerx.com. https://www.leveragerx.com/. Accessed 20 May 2021.
      HealthIQ.com. https://www.healthiq.com/. Accessed 20 May 2021.

77   "Fact Sheet Social Security." Social Security Administration. https://www.ssa.gov/news/press/factsheets/colafacts2021.pdf. Accessed 20 May 2021.

INDEX

Made in the USA
Columbia, SC
21 March 2022

57835420R00215